CHANTING HARE KRISHNA

Books by His Divine Grace

A.C. Bhaktivedanta Swami Prabhupāda

Bhagavad-gītā As It Is

Śrīmad-Bhāgavatam (completed by disciples)

Śrī Caitanya-caritāmṛta

Kṛṣṇa, the Supreme Personality of Godhead

Teachings of Lord Caitanya

The Nectar of Devotion

The Nectar of Instruction

Śrī Īśopaniṣad

Light of the Bhāgavata

Easy Journey to Other Planets

Teachings of Lord Kapila, the Son of Devahūti

Teachings of Queen Kuntī

Message of Godhead

The Science of Self-Realization

The Perfection of Yoga

Beyond Birth and Death

Perfect Questions, Perfect Answers

Available from krishna.com and blservices.com

Chanting Hare Krishna

The Art of Mystic Meditation, Kirtan, and Bhakti Yoga

Revised Edition

Compiled from the teachings of

HIS DIVINE GRACE
A. C. BHAKTIVEDANTA SWAMI PRABHUPĀDA
Founder-*Ācārya* of the International Society
for Krishna Consciousness

THE BHAKTIVEDANTA BOOK TRUST

Readers interested in the subject matter of this book are invited by the International Society for Krishna Consciousness to visit any ISKCON center (see address list in back of book) or contact one of the following information centers:

ISKCON Reader Services UK
+44 (0)1923 851000
readerservices@pamho.net

ISKCON Reader Services Ireland
+44 (0)28 677 23878
tp@krishnaisland.com

Compiled and edited by Advaita Candra Dāsa, Dānakelī Dāsī, Dharmasetu Dāsa, Mahāmāyā Dāsī, Pyāri Mohana Dāsa, and Śrutadeva Dāsa

Book design by Yamarāja Dāsa

ISBN 978-91-7149-856-4

www.krishna.com
www.bbt.se
www.bbtmedia.com

Printed in 2015

Contents

PRONUNCIATION GUIDE

The system of transliteration used in this book conforms to a system that scholars have accepted to indicate the pronunciation of each sound in the Sanskrit language.

The short vowel **a** is pronounced like the **u** in b**u**t, long **ā** like the **a** in f**a**r. Short **i** is pronounced as in p**i**n, long **ī** as in p**i**que, short **u** as in p**u**ll, and long **ū** as in r**u**le. The vowel **ṛ** is pronounced like the **ri** in **ri**m, **e** like the **ey** in th**ey**, **o** like the **o** in g**o**, **ai** like the **ai** in **ai**sle, and **au** like the **ow** in h**ow**. The *anusvāra* (**ṁ**) is pronounced like the **n** in the French word *bo***n**, and *visarga* (**ḥ**) is pronounced as a final **h** sound. At the end of a couplet, **aḥ** is pronounced **aha**, and **iḥ** is pronounced **ihi**.

The guttural consonants – **k, kh, g, gh,** and **ṅ** – are pronounced from the throat in much the same manner as in English. **K** is pronounced as in **k**ite, **kh** as in Ec**kh**art, **g** as in **g**ive, **gh** as in di**g h**ard, and **ṅ** as in si**ng.**

The palatal consonants – **c, ch, j, jh,** and **ñ** – are pronounced with the tongue touching the firm ridge behind the teeth. **C** is pronounced as in **ch**air, **ch** as in staun**ch-h**eart, **j** as in **j**oy, **jh** as in he**dgeh**og, and **ñ** as in ca**ny**on.

The cerebral consonants – **ṭ, ṭh, ḍ, ḍh,** and **ṇ** – are pronounced with the tip of the tongue turned up and drawn back against the dome of the palate. **ṭ** is pronounced as in **t**ub, **ṭh** as in ligh**t-h**eart, **ḍ** as in **d**ove, **ḍh** as in re**d-h**ot, and **ṇ** as in **n**ut. The dental consonants – **t, th, d, dh,** and **n** – are pronounced in the same manner as the cerebrals, but with the forepart of the tongue against the teeth.

The labial consonants – **p, ph, b, bh,** and **m** – are pronounced with the lips. **P** is pronounced as in **p**ine, **ph** as in u**ph**ill, **b** as in **b**ird, **bh** as in ru**b-h**ard, and **m** as in **m**other.

The semivowels – **y, r, l,** and **v** – are pronounced as in **y**es, **r**un, **l**ight, and **v**ine respectively. The sibilants – **ś, ṣ,** and **s** – are pronounced, respectively, as in the German word **s**_prechen_ and the English words **sh**ine and **s**un. The letter **h** is pronounced as in **h**ome.

NOTE: In this book, sometimes Krishna is spelled as it sounds (Krishna) or sometimes with the Sanskrit spelling (Kṛṣṇa) depending on where the quote is coming from and when it was originally written. Both are pronounced in the same way.

Preface

Invocation Prayers

nama oṁ viṣṇu-pādāya kṛṣṇa-preṣṭhāya bhū-tale
śrīmate bhaktivedānta-svāmin iti nāmine

We offer our respectful obeisances unto His Divine Grace A.C. Bhaktivedanta Swami Prabhupāda, who is very dear to Lord Krishna, having taken shelter at His lotus feet.

namas te sārasvate deve gaura-vāṇī-pracāriṇe
nirviśeṣa-śūnyavādi-pāścātya-deśa-tāriṇe

Our respectful obeisances are unto you, O spiritual master, servant of Sarasvatī Gosvāmī. You are kindly preaching the message of Lord Caitanyadeva and delivering the Western countries, which are filled with impersonalism and voidism.

vāñchā-kalpa-tarubhyaś ca kṛpā-sindhubhya eva ca
patitānāṁ pāvanebhyo vaiṣṇavebhyo namo namaḥ

We offer respectful obeisances unto all the Vaiṣṇava devotees of the Lord, who can fulfill the desires of everyone, just like desire trees, and are full of compassion for the fallen conditioned souls.

śrī-kṛṣṇa-caitanya prabhu-nityānanda
śrī-advaita gadādhara śrīvāsādi-gaura-bhakta-vṛnda

We offer our obeisances to Śrī Kṛṣṇa Caitanya, Prabhu Nityānanda, Śrī Advaita, Gadādhara, Śrīvāsa and all others in the line of devotion.

hare kṛṣṇa hare kṛṣṇa kṛṣṇa kṛṣṇa hare hare
hare rāma hare rāma rāma rāma hare hare
iti ṣoḍaśakaṁ nāmnāṁ kali-kalmaṣa-nāśanam
nātaḥ paratаropāyaḥ sarva-vedeṣu dṛśyate

"The sixteen words Hare Kṛṣṇa, Hare Kṛṣṇa, Kṛṣṇa Kṛṣṇa, Hare Hare/ Hare Rāma, Hare Rāma, Rāma Rāma, Hare Hare are especially meant for counteracting the contaminations of Kali (the present age of quarrel and hypocrisy). These sixteen names composed of thirty-two syllables are the only means to counteract the evil effects of Kali-yuga. After searching through all the Vedic literature, one cannot find a method of religion more sublime for this age than the chanting of Hare Kṛṣṇa."

(*Kali-santaraṇa Upaniṣad*)

Of course, there are many books by Śrīla Prabhupāda and his disciples on the chanting of Hare Krishna, and one may question the necessity for another one. This present edition can be explained in the following way. This book is a humble attempt by the publishers to put Śrīla Prabhupāda's instructions on chanting in a format that takes the reader progressively from the most basic teachings through different stages and types of chanting, and ultimately to the perfection of chanting and the final test at the time of death. Naturally, it is not meant to include all of Śrīla Prabhupāda's instructions, as that would take many volumes, and they can already be found in other books and in the Bhaktivedanta Vedabase. We should mention here that we are deeply indebted to the Bhaktivedanta Archives for their tremendous work of making Śrīla Prabhupāda available through the Vedabase, without which this book would never have been possible. However, what is being attempted here is a shortened and concise gathering of *some* of Śrīla Prabhupāda's instructions to make a book that is both easy to approach and an easy-to-read guide on chanting. We are hopeful that the audience will find it both elucidatory and inspiring, be one a total newcomer to chanting or even an advanced and longtime disciple of Śrīla Prabhupāda. Our goal is to provide a collection of Śrīla Prabhupāda's teachings that will encourage the newcomer to take up chanting; the serious chanter to understand the significance of initiation and the ten offenses; the newly initiated to practice more strictly, seriously, and sincerely; the practiced devotees to chant more themselves and then take to the streets to spread the glories of the holy names to others; and the older, senior devotees to relish and increase their taste in chanting the holy names in preparing for the time of death.

Śrīla Prabhupāda named his movement the International Society for Krishna Consciousness. Yet everyone knew it as, and Śrīla Prabhupāda himself called it, "the Hare Krishna movement." He took pride in calling his disciples "the Hare Krishna people."

"In 1966 this movement was registered in New York, and from 1966 it is spreading. So within four or five years it has spread all over the world. We have got branches in every part of the globe. And at least, these people know there is a movement, Kṛṣṇa consciousness, and we are welcome everywhere as Kṛṣṇa conscious people, 'Hare Kṛṣṇa People.' Our name is 'Hare Kṛṣṇa People.' "

(Lecture on *The Nectar of Devotion*,
November 8, 1972, Vṛndāvana, India)

"Actually we experienced this when we came to preach the Hare Kṛṣṇa movement in the West. When we came to New York in 1965, we never expected that the Hare Kṛṣṇa *mahā-mantra* would be accepted in this country. Nonetheless, we invited people to our storefront to join in chanting the Hare Kṛṣṇa mantra, and the Lord's holy name is so attractive that simply by coming to our storefront in New York, fortunate young people became Kṛṣṇa conscious. ”

(*Śrī Caitanya-caritāmṛta, Madhya-līlā* 17.145, purport)

“The *Caitanya-bhāgavata* confirms that Śrī Caitanya Mahāprabhu, by His birth, has made the whole world peaceful, as in the past Nārāyaṇa protected this earth in His incarnation as Varāha. Because of His protecting and maintaining this world in the present Kali-yuga, Lord Caitanya Mahāprabhu is known as Viśvambhara, which refers to one who feeds the entire world. The movement inaugurated by Śrī Caitanya Mahāprabhu when He was present five hundred years ago is again being propagated all over the world, and factually we are seeing its practical results. People are being saved, protected, and maintained by this Hare Kṛṣṇa movement. Thousands of followers, especially Western youths, are taking part in this Hare Kṛṣṇa movement, and how safe and happy they feel can be understood from the expressions of gratitude in their hundreds and thousands of letters.”

(*Śrī Caitanya-caritāmṛta, Ādi-līlā* 14.19, purport)

And in a conversation with a professor of Indian History that took place in Melbourne, Australia, on May 20, 1975 there was this exchange:

> **Dr. Copeland:** And you’ve been rather successful in institutionalizing your religion, getting a large number of temples constructed or built or taken over, and a large number of followers.
> **Prabhupāda:** Yes.
> **Dr. Copeland:** Why do you think you are so successful?
> **Prabhupāda:** I don’t think I am successful, but people say.
> **Dr. Copeland:** [*laughs*] Very good.
> **Prabhupāda:** I will be successful when everyone will chant Hare Kṛṣṇa.

Śrīla Prabhupāda left behind an amazing legacy of books, lectures, letters, and recorded conversations to guide his disciples and all future followers for the years to come. These writings and recordings are the sole source material for this book. Presented as it was spoken and written at the time, with only minor editing, we hope you will experience the potency of Śrīla Prabhupāda's words as if you were sitting right there in front of him when he first delivered his message.

In conclusion, to paraphrase Śrīla Prabhupāda in his preface to *Bhagavad-gītā As It Is,* we hope that people will derive the greatest benefit by studying this book *Chanting Hare Krishna* as we have presented it here. And if even one person takes up this chanting with all sincerity and seriousness, we shall consider our attempt a success. Hare Krishna.

The Publishers

PROLOGUE

A Short Sketch of the Life of Lord Caitanya

(Condensed from the Introduction to *Śrīmad-Bhāgavatam*)

Lord Śrī Caitanya Mahāprabhu, the great apostle of love of God and the father of the congregational chanting of the holy name of the Lord, advented Himself at Śrīdhāma Māyāpur, a quarter in the city of Navadvīpa in Bengal, on the Phālgunī Pūrṇimā evening in the year 1407 Śakābda (corresponding to February 1486 by the Christian calendar). It was by the will of the Lord that there was a lunar eclipse on that evening. During the hours of eclipse it was the custom of the Hindu public to take bath in the Ganges or any other sacred river and chant the Vedic mantras for purification. When Lord Caitanya was born during the lunar eclipse, all India was roaring with the holy sound of Hare Kṛṣṇa, Hare Kṛṣṇa, Kṛṣṇa Kṛṣṇa, Hare Hare/ Hare Rāma, Hare Rāma, Rāma Rāma, Hare Hare. These sixteen names of the Lord are mentioned in many *Purāṇas* and *Upaniṣads,* and they are described as the *Tāraka-brahma nāma* of this age. It is recommended in the *śāstras* (revealed scriptures) that offenseless chanting of these holy names of the Lord can deliver a fallen soul from material bondage. There are innumerable names of the Lord both in India and outside, and all of them are equally good because all of them indicate the Supreme Personality of Godhead. But because these sixteen are especially recommended for this age, people should take advantage of them and follow the path of the great *ācāryas* [saintly teachers] who attained success by practicing the rules of the *śāstras*.

The simultaneous occurrence of the Lord's appearance and the lunar eclipse indicated the distinctive mission of the Lord. This mission was to preach the importance of chanting the holy names of the Lord in this age of Kali (quarrel). In this present age, quarrels take place even over trifles, and therefore the *śāstras* have recommended for this age a common platform for realization, namely chanting the holy names of the Lord. People can hold meetings to glorify the Lord in their respective languages and with melodious songs, and if such performances are executed in an offenseless manner, it is certain that the participants will gradually attain spiritual perfection without having to undergo more rigorous methods. At such meetings everyone, the learned and the foolish, the rich and the poor, the Hindus and the Muslims, the Englishmen and the Indians, and the *caṇḍālas* [dog-eaters] and the *brāhmaṇas* [priestly class], can all hear the transcendental sounds and thus cleanse the dust of material association from the mirror of the heart. To confirm the Lord's mission, all the people of the world will accept the holy name of the Lord as the common platform for the universal religion of mankind. In other words, the advent of the holy name took place along with the advent of Lord Śrī Caitanya Mahāprabhu.

When the Lord was on the lap of His mother, He would at once stop crying as soon as the ladies surrounding Him chanted the holy names and clapped their hands. This peculiar incident was observed by the neighbors with awe and veneration. Sometimes the young girls took pleasure in making the Lord cry and then stopping Him by chanting the holy name. So from His very childhood the Lord began to preach the importance of the holy name. In His early age Lord Śrī Caitanya was known as Nimāi. This name was given by His beloved mother because the Lord took His birth beneath a *nīm* tree in the courtyard of His paternal house. When the Lord was offered solid food at the age of six months in the *anna-prāśana* ceremony, the Lord indicated His future activities. At this time it was customary to offer the child both coins and books in order to get some indication of the future tendencies of the child. The Lord was offered on one side coins and on the other the *Śrīmad-Bhāgavatam*. The Lord accepted the *Bhāgavatam* instead of the coins.

[Later on in life] the Lord was then married with great pomp and gaiety, and at this time He began to preach the congregational chanting of the holy name of the Lord at Navadvīpa. Some of the *brāhmaṇas* became envious of His popularity, and they put many hindrances on His path. They were so jealous that they finally took the matter before the Muslim magistrate at Navadvīpa. Bengal was then governed by Pāṭhānas, and the governor of the province was Nawab Hussain Shah. The Muslim magistrate of Navadvīpa took up the complaints of the *brāhmaṇas* seriously, and at first he warned the followers of Nimāi Paṇḍita not to chant loudly the name of Hari. But Lord Caitanya asked His followers to disobey the orders of the Kazi, and they went on with their *saṅkīrtana* (chanting) party as usual. The magistrate then sent constables who interrupted a *saṅkīrtana* and broke some of the *mṛdaṅgas* (drums). When Nimāi Paṇḍita heard of this incident He organized a party for civil disobedience. He is the pioneer of the civil disobedience movement in India for the right cause. He organized a procession of one hundred thousand men with thousands of *mṛdaṅgas* and *karatālas* (hand cymbals), and this procession passed over the roads of Navadvīpa in defiance of the Kazi who had issued the order. Finally the procession reached the house of the Kazi, who went upstairs out of fear of the masses. The great crowds assembled at the Kazi's house displayed a violent temper, but the Lord asked them to be peaceful.

At this time the Kazi came down and tried to pacify the Lord and the two learned scholars began a long discussion on the Koran and Hindu *śāstras*. [The Lord told the Kazi that] in Kali-yuga only the *saṅkīrtana-yajña* is recommended for all practical purposes. Speaking in this way, the Lord finally convinced the Kazi, who became the Lord's follower. The Kazi thenceforth declared that no one should hinder the *saṅkīrtana* movement which was started by the Lord, and the Kazi left this order in his will for the sake of progeny. The Kazi's tomb still exists in the area of Navadvīpa, and Hindu pilgrims go there to show their respects. The Kazi's descendants are residents, and they never objected to *saṅkīrtana,* even during the Hindu-Muslim riot days.

Once Nityānanda Prabhu and Śrīla Haridāsa Ṭhākura [two close associates of the Lord] were walking down a main road, and on the way they saw a roaring crowd assembled. Upon inquiring from passers-by, they understood that two brothers, named Jagāi and Mādhāi, were creating a public disturbance in a drunken state. They also heard that these two brothers were born in a respectable *brāhmaṇa* family, but because of low association they had turned into debauchees of the worst type. They were not only drunkards but also meat-eaters, woman-hunters, dacoits and sinners of all description. Śrīla Nityānanda Prabhu heard all of these stories and decided that these two fallen souls must be the first to be delivered. If they were delivered from their sinful life, then the good name of Lord Caitanya would be even still more glorified. Thinking in this way, Nityānanda Prabhu and Haridāsa pushed their way through the crowd and asked the two brothers to chant the holy name of Lord Hari. The drunken brothers became enraged upon this request and attacked Nityānanda Prabhu with filthy language. Both brothers chased them a considerable distance. In the evening the report of the preaching work was submitted to the Lord, and He was glad to learn that Nityānanda and Haridāsa had attempted to deliver such a stupid pair of fellows.

The next day Nityānanda Prabhu went to see the brothers, and as soon as He approached them one of them threw a piece of earthen pot at Him. This struck Him on the forehead, and immediately blood began to flow. But Nityānanda Prabhu was so kind that instead of protesting this heinous act, He said, "It does not matter that you have thrown this stone at Me. I still request you to chant the holy name of Lord Hari."

One of the brothers, Jagāi, was astonished to see this behavior of Nityānanda Prabhu, and he at once fell down at His feet and asked Him to pardon his sinful brother. When Mādhāi again attempted to hurt Nityānanda Prabhu, Jagāi stopped him and implored him to fall down at His feet. In the meantime the news of Nityānanda's injury reached the Lord, who at once hurried to the spot in a fiery and angry mood. The Lord immediately invoked His Sudarśana *cakra* (the Lord's ultimate weapon, shaped like a wheel) to kill the sinners, but Nityānanda Prabhu reminded Him of His mission. The mission of the Lord was to deliver the hopelessly fallen souls of Kali-yuga, and the brothers Jagāi and Mādhāi were typical examples of these fallen souls. Ninety percent of the population of this age resembles these brothers, despite high birth and mundane respectability. According to the verdict of the revealed scriptures, the total population of the world in this age will be of the lowest *śudra* [laborer class] quality, or even lower. It should be noted that Śrī Caitanya Mahāprabhu never acknowledged the stereotyped caste system by birthright; rather, He strictly followed the verdict of the *śāstras* in the matter of one's *svarūpa,* or real identity.

When the Lord was invoking His Sudarśana *cakra* and Śrī Nityānanda Prabhu was imploring Him to forgive the two brothers, both the brothers fell down at the lotus feet of the Lord and begged His pardon for their gross behavior. The Lord was also asked by Nityānanda Prabhu to accept these repenting souls, and the Lord agreed to accept them on one condition, that they henceforward completely give up all their sinful activities and habits of debauchery. Both the brothers agreed and promised to give up all their sinful habits, and the kind Lord accepted them and did not again refer to their past misdeeds.

During His householder life, the Lord did not display many of the miracles which are generally expected from such personalities, but He did once perform a wonderful miracle in the house of Śrīnivāsa Ṭhākura while *saṅkīrtana* was in full swing. He asked the devotees what they wanted to eat, and when He was informed that they wanted to eat mangoes, He asked for a seed of a mango, although this fruit was out of season. When the seed was brought to Him, He sowed it in the yard of Śrīnivāsa, and at once a creeper began to grow out of the seed. Within no time this creeper became a full-grown mango tree heavy with more ripened fruits than the devotees could eat. The tree remained in Śrīnivāsa's yard, and from then on the devotees used to take as many mangoes from the tree as they wanted.

The Lord left only eight *ślokas* [verses] of His instructions in writing, and they are known as the *Śikṣāṣṭaka*. All other literatures of His divine cult were extensively written by the Lord's principal followers, the six Gosvāmīs of Vṛndāvana, and their followers. The cult of Caitanya philosophy is richer than any other, and it is admitted to be the living religion of the day with the potency for spreading as *viśva-dharma,* or universal religion. We are glad that the matter has been taken up by some enthusiastic sages like Bhaktisiddhānta Sarasvatī Gosvāmī Mahārāja and his disciples. We shall eagerly wait for the happy days of *Bhāgavata-dharma,* or *prema-dharma,* inaugurated by the Lord Śrī Caitanya Mahāprabhu.

INTRODUCTION

Who Is Śrīla Prabhupāda?

Śrīla Prabhupāda appeared in this world in 1896, in Calcutta, India. His father, Gour Mohan De, and his mother, Rajani, were great devotees of Lord Kṛṣṇa (Vaiṣṇavas), and from birth they trained their son in devotional service. They named him Abhay Charan: one who is fearless, having taken shelter at the lotus feet of Lord Kṛṣṇa. Gour Mohan desired his son to become a pure Vaiṣṇava and always prayed to Rādhārāṇī that She bless Abhay.

As a baby, an astrologer read his chart. "When this child reaches the age of seventy, he will cross the ocean, become a great exponent of religion, and open 108 temples." Who could have envisioned that this and much more would actually happen?

When Abhay was only five he wanted to hold a Ratha-yātrā festival in the neighborhood. (Ratha-yātrā is a festival in which the Deity form of the Lord is seated in a chariot and pulled through the streets). His father arranged for a cart, and Abhay's desire was fulfilled. At six years of age Abhay's father gave him a set of Rādhā-Kṛṣṇa Deities to worship. He learned *mṛdaṅga* and other Vaiṣṇava arts, even cooking. During his studies at Scottish Churches College in Calcutta, his father arranged for his marriage. After graduating he refused to accept his degree as he had become a sympathizer of Gandhi's policy of non-cooperation with the British. Still his father secured for him a good job in pharmaceuticals.

In 1922, when Abhay was twenty-five, a most significant eventoccurred. He met his spiritual master, Śrīla Bhaktisiddhānta Sarasvatī Mahārāja. Even before any formal introduction, as Abhay and his friend were offering their obeisances, Śrīla Bhaktisiddhānta addressed them, "You are educated young men. Why don't you preach Lord Caitanya's message throughout the whole world?" Abhay was shocked by his boldness. He sat and listened to the lecture. Afterwards, as Abhay was a follower of Gandhi at that time, he challenged Śrīla Bhaktisiddhānta that with India still under British rule, who would listen to Caitanya's message? Śrīla Bhaktisiddhānta soundly defeated him. "Kṛṣṇa consciousness doesn't have to wait for a change in politics, nor is it dependent on who rules. Kṛṣṇa consciousness is so important—so exclusively important—that it cannot wait." Abhay was convinced that he had at last met his guru. "I accepted him as my spiritual master immediately. Not officially, but in my heart. I was thinking that I have met a very nice saintly person."

In this way Abhay, now a married man, carried on as a householder, always thinking of Kṛṣṇa and his spiritual master, but doing business to maintain his family. In 1933 at Allahabad, he took formal initiation, and his relationship with his spiritual master's mission continued to deepen and unfold. Then, fifteen years after their first meeting, Śrīla Bhaktisiddhānta passed away from this mortal world on January 1, 1937. He had been spending his last days reading *Caitanya-caritāmṛta* and chanting on his beads. When a doctor had visited him, wanting to give him an injection, Śrīla Bhaktisiddhānta had protested, "Why are you disturbing me in this way? Simply chant Hare Kṛṣṇa, that's all."

As the years passed by, and with his children grown up, Abhay's desire and determination to serve his spiritual master's mission increased. Abhay spent more and more of his time working to spread the message of Kṛṣṇa consciousness. For years he had spent much of his time away from home, traveling on business. Now he would dedicate his whole time to preaching. In 1954 he left the business to his family and moved to Jhansi. After his efforts in Jhansi failed to materialize he eventually moved to Vṛndāvana, the holy birth place of Lord Kṛṣṇa. There he spent his time writing books and performing *bhajana* (worship of the Lord).

Soon after, Abhay, now A.C. Bhaktivedanta Swami, moved to the Rādhā-Dāmodara Temple in Vṛndāvana, where he began the momentous task of translating and writing commentary to the *Śrīmad-Bhāgavatam,* the most important book for Vaiṣṇavas. Living as a mendicant, he struggled to publish and print the First Canto, complete in three volumes. Finally in 1965, with the books printed, he felt confident it was the time to go to the West to preach. With much difficulty, he eventually secured a free passage by cargo ship to New York from Mrs. Morarji, owner of Scindia Steamship Company. After obtaining his passport and visa, he boarded the Jaladuta steamship in Calcutta on August 13, 1965. Several trunks of *Śrīmad-Bhāgavatams* were loaded aboard en route.

On the journey, Bhaktivedanta Swami suffered two heart attacks. He thought he would die should another one occur, but Kṛṣṇa appeared to him in a dream, rowing a boat and telling him not to fear, but to come along. The rest of the journey was smooth. On the voyage he wrote his famous poem "Prayer to the Lotus Feet of Kṛṣṇa," in which he revealed his complete dependence on the Lord and his feeling of total humility. Upon arrival in Boston on September 17, 1965, he wrote another poem, "*Markine Bhagavat Dharma:* Preaching Kṛṣṇa Consciousness in America." In this poem, Śrīla Prabhupāda petitions the Lord for His mercy to guide him. Feeling completely incapable alone, he knew only Kṛṣṇa could fulfill his mission. Forty-three years after receiving the order from his spiritual master to preach in the West, he was now there, in New York. He was sixty-nine years of age, alone and penniless, with nowhere to stay. He didn't know which way to turn. Who would have thought that such great things were about to unfold? To material vision it seems almost inconceivable.

For almost a year "Swamiji," as he was called at that time, moved around New York with no fixed place to live or teach. Staying in a loft in the infamous Bowery section of New York, full of homeless bums and alcoholics, he gradually attracted a few youths to his teachings and *kirtana* (chanting). Hippies, musicians, people of all sorts joined in the musical meditation and were beginning to feel something extraordinary from the singing of the Lord's holy names. In June of 1966 he moved to a small storefront at 26 Second Avenue, accompanied by a small band of sympathizers. In July of 1966, Śrīla Prabhupāda officially registered ISKCON (The International Society for Krishna Consciousness). Prabhupāda simply taught the *Bhagavad-gītā* as it is, distributed *prasāda* (food offered to Kṛṣṇa), and chanted the *mahā-mantra*—Hare Kṛṣṇa, Hare Kṛṣṇa, Kṛṣṇa Kṛṣṇa, Hare Hare/ Hare Rāma, Hare Rāma, Rāma Rāma, Hare Hare. More young people began to take interest, and soon he had a small group of serious followers.

For the first time in history, the holy names of Kṛṣṇa were being distributed in public in the world outside of India. In the streets and parks, wherever possible, Śrīla Prabhupāda would chant with his small band of followers and others would join in. Lord Caitanya had predicted that His holy name would be heard in every town and village of the world, but previously nobody had even remotely attempted to spread it. Yet Prabhupāda came to conquer the West armed with only one weapon—complete and unflinching faith in the holy names. Gradually his Hare Krishna movement spread to San Francisco, Montreal, and beyond. People were chanting in Russia, Australia, even Africa. The Beatles produced the "Hare Krishna Mantra" hit record. Hare Krishna would become a household word.

In May 1968, while in Boston, Prabhupāda had been dictating a letter and had mentioned to his secretary that Swamiji was a third-class title for the spiritual master. "Then why do we call you Swamiji?" his secretary had asked.

"The spiritual master," Prabhupāda had replied, "is usually addressed by names like Gurudeva, Viṣṇupāda, or Prabhupāda."

"May we call you Prabhupāda?" his secretary had asked.

Prabhupāda had replied, "Yes," and his disciples had switched from "Swamiji" to "Prabhupāda." One of the devotees had inquired further from Prabhupāda about the meaning of the word and had published a statement in their monthly *Back to Godhead* magazine:

> The word Prabhupāda is a term of the utmost reverence in Vedic religious circles, and it signifies a great saint even among saints. The word actually has two meanings: first, one at whose feet (*pada*) there are many Prabhus (a term meaning "master," which the disciples of a Guru use in addressing each other). The second meaning is one who is always found at the Lotus Feet of Krishna (the Supreme Master).

Although Śrīla Prabhupāda gave a way of transcendental realization by which even a child can very easily make advancement in spiritual life—simply by chanting Hare Kṛṣṇa—he also left the world a unique library of profound philosophical literature, literature studied and praised by scholars and intellectuals, eagerly acquired by professors and librarians, and treasured by devotees of Vedic philosophy and culture.

Śrīla Prabhupāda was the author of nearly seventy volumes of translations and summary studies of, and commentary on, India's immortal Vedic scriptures. His books have already been translated into more than sixty languages. His books are unique because they present the Vedic literature as it is, without personally motivated interpretations. Consequently, his books, apart from their immense scholarly and literary value, offer one the opportunity to understand and actually attain the perfection of self-realization and ultimately realize the Absolute Truth, the Personality of Godhead, and see Him face to face. In other words, by reading his books, not only can one gain access to a wealth of Vedic history, poetry, philosophy, culture, and guidance in down-to-earth, practical affairs, but also one can traverse the path to the highest perfection of human life. Those who have lost their spiritual vision due to the darkness of the present age of quarrel can get light from the books of His Divine Grace Śrīla Prabhupāda. He truly built a house for the whole world to live in.

Between 1965 and 1977, wherever Śrīla Prabhupāda went, on his fourteen journeys around the globe, he constantly spread the chanting of the Hare Kṛṣṇa mantra, and when he finally departed he was surrounded by loving disciples from around the world loudly yet sweetly chanting these names of God he had given them. He began his movement by chanting Hare Kṛṣṇa, and when he left, "Hare Kṛṣṇa" were the last words he spoke. Śrīla Prabhupāda passed away from this mortal world in November of 1977.

* * *

"I have no devotion, nor do I have any knowledge, but I have strong faith in the holy name of Kṛṣṇa."

— A. C. Bhaktivedanta Swami, on board the ship Jaladuta,
Commonwealth Pier, Boston, Massachusetts, U.S.A.
dated 18th of September, 1965

Painting by Muralidhara Dāsa

1
THE HARE KṚṢṆA MAHĀ-MANTRA

One Can at Once Feel Transcendental Ecstasy

This transcendental vibration by the chanting of Hare Kṛṣṇa, Hare Kṛṣṇa, Kṛṣṇa Kṛṣṇa, Hare Hare/ Hare Rāma, Hare Rāma, Rāma Rāma, Hare Hare is the sublime method for reviving our Kṛṣṇa consciousness. As living spiritual souls we are all originally Kṛṣṇa conscious entities, but due to our association with matter since time immemorial, our consciousness is now polluted by the material atmosphere. In this polluted concept of life, we are all trying to exploit the resources of material nature, but actually we are becoming more and more entangled in her complexities. This illusion is called *māyā,* or hard struggle for existence for winning over the stringent laws of material nature. This illusory struggle against the material nature can at once be stopped by revival of our Kṛṣṇa consciousness.

Kṛṣṇa consciousness is not an artificial imposition on the mind. This consciousness is the original energy of the living entity. When we hear the transcendental vibration, this consciousness is revived. And the process is recommended by authorities for this age. By practical experience also, we can perceive that by chanting this *mahā-mantra,* or the Great Chanting for Deliverance, one can at once feel transcendental ecstasy from the spiritual stratum. When one is factually on the plane of spiritual understanding, surpassing the stages of sense, mind, and intelligence, one is situated on the transcendental plane.

This chanting of Hare Kṛṣṇa, Hare Kṛṣṇa, Kṛṣṇa Kṛṣṇa, Hare Hare/ Hare Rāma, Hare Rāma, Rāma Rāma, Hare Hare is directly enacted from the spiritual platform, surpassing all lower status of consciousness, namely sensual, mental, and intellectual. There is no need of understanding the language of the mantra, nor is there any need of mental speculation nor any intellectual adjustment for chanting this *mahā-mantra.* It springs automatically from the spiritual platform, and as such, anyone can take part in this transcendental sound vibration, without any previous qualification, and dance in ecstasy. We have seen it practically. Even a child can take part in the chanting, or even a dog can take part in it. The chanting should be heard from the lips of a pure devotee of the Lord, so that immediate effect can be achieved. As far as possible, chanting from the lips of a nondevotee should be avoided, as much as milk touched by the lips of a serpent causes poisonous effect.

The word Harā is a form of addressing the energy of the Lord.

Both Kṛṣṇa and Rāma are forms of addressing directly the Lord, and they mean the highest pleasure, eternal. Harā is the supreme pleasure potency of the Lord. This potency, when addressed as Hare, helps us in reaching the Supreme Lord. The material energy, called as *māyā,* is also one of the multi-potencies of the Lord, as much as we are also marginal potency of the Lord. The living entities are described as superior energy than matter. When the superior energy is in contact with inferior energy, it becomes an incompatible situation. But when the supreme marginal potency is in contact with the spiritual potency, Harā, it becomes the happy, normal condition of the living entity.

The three words, namely Harā, Kṛṣṇa, and Rāma, are transcendental seeds of the *mahā-mantra,* and the chanting is a spiritual call for the Lord and His internal energy, Harā, for giving protection to the conditioned soul. The chanting is exactly like a genuine cry by the child for the mother. Mother Harā helps in achieving the grace of the supreme father, Hari, or Kṛṣṇa, and the Lord reveals Himself to such a sincere devotee.

No other means, therefore, of spiritual realization is as effective in this age as chanting the *mahā-mantra:* Hare Kṛṣṇa, Hare Kṛṣṇa, Kṛṣṇa Kṛṣṇa, Hare Hare/ Hare Rāma, Hare Rāma, Rāma Rāma, Hare Hare.

(Explanation on the Happening record album, New York City, December 1966)

Cleanse Away All Misgivings Within Our Hearts

Hare Kṛṣṇa, Hare Kṛṣṇa, Kṛṣṇa Kṛṣṇa, Hare Hare is the transcendental process for reviving our original pure consciousness. By chanting this transcendental vibration, we can cleanse away all misgivings within our hearts. The basic principle of all such misgivings is the false consciousness that I am the lord of all I survey.

In the beginning, there may not be the presence of all

transcendental ecstasies, which are eight in number. But there is no doubt that chanting for a while takes one immediately to the spiritual platform, and one shows the first symptom of this in the urge to dance along with the chanting of the mantra. We have seen this practically. Even a child can take part in the chanting and dancing. Of course, for one who is too entangled in material life, it takes a little more time to come to the standard point, but even such a materially engrossed man is raised to the spiritual platform very quickly.

(From *Kṛṣṇa Consciousness, the Topmost Yoga System*)

The Very High Level

Kṛṣṇa means all-attractive. And another meaning of Kṛṣṇa is that those who are struggling very hard in this material world, Kṛṣṇa can give them liberation. Similarly Rāma, Rāma means pleasure. So one who gives transcendental pleasure, He's called Rāma. So this Kṛṣṇa name, Rāma name, are God's names. That is on the very high level. Therefore we chant Hare Kṛṣṇa, Hare Kṛṣṇa, Kṛṣṇa Kṛṣṇa, Hare Hare/ Hare Rāma, Hare Rāma, Rāma Rāma, Hare Hare. And Harā, Harā also means one who can take away all our miserable conditions and put us into the transcendental position. This is Harā. So these three names are there, Harā, Kṛṣṇa, and Rāma.

(Lecture on *Śrīmad-Bhāgavatam* 6.1.21, Los Angeles, 1970)

The Spiritual Vision to See God

Now some of you members have asked me to explain the meaning of this chanting, Hare Kṛṣṇa, Hare Kṛṣṇa, Kṛṣṇa Kṛṣṇa, Hare Hare/ Hare Rāma, Hare Rāma, Rāma Rāma, Hare Hare. This sound is transcendental sound, sound incarnation of the Absolute Truth. Just try to understand what is incarnation. The Sanskrit word is *avatāra*, and that is translated into English as "incarnation." The root meaning of *avatāra* is "that which comes from the transcendental sky, the spiritual sky, to the material sky." That is called *avatāra. Avatāraṇa. Avatāraṇa* means "coming from up to down." That is called *avatārana*. And *avatāra* is understood that when God or His bona fide representative comes from that sky to this material plane, that is called *avatāra*.

So this is the meaning in a nutshell of this spiritual vibration Hare Kṛṣṇa, Hare Kṛṣṇa, Kṛṣṇa Kṛṣṇa, Hare Hare/ Hare Rāma, Hare Rāma, Rāma Rāma, Hare Hare. Now, according to grammatical rules, when somebody is addressed, just like in your English language, it is a note of address, "O Mr. such-and-such." Similarly, in Sanskrit grammar, the same note of address, which is called *sambodhana,* that is expressed in this way. So Hare, Hare is the note of address form of the sound Harā. Harā means the potency of the Supreme Lord. The Supreme Lord is represented everywhere by His potency.

So the incarnation of God means the expansion which is as good as God Himself. That is called incarnation. So this Hare Kṛṣṇa, Hare Kṛṣṇa, Kṛṣṇa Kṛṣṇa, Hare Hare/ Hare Rāma, Hare Rāma, Rāma Rāma, Hare Hare is the expansion, incarnation, sound incarnation of God, not representation. God presents Himself in this form of sound because we cannot see God with our present eyes. Because this is not our proper eyes. They are material eyes. You don't think that this eye, the transparent thing which is floating in this hole, that is not seeing. If you take this eye out, you cannot see. It is simply a lens only. So none of this body is actually the thing which is taking part. So therefore with these eyes, with these material eyes, you cannot see. The present senses cannot have any knowledge of the Supreme God. But how then can we have knowledge? If my senses are unfit, then how can I make them fit? Oh, that is the thing.

You have to spiritualize, spiritualize these material sense organs. And then when you spiritualize, then you can have the spiritual vision to see God and yourself. The same example which

I have recited many times: just like the iron rod. Iron rod, you put into the fire. It gets warm—warm, warmer, warmer. And when it is red-hot, then it is no longer iron. Iron it is, but it does not act as iron, but it acts as fire. That iron rod which is red-hot in association with fire, you can take that rod and touch anything; it will burn. That means it is no longer acting as iron; it is acting as fire. Similarly, if you associate with this transcendental incarnation, sound incarnation of God, then you will be gradually godly. You will be godly. You can become godly with God's association, not by any other material, extraneous things. No. Just like you can have fire only in association with fire, not with water. If you want to get yourself warm, then you have to associate with fire, not with water, not with air. Similarly, if you want to spiritualize your vision, if you want to spiritualize your action, if you want to spiritualize the whole constitution of your existence, then you have to associate with the supreme spirit. And that supreme spirit is very kind because He is everything. That we have already explained. Everything is interrelated with the Supreme; therefore He is interrelated with sound also. So by God's inconceivable potency, He can be present before you in sound incarnation. That is His potency. He can do that. And therefore this name, Kṛṣṇa, and the Supreme Lord Kṛṣṇa, there is no difference.

(Lecture on the *Mahā-mantra*,
New York, September 8, 1966)

Always In Kṛṣṇa's Company

Since the Lord is absolute, there is no difference between His name and His actual form. In the material world there is a difference between form and name. The mango fruit is different from the name of the mango. One cannot taste the mango fruit simply by chanting "mango, mango, mango." But the devotee who knows that there is no difference between the name and the form of the Lord chants Hare Kṛṣṇa, Hare Kṛṣṇa, Kṛṣṇa Kṛṣṇa, Hare Hare/

Hare Rāma, Hare Rāma, Rāma Rāma, Hare Hare and realizes that he is always in Kṛṣṇa's company.

(*Kṛṣṇa,* "Prayers by the Demigods for Lord Kṛṣṇa in the Womb")

We Should Simply Cry

Kṛṣṇa is complete spirit and He's absolute, therefore His name is also spirit; His name, His form, His quality, His, I mean to say, opulence, His paraphernalia—everything is spiritual. But at the present moment, due to our material bondage or condition, we cannot understand what is spiritual. But this ignorance can be removed by this process, chanting Hare Kṛṣṇa. How it is? I'll give you example. Just like a man is sleeping. How you can awaken him? By vibration of sound. "Mr. such-and-such, just get up. Get up! The time is up." Although he is now practically unconscious, he cannot see, still, that hearing process is so prominent that a sleeping man can be awakened by vibration of sound. Similarly, the spirit soul, although it is now overpowered by this material bondage or material conditions, that spiritual consciousness can be revived by this transcendental vibration, Hare Kṛṣṇa, Hare Kṛṣṇa, Kṛṣṇa Kṛṣṇa, Hare Hare/ Hare Rāma, Hare Rāma, Rāma Rāma, Hare Hare.

Now, this is Sanskrit word. Some of you do not know what is the meaning of this Hare Kṛṣṇa. This meaning of Hare Kṛṣṇa, it is just addressing the Supreme Lord and His energy, Harā. Harā is the energy, and Kṛṣṇa is the Supreme Lord. So we are addressing, Hare Kṛṣṇa, Hare Kṛṣṇa: "O the energy of the Lord, O the Lord, please accept me." That's all. "Please accept me." We have no other prayer. "Please accept me." Lord Caitanya taught that we should simply cry, and we shall simply pray for accepting us. That's all. So this vibration is simply a cry for addressing the Supreme Lord, requesting Him, "Please accept me. Please accept me."

(Lecture on *Bhagavad-gītā* 8.21–22, New York, November 19, 1966)

That Is Spiritual Enjoyment

So the holy name of Kṛṣṇa is spiritual. You can get the same benefit by chanting the name as you get personally talking with Kṛṣṇa. That is also possible. But this will be gradually realized. As you chant the name of Hare Kṛṣṇa, so gradually you relish some transcendental pleasure. Just like these boys and girls, while chanting, they're dancing in joyfulness. They are not crazy fellows, that they're chanting. Actually, they're getting some pleasure, transcendental pleasure. Therefore they're dancing. It is not that it is dog-dance. No. It is really spiritual dance, the soul's dance. Therefore, He's called *rasa-vigraha,* reservoir of all pleasure.

There is contamination in the material world. Material, any name you chant, because it is materially contaminated, you cannot continue it for very long. This is another experience. But this chanting of Hare Kṛṣṇa mantra, if you go on chanting for twenty-four hours, you'll never feel fatigued. That is the test. You go on chanting. These boys can chant twenty-four hours, without eating anything, without drinking water. It is so nice. Because it is complete, spiritual, *śuddha. Śuddha* means pure. Not materially contaminated. Material pleasure, any pleasure, the highest pleasure in the material world is sex. But you cannot enjoy it twenty-four hours. That is not possible. You can enjoy it for few minutes. That's all. Even if you are forced to enjoy, you'll reject it: "No, no more." That is material. But spiritual means there is no end. You can enjoy perpetually, twenty-four hours. That is spiritual enjoyment.

(Lecture on *Bhagavad-gītā* 7.1, Uppsala University, Uppsala, September 8, 1973)

All Fear Is Vanished

This sound of the Lord is identical with the Lord, as we have tried to explain by the nondual position of the Lord. The material existence of our present status is full of fear. Out of the four problems of material existence, namely the food problem, the shelter problem, the fear problem and the mating problem, the fear problem gives us more trouble than the others. We are always fearful due to our ignorance of the next problem. The whole material existence is full of problems, and thus the fear problem is always prominent. This is due to our association with the illusory energy of the Lord, known as *māyā,* or external energy. Yet all fear is vanished as soon as there is the sound of the Lord, represented by His holy name, as it was sounded by Lord Śrī Caitanya Mahāprabhu in the following sixteen words: Hare Kṛṣṇa, Hare Kṛṣṇa, Kṛṣṇa Kṛṣṇa, Hare Hare/ Hare Rāma, Hare Rāma, Rāma Rāma, Hare Hare. We can take advantage of these sounds and be free from all threatening problems of material existence.

(*Śrīmad-Bhāgavatam* 1.11.3, Purport)

Grateful

Any person who is conscious of his friend's beneficent activities and never forgets his service is called grateful. The *mahā-mantra* (Hare Kṛṣṇa, Hare Kṛṣṇa, Kṛṣṇa Kṛṣṇa, Hare Hare/ Hare Rāma, Hare Rāma, Rāma Rāma, Hare Hare) is also simply an address to the Lord and His energy. So to anyone who is constantly engaged in addressing the Lord and His energy, we can imagine how much the Supreme Lord is obliged. It is impossible for the Lord to ever forget such a devotee. It is clearly stated in this verse that anyone who addresses the Lord immediately attracts the attention of the Lord, who always remains obliged to him.

(*The Nectar of Devotion,* "Qualities of Śrī Kṛṣṇa")

2
WHY DON'T YOU TRY IT?

This Mystic Meditation

He who meditates on Me as the Supreme Personality of Godhead, his mind constantly engaged in remembering Me, undeviated from the path, he, O Pārtha, is sure to reach Me.

PURPORT

In this verse Lord Kṛṣṇa stresses the importance of remembering Him. One's memory of Kṛṣṇa is revived by chanting the *mahā-*

mantra, Hare Kṛṣṇa. By this practice of chanting and hearing the sound vibration of the Supreme Lord, one's ear, tongue, and mind are engaged. This mystic meditation is very easy to practice, and it helps one attain the Supreme Lord.

(*Bhagavad-gītā* 8.8)

Simply and Melodiously

Hare Kṛṣṇa, Hare Kṛṣṇa, Kṛṣṇa Kṛṣṇa, Hare Hare/ Hare Rāma, Hare Rāma, Rāma Rāma, Hare Hare—these sixteen words. Anyone, any illiterate man or any rich man, any poor man or any man of any country, these sixteen words anyone can learn. You see? Hare Kṛṣṇa, Hare Kṛṣṇa, Kṛṣṇa Kṛṣṇa, Hare Hare/ Hare Rāma, Hare Rāma, Rāma Rāma, Hare Hare. And chant. Go on chanting it. There is no expenditure.

Suppose if you are moving on the street and if you go on chanting Hare Kṛṣṇa, Hare Kṛṣṇa, Kṛṣṇa Kṛṣṇa, Hare Hare/ Hare Rāma, Hare Rāma, Rāma Rāma, Hare Hare. There is no expenditure and there is no loss. Suppose you are sitting on the bus, on the car, for two hours. For two hours, if you go on chanting, "Hare Kṛṣṇa, Hare Kṛṣṇa," then tremendous result. So why don't you try it? There is no expenditure; there is no loss, neither loss of time, neither loss of money, neither loss of energy. There is no loss. Simply and melodiously, in a singing way, if you go on, "Hare Kṛṣṇa, Hare Kṛṣṇa, Kṛṣṇa Kṛṣṇa, Hare Hare/ Hare Rāma, Hare Rāma, Rāma Rāma, Hare Hare," you will be directly associating with the Supreme Lord.

Now, suppose, theoretically accepting that if I am directly associating with the Supreme Lord, then what else I want more? In the *Bhagavad-gītā* it is said, if you actually get the association of the Lord, then what else you have got to gain? You have got everything with you. So that is a fact. It is a question of realization only. And as soon as we get advanced in this chanting of this Hare Kṛṣṇa, Hare Kṛṣṇa, Kṛṣṇa Kṛṣṇa, Hare Hare, then we shall gradually realize that actually God is with us. God is dancing on my tongue in the form of sound.

(Lecture on *Bhagavad-gītā* 3.16–17, New York, May 25, 1966)

You Will Be Happy, You Will Be Prosperous

So if you take this advantage of Hare Kṛṣṇa, Hare Kṛṣṇa, Kṛṣṇa Kṛṣṇa, Hare Hare/ Hare Rāma, Hare Rāma, Rāma Rāma, Hare Hare, in whatever position you may be, you will never be unhappy. You will always be prosperous. So why don't you take this advantage? Be situated. Oh, you are medical practitioner? That's all right. You are engineer? That's all right. You are a clerk? That's all right. You are a real estate man? That's all right. Never mind whatever you are doing. Everyone has to do something to keep his body and soul together. That is the law of nature. So we may do whatever by God's grace, or by Nature we are situated. That doesn't matter. But if you take this formula, always think of Kṛṣṇa, then the result will be that you will never be unhappy. Just try. Make an experiment.

Why don't you try it? This is our mission. We don't say that you change your life. We simply say that in whatever position you are, you please chant. That's all. You please chant. You will be happy. You will be prosperous. Kṛṣṇa will be pleased upon you, and you will be never in scarcity. Is it not a very nice thing? You will never be unhappy. You will never be in scarcity. It is guaranteed here. Hare Kṛṣṇa, Hare Kṛṣṇa, Kṛṣṇa Kṛṣṇa, Hare Hare/ Hare Rāma, Hare Rāma, Rāma Rāma, Hare Hare. You will not be deviated from what you are doing, but at the same time, you will be able to hear this sound, transcendental sound vibration. So this is the formula given by the Lord Himself. Please try to follow it always. Always chant Hare Kṛṣṇa. There is no rule, no regulation. Never mind what you are doing. Simply chant and hear. We are anxious that everyone may take up this simple thing.

(Lecture on *Bhagavad-gītā* 9.22–23, New York, December 8, 1966)

The Easiest Type of Meditation

Devotee: What should you be thinking about when you're chanting? What do you think about when you're chanting?

Prabhupāda: Chanting? You simply hear. When you say "Hare Kṛṣṇa," you try to hear the very sound, "Hare Kṛṣṇa." That's all. Nothing more. This is meditation. Your tongue and your ear should be engaged in sounding this transcendental vibration, "Hare Kṛṣṇa." Best meditation. This is also accepted in *Bhagavad-gītā:* the best meditation. You don't keep your mind elsewhere. You keep your mind on the chanting, "Hare Kṛṣṇa," and hear. So this is responsive. When I was chanting, you were hearing; when you were chanting, I was hearing. So it is exchange. I hear your chanting, you hear my chanting. This is the process. So there is no possibility of thinking anything else. Best and the easiest type of meditation. Fully. Factual. You at once become on the transcendental plane. You see? So practice it and you'll see how spiritually you are making advancement. And it is very simple. When you are walking on the street, you can chant Hare Kṛṣṇa. There is not tax. There is no expenditure. There is no loss. But the gain is very great. Why don't you try it? If without any loss, without any expenditure, you gain something, the supermost sublime thing, spiritual realization, why don't you try for it? We are not asking any money. We are not asking $250 for paying for hearing. No. It is freely distributed. Please take it and try it. Make an experiment. There is no business here. You simply chant Hare Kṛṣṇa and try to hear the sound, that's all. Nothing more.

(Lecture on *Śrī Caitanya-caritāmṛta, Madhya-līlā* 6.254 / Los Angeles, January 8, 1968)

Powerful Beyond Our Conception

And if there is chanting of Hare Krishna, oh, he will hear and become advanced. This sound vibration is not material, it is spiritual, and powerful beyond our conception. So it cannot be hindered in any way by something material; it surpasses all these material barriers. So you can know it that when you are chanting, you are also giving benefit to even the child in the womb.

(Letter to Mukunda Dāsa and Janakī Devī Dāsī, February 28, 1968)

That Is Not Possible in This Age

So these things are not possible. Because our mind is so disturbed, we are engaged in so many outside work, it is not possible to concentrate. The so-called meditation going on in a class, that is not meditation. Meditation cannot be performed in that way. It must be in a very solitary place, sacred place, and you have to do it alone. You see? So these facilities are not available at the present age. Besides that, that meditation process will take you a very long time to realize yourself. So meditation is there in our process, but it is a very quick process. What is that? We loudly chant Hare Kṛṣṇa. So even if your mind is diverted to some other subject, you will be forced to hear Hare Kṛṣṇa. You have to apply your mind. Either you take it, "Oh, somebody is disturbing," or you are enjoying, you are forced to turn your mind to this side. And if we go on chanting for a short time, the meditation is always there. And with the dancing, the breathing is also there, but it is a shortcut policy. That policy, the yogic meditation or breathing exercise, *samādhi,* it is already there in our process. But we don't take in that prescribed way of meditation because that is not possible in this age. It is very difficult. So meditation and breathing exercise is not a part of our program, but it is automatically performed by this process of chanting Hare Kṛṣṇa, Hare Kṛṣṇa, Kṛṣṇa Kṛṣṇa, Hare Hare/ Hare Rāma, Hare Rāma, Rāma Rāma, Hare Hare. That is automatically done. It is such a nice process.

(Radio interview, San Francisco, March 9, 1968)

Just Try It and You Will Understand Everything

Fortunately we have got these instructions of *Bhagavad-gītā,* and the teacher is Lord Caitanya. If we follow these principles and try to understand it with all our knowledge, all our logic and argument, then our life is successful. Here is an opportunity, the movement of Kṛṣṇa consciousness. And it is very easy. You simply sit down. If you don't like to come to this temple, it doesn't matter. At your home, you sit down with your friends, with your boyfriend or girlfriend or family members, children. Sit down and chant Hare Kṛṣṇa. If you have got a nice musical instrument it is all right. Otherwise, God has given you these hands. You can clap, Hare Kṛṣṇa. Very easy. Just try it and you will understand everything gradually . . . God, the living entity, the material nature, the time, and the activities. If you can thoroughly study these five principles, then you become perfectly advanced in knowledge and your life is successful. And all this will be possible simply by this chanting Hare Kṛṣṇa.

(Lecture on *Bhagavad-gītā* 4.8, Montreal, June 14, 1968)

The Name Kṛṣṇa, or the Name Allah, Or the Name Jehovah

So anyone can take it by heart, these three words, and chant it. It is universal. Is it very difficult? It is not at all difficult. Lord Caitanya said that there are innumerable names of God according to different languages, different countries, different societies. And each and every one of them has the potency of God Himself. If there is any God, so God is Absolute. Therefore, there is no difference between His name and He Himself. Just like in the material world, in the world of duality there is difference between the name "water" and the substance water. The name "water" is different from the substance water. If you are thirsty, if you simply chant "water, water, water, water," your thirstiness will not be quenched. You require the substance water. That is material, but spiritually, the name Kṛṣṇa or the name Allah or the name Jehovah is as good as the Supreme Personality of Godhead.

(Public lecture, Montreal, June 15, 1968)

Just See the Result

Guest: How many minutes do you recommend a day? How many minutes do you chant?

Prabhupāda: Constantly, without any cessation. Is it very difficult? You can chant while you are walking in the street, "Hare Kṛṣṇa." Who checks you? There is no tax, there is no price, and if there is some gain, why don't you try it? If there is any gain by chanting Hare Kṛṣṇa, oh, it is better to give it a trial. We are not charging anything; the government is not taxing anything. You can chant: Hare Kṛṣṇa, Hare Kṛṣṇa, Kṛṣṇa Kṛṣṇa, Hare Hare/ Hare Rāma, Hare Rāma, Rāma Rāma, Hare Hare. Just see the result. At least for one week you chant. It is very nice thing. One does not require to be highly educated or very rich or very beautiful or very famous. No. Anyone. Anyone. Simply God has given us this tongue, we can vibrate nicely. Chant Hare Kṛṣṇa, just see the result. Yes. So our only appeal to you, all people of the world, that we are embarrassed with so many problems. So we say this is the only solution. There is no price; there is no tax; there is no, I mean to say, imposition of previous qualifications. Simply chant Hare Kṛṣṇa. This is our propaganda. And see the result. So we request everyone to chant this transcendental vibration and see the result. There is no question that you have to change your religion, you have to change your dress, change your occupation. No. Simply go on chanting.

(Lecture on *Śrīmad-Bhāgavatam* 7.9.10, Montreal, July 9, 1968)

What Is That Test?

These are some of the practical examples. There are persons who criticize the chanting of Hare Kṛṣṇa mantra. Because the glories of the holy name are described here, sometimes those who are not in the line, they think, "It is too much. It is too much." So it is advised, "No, it is not too much. You can test it." Test it. What is that test? When you fall down from a high place. Suppose from the roof you may fall down, you may slip and fall down. By falling down you may break your bones. Or you may be bitten by some animal—cats, dogs, a snake. There are so many, domestic. Or you may be burned or you may be injured by others. Then during this time you can test, practical. What is that test? Try to chant Hare Kṛṣṇa. If anyone does so, you'll immediately feel that from the injuries you are not feeling pain. This is practical. Even from a snakebite you may be saved. The author never says that you may be saved from death, but the suggestion is that you may not feel much pain. This is practical.

(*Śrīmad-Bhāgavatam* 6.2.15, Vṛndāvana, September 18, 1975)

Your Heart Is Hankering After So Many Pleasures

So we are praying to the energy of the Supreme Lord and the Supreme Lord, "Please pick me up. Please pick me up. I am in this bodily concept of life. I am in this material existence. I am suffering. Please pick me up to the spiritual platform so that I will be happy." Because, as I explained just a minute before, as soon as you come to the transcendental platform, you become joyful, happy. That is the sign.

So our request—that you give a try. You simply chant at home or anywhere. There is no restriction that "You have to chant this Hare Kṛṣṇa mantra in such-and-such place, in such-and-such condition." There is no restriction of time and, I mean to say, circumstances or atmosphere. Anywhere, at any time, you can meditate. No meditation is possible while you are walking on the street. But this meditation is possible: Hare Kṛṣṇa, Hare Kṛṣṇa, Kṛṣṇa Kṛṣṇa, Hare Hare/ Hare Rāma, Hare Rāma, Rāma Rāma, Hare Hare. And go on with your work. You are working with your hands? You can chant Hare Kṛṣṇa, Hare Kṛṣṇa, Kṛṣṇa Kṛṣṇa, Hare Hare. So this is very nice. So kindly accept this Kṛṣṇa consciousness movement. At the same time, Lord Caitanya Mahāprabhu says that the Lord's name is not limited with Kṛṣṇa. Kṛṣṇa is the perfect name. Kṛṣṇa means all-attractive. And Rāma means the supreme pleasure. So if God is not all-attractive and supreme pleasure, then what is the meaning of God? God must be. He must be the supreme pleasure. Otherwise how you can be satisfied with Him? Your heart is hankering after so many, so many pleasures. If God cannot satisfy you with all the pleasures, Rāma, then how can He be God? Therefore these two names, Rāma and Kṛṣṇa, all-attractive. If Kṛṣṇa cannot be attractive to any person, then how can He be God? He is attractive, actually.

We are chanting Hare Kṛṣṇa. So if you think, "Oh, this is Indian name. This is Hindu name. Why shall we chant? Why shall I chant the Hindu name . . . ?" There are some sectarian people, they may think like that. But Lord Caitanya says, "It doesn't matter. If you have got any bona fide name of God, you chant that. But you chant God's name." That is the prescription of this movement. And do not think that this movement is a proselytizing movement from Christian to Hindu, or Hindu to . . . No. You remain Christian, Hindu, Jew, or Mohammedan. It doesn't matter. Our process is that if you are ready to perfect your human form of life, then try to learn, develop your dormant love of Godhead. That is perfection of life. You profess any type of religion—then just test whether your religion is perfect or you are perfect, whether you have developed your love for God more than any other love. We have distributed our love in so many things. When all that love will be concentrated simply on God, that is perfection of life. Love is there, but because we do not know, because we have forgotten our relationship with God, therefore we are imposing our love on dog. That has been our disease.

So we have to transfer our love from so many dogs to God. That is the perfection of life. And we are not teaching any particular type of religion. We are simply teaching that you love God. And this is possible simply by chanting these three names: Hare, Kṛṣṇa, and Rāma. Rāma means the supreme pleasure, Kṛṣṇa means all-attractive, and Hare means the energy. Then it is perfect.

(Lecture at Northeastern University, Boston, April 30, 1969)

Painting by Pāṇḍu Dāsa

3

That Will Solve All the Problems

Come Back Home, Back to Godhead

In the beginning of creation, the Lord of all creatures sent forth generations of men and demigods, along with sacrifices for Viṣṇu, and blessed them by saying, "Be thou happy by this *yajña* [sacrifice] because its performance will bestow upon you everything desirable for living happily and achieving liberation."

PURPORT

The material creation by the Lord of creatures (Viṣṇu) is a chance offered to the conditioned souls to come back home—back to

Godhead. All living entities within the material creation are conditioned by material nature because of their forgetfulness of their relationship to Viṣṇu, or Kṛṣṇa, the Supreme Personality of Godhead. The Vedic principles are to help us understand this eternal relation, as it is stated in the *Bhagavad-gītā: vedaiś ca sarvair aham eva vedyaḥ.* The Lord says that the purpose of the *Vedas* is to understand Him.

The Lord created this material world to enable the conditioned souls to learn how to perform *yajñas* (sacrifices) for the satisfaction of Viṣṇu, so that while in the material world they can live very comfortably without anxiety, and after finishing the present material body they can enter into the kingdom of God. That is the whole program for the conditioned soul. By performance of *yajña,* the conditioned souls gradually become Kṛṣṇa conscious and become godly in all respects. In the Age of Kali, the *saṅkīrtana-yajña* (the chanting of the names of God) is recommended by the Vedic scriptures, and this transcendental system was introduced by Lord Caitanya for the deliverance of all men in this age. *Saṅkīrtana-yajña* and Kṛṣṇa consciousness go well together. Lord Kṛṣṇa in His devotional form (as Lord Caitanya) is mentioned in the *Śrīmad-Bhāgavatam* as follows, with special reference to the *saṅkīrtana-yajña:* "In this Age of Kali, people who are endowed with sufficient intelligence will worship the Lord, who is accompanied by His associates, by performance of *saṅkīrtana-yajña.*" Other *yajñas* prescribed in the Vedic literatures are not easy to perform in this Age of Kali, but the *saṅkīrtana-yajña* is easy and sublime for all purposes.

(*Bhagavad-gītā* 3.10)

We Are Searching After That Joyfulness

Thank you very much for coming here and participating in this great movement known as the Hare Kṛṣṇa saṅkīrtana movement. This *saṅkīrtana* movement was started five hundred years ago by Lord Caitanya Mahāprabhu in India, in the state of West Bengal, in the district of Nadia. His mission was that this Hare Kṛṣṇa movement, or God consciousness, should be spread all over the world. As many towns and villages as there are on the surface of the globe, this Hare Kṛṣṇa movement would be spread all over. His prediction is now being carried out by some of the devotees, and you may kindly take advantage of this movement.

The purpose of this movement is to cleanse the heart. We have created so many problems in our life simply on the platform of misunderstanding. Therefore this movement is meant for cleansing the misunderstanding of the heart. What is that misunderstanding? The misunderstanding is that we are accepting this material body as the self. We are all living entities, spirit souls, encaged in this material body. We are transmigrating from one body to another. There are 8,400,000 species of life, and this human form of life is the greatest opportunity for self-realization. Self-realization means to know that "I am not this body. I am spirit soul. I am part and parcel of God." God is by nature joyful. Therefore, as we are part and parcel of God, our aim of life is joy. We are searching after that joyfulness within this material world, but that is not possible. Just like a fish, if it is taken from the water and put on the land, in any condition the fish will never feel joyfulness. Similarly, we are spirit souls. Somehow or other, we have come in contact with this material world. Therefore in this material world we cannot have joyfulness. This material world is not befitting our spiritual self. Spiritual self requires spiritual joy. That is beyond these material senses. Therefore this Kṛṣṇa consciousness movement is meant for clearing or cleansing or purifying the senses. As soon as we purify our senses, then actually we can enjoy our spiritual sense enjoyment.

At the present moment, on account of our ignorance, or in ignorance of our self-realization, we are thinking in relationship with this body. I am born in India, so I am thinking, "I am Indian." You are born in England; therefore you are thinking, "Englishmen." Or another is thinking some other thing. But actually, we are neither Indian nor Englishmen nor Japanese nor German. We are spirit soul, part and parcel of God. Therefore, that is self-realization. Unless we realize our self, all activities that we are enacting, they are meant for our defeat.

Therefore, practically we see that in spite of advancement of education, in spite of economic development, in spite of so many philosophical speculations, we are in the same problematic atmosphere. That is the defect of the present civilization, because they do not know what we are. We are spirit soul. So we must realize. And five thousand years ago, the Lord Himself, Lord Kṛṣṇa, spoke the philosophy, or the knowledge in the *Bhagavad-gītā.* We are publishing all these literatures translated into English and other languages. If you want to read them, if you want to understand this scientific, spiritual movement through your scientific knowledge, philosophical speculation, we have got dozens of books. You can read them and you can understand them. Otherwise, it is very simple method. You can simply chant this Hare Kṛṣṇa *mahā-mantra.* It is only sixteen words: Hare Kṛṣṇa, Hare Kṛṣṇa, Kṛṣṇa Kṛṣṇa, Hare Hare/ Hare Rāma, Hare Rāma, Rāma Rāma, Hare Hare.

So there is no expenditure. If you chant Hare Kṛṣṇa mantra, there is no loss on your part, neither we are charging anything. We are distributing this *mahā-mantra* free of charges, and anyone can chant. There is no difficulty. We are spreading this movement all over the world. So our only request is that in whatever condition you may be, it doesn't matter, please try to chant these sixteen words whenever you have got time. You have got enough time. You can chant Hare Kṛṣṇa mantra when you are walking on the street, when you are traveling in the bus, or when you are sitting alone. There is no loss, but the gain is very great. Therefore our only request is that you take this *mahā-mantra:* Hare Kṛṣṇa, Hare Kṛṣṇa, Kṛṣṇa Kṛṣṇa, Hare Hare/ Hare Rāma, Hare Rāma, Rāma Rāma, Hare Hare.

So this movement is a very important movement. We are trying to educate people how to transfer one from this world of darkness to the world of light. Take advantage of this opportunity and make your life successful.

(Ratha-yātrā festival / London, July 13, 1972)

These Four Things Will Make One Happy

The best process for making the home pleasant is Kṛṣṇa consciousness. If one is in full Kṛṣṇa consciousness, he can make his home very happy, because this process of Kṛṣṇa consciousness is very easy. One need only chant Hare Kṛṣṇa, Hare Kṛṣṇa, Kṛṣṇa Kṛṣṇa, Hare Hare/ Hare Rāma, Hare Rāma, Rāma Rāma, Hare Hare, accept the remnants of foodstuffs offered to Kṛṣṇa, have some discussion on books like *Bhagavad-gītā* and *Śrīmad-Bhāgavatam,* and engage oneself in Deity worship. These four things will make one happy. One should train the members of his family in this way. The family members can sit down morning and evening and chant together Hare Kṛṣṇa, Hare Kṛṣṇa, Kṛṣṇa Kṛṣṇa, Hare Hare/ Hare Rāma, Hare Rāma, Rāma Rāma, Hare Hare. If one can mold his family life in this way to develop Kṛṣṇa consciousness, following these four principles, then there is no need to change from family life to renounced life.

(*Bhagavad-gītā* 13.10, purport)

So I Cannot Give You
Any Better Advice for Your Problem

Lord Sri Chaitanya Mahaprabhu, the incarnation of Godhead in this age has delivered the medicine for all problems of the world by His introducing the Sankirtan movement. Sankirtan means to chant the Holy names of the Lord and to give up all other engagements. The chanting is a process of purification. Just like we use soap to cleanse the body, this is material, but the chanting is spiritual cleansing. The three stages of cleansing are first to clean the mirror of the mind. In the Bhagavad Gita it is said, "The mind is the best friend and the worst enemy. For one who has learned to control the mind it is the best of friends but for one who has failed to do so it is the worst enemy." Due to long term association, the mind absorbed in material things has become contaminated, or dirty, the chanting process purifies the mind.

Then the next stage, when the mind is cleansed one becomes free from the symptoms of material existence. Material existence means to be always hankering and lamenting. I must have a new automobile, I must have more money, I must have good wife, I must have this, I must have that. Then when I have the thing, I lament, I have lost my wife, I have lost my money, I have lost my car, simply lamenting. So the second stage is to be free from this anxiety.

The third stage is: "He never laments nor desires to have anything; he is equally disposed to every living entity. In that state he attains pure devotional service unto me." (*Bg.* 18.54)

The next verse continues, "And when one is in full consciousness of the Supreme Lord by such devotion, he can enter into the kingdom of God." It is further stated in the *Gita* that when one is so situated even in the midst of greatest danger he is not disturbed. In other words when one has achieved perfection in chanting the Holy name of God he is always joyful, even death does not disturb him, what to speak of other things.

The conclusion is that one should learn the art of chanting the Holy name of Krishna 24 hours a day and that alone is the remedy for all problems of material existence. How is it possible to chant 24 hours a day? Lord Chaitanya gave the hint, "One can chant the holy name of God in a humble state of mind, thinking himself lower than the straw in the street, more tolerant than a tree, devoid of all kinds of sense of false prestige, and always ready to offer all respects to others. In such a humble state of mind one can chant the Holy name of God constantly."

So I cannot give you any better advice for your problem, simply chant Hare Krishna and everything will be all right.

(Letter to Susan Beckman, August 29, 1973)

If the Surface of the Globe Is Overflooded with the Chanting

The Kṛṣṇa consciousness movement has started performing *saṅkīrtana-yajña* in different places, and it has been experienced that wherever *saṅkīrtana-yajña* is performed, many thousands of people gather and take part in it. Imperceptible auspiciousness achieved in this connection should be continued all over the world. The members of the Kṛṣṇa consciousness movement should perform *saṅkīrtana-yajñas* one after another, so much that all the people of the world will either jokingly or seriously chant Hare Kṛṣṇa, Hare Kṛṣṇa, Kṛṣṇa Kṛṣṇa, Hare Hare/ Hare Rāma, Hare Rāma, Rāma Rāma, Hare Hare, and thus they will derive the benefit of cleansing the heart. The holy name of the Lord (*harer nāma*) is so powerful that whether it is chanted jokingly or seriously the effect of vibrating this transcendental sound will be equally distributed. It is not possible at the present moment to perform repeated *yajñas* as Mahārāja Barhiṣat performed, but it is within our means to perform *saṅkīrtana-yajña,* which does not cost anything. One can sit down anywhere and chant Hare Kṛṣṇa, Hare Kṛṣṇa, Kṛṣṇa Kṛṣṇa, Hare Hare/ Hare Rāma, Hare Rāma, Rāma Rāma, Hare Hare. If the surface of the globe is overflooded with the chanting of the Hare Kṛṣṇa mantra, the people of the world will be very, very happy.

(*Śrīmad-Bhāgavatam* 4.24.10, purport)

He Was Never Distressed, But Always Happy

Everyone in this material world is distressed by miserable

conditions, but Śrīla Prabodhānanda Sarasvatī says that this world is full of happiness. How is this possible? He answers, a devotee accepts the distress of this material world as happiness only due to the causeless mercy of Śrī Caitanya Mahāprabhu. By His personal behavior, Śrī Caitanya Mahāprabhu showed that He was never distressed, but always happy in chanting the Hare Kṛṣṇa *mahā-mantra*. One should follow in the footsteps of Śrī Caitanya Mahāprabhu and engage constantly in chanting the *mahā-mantra*—Hare Kṛṣṇa, Hare Kṛṣṇa, Kṛṣṇa Kṛṣṇa, Hare Hare/ Hare Rāma, Hare Rāma, Rāma Rāma, Hare Hare. Then he will never feel the distresses of the world of duality. In any condition of life one will be happy if he chants the holy name of the Lord.

(*Śrīmad-Bhāgavatam* 6.17.30, purport)

Seeing the Supreme Personality of Godhead Directly

The vibration of the Lord's voice appeared in the presence of all the devotees, and although the person vibrating the sound was unseen to them, they were meeting or seeing the Lord because they were offering prayers and because the vibration of the Lord was present. Contrary to the laws of the material world, there is no difference between seeing the Lord, offering prayers and hearing the transcendental vibration. Pure devotees, therefore, are fully satisfied by glorifying the Lord. Such glorification is called *kīrtana*. Performing *kīrtana* and hearing the vibration of the sound Hare Kṛṣṇa is actually seeing the Supreme Personality of Godhead directly.

(*Śrīmad-Bhāgavatam* 7.4.26, purport)

There Is One Chance, One Opportunity

Now is the time to invoke the mode of goodness of the living enti-

ties who have accepted material bodies. The mode of goodness is meant to establish the Supreme Lord's rule, which will maintain the existence of the creation. Therefore, this is the opportune moment to take shelter of the Supreme Personality of Godhead. Because He is naturally very kind and dear to the demigods, He will certainly bestow good fortune upon us.

PURPORT

The material world is conducted by the three modes of nature, namely *sattva-guṇa, rajo-guṇa,* and *tamo-guṇa.* By *rajo-guṇa* [passion] everything material is created, by *sattva-guṇa* [goodness] everything material is maintained properly, and by *tamo-guṇa* [ignorance], when the creation is improperly situated, everything is destroyed.

From this verse we can understand the situation of Kali-yuga, through which we are now passing. Just before the beginning of Kali-yuga—or, in other words, at the end of Dvāpara-yuga—Lord Śrī Kṛṣṇa appeared and left His instructions in the form of *Bhagavad-gītā,* in which He asked all living entities to surrender unto Him. Since the beginning of Kali-yuga, however, people have practically been unable to surrender to the lotus feet of Kṛṣṇa, and therefore, after some five thousand years, Kṛṣṇa came again as Śrī Caitanya Mahāprabhu just to teach the entire world how to surrender unto Him, unto Śrī Kṛṣṇa, and thus be purified.

Surrendering unto the lotus feet of Kṛṣṇa means achieving complete purification. Kṛṣṇa says in *Bhagavad-gītā* (18.66): "Abandon all varieties of religion and just surrender unto Me. I shall deliver you from all sinful reaction. Do not fear." Thus as soon as one surrenders unto the lotus feet of Kṛṣṇa, one certainly becomes free from all contamination.

Kali-yuga is full of contamination. This is described in the *Śrīmad-Bhāgavatam* (12.3.51): This age of Kali is full of unlimited faults. Indeed, it is just like an ocean of faults (*doṣa-nidhi*). But there is one chance, one opportunity. *Kīrtanād eva kṛṣṇasya mukta-saṅgaḥ paraṁ vrajet:* simply by chanting the Hare Kṛṣṇa mantra, one can be freed from the contamination of Kali-yuga and, in his original spiritual body, can return home, back to Godhead. This is the opportunity of Kali-yuga.

When Kṛṣṇa appeared, He gave His orders, and when Kṛṣṇa Himself appeared as a devotee, as Śrī Caitanya Mahāprabhu, He showed us the path by which to cross the ocean of Kali-yuga. That is the path of the Hare Kṛṣṇa movement. When Śrī Caitanya Mahāprabhu appeared, He ushered in the era for the *saṅkīrtana* movement. It is also said that for ten thousand years this era will continue. This means that simply by accepting the *saṅkīrtana* movement and chanting the Hare Kṛṣṇa *mahā-mantra,* the fallen souls of this Kali-yuga will be delivered. After the Battle of Kurukṣetra, at which *Bhagavad-gītā* was spoken, Kali-yuga continues for 432,000 years, of which only 5,000 years have passed. Thus there is still a balance of 427,000 years to come. Of these 427,000 years, the 10,000 years of the *saṅkīrtana* movement inaugurated by Śrī Caitanya Mahāprabhu 500 years ago provide the opportunity for the fallen souls of Kali-yuga to take to the Kṛṣṇa consciousness movement, chant the Hare Kṛṣṇa *mahā-mantra* and thus be delivered from the clutches of material existence and return home, back to Godhead.

Chanting of the Hare Kṛṣṇa *mahā-mantra* is potent always, but it is especially potent in this age of Kali. Therefore Śukadeva Gosvāmī, while instructing Mahārāja Parīkṣit, stressed this chanting of the Hare Kṛṣṇa mantra: "My dear King, although Kali-yuga is full of faults, there is still one good quality about this age. It is that simply by chanting the Hare Kṛṣṇa *mahā-mantra,* one can become free from material bondage and be promoted to the transcendental kingdom." (*Bhāg.* 12.3.51) Those who have accepted the task of spreading the Hare Kṛṣṇa *mahā-mantra* in full Kṛṣṇa consciousness should take this opportunity to deliver people very easily from the clutches of material existence. Our duty, therefore, is to follow the instructions of Śrī Caitanya Mahāprabhu and preach the Kṛṣṇa consciousness movement all over the world very sincerely. This is the best welfare activity for the peace and prosperity of human society.

Śrī Caitanya Mahāprabhu's movement consists of spreading *kṛṣṇa-saṅkīrtana. Paraṁ vijayate śrī-kṛṣṇa-saṅkīrtanam:* "All glories to the Śrī Kṛṣṇa *saṅkīrtana*!" Why is it so glorious? This has also been explained by Śrī Caitanya Mahāprabhu. *Ceto-darpaṇa-mārjanam:* by the chanting of the Hare Kṛṣṇa *mahā-mantra,* one's heart is cleansed.

(*Śrīmad-Bhāgavatam* 8.5.23)

Either You Work Hard or Not Hard, It Doesn't Matter

That is the nature of this material world. You think that by simply working hard you will be very happy. That is not possible. You can simply work hard—you will get whatever you are destined to get, either you work hard or not hard. It doesn't matter. In the material world, there are two things: something gained and something lost. So gain or loss, you will get it as you are destined. Every one of us, we are destined to certain extent of gain and certain extent of loss. That is destined. So therefore *śāstra* says, "Don't try for this destined gain or loss. You are working so hard to make some gain. Even if you do not work hard, you will get that gain. Don't try for it. Better utilize the time for chanting Hare Kṛṣṇa." That is the injunction of *śāstra.*

So Prahlāda Mahārāja recommends that there are so many processes how to get out of this material world, but Prahlāda Mahārāja and all the devotees, especially Caitanya Mahāprabhu, He has recommended that "Chant Hare Kṛṣṇa." And that you benefit. Very easy, you take it and chant it sincerely, without any offense. So we are so fallen, it is not possible to execute all these processes. Therefore Caitanya Mahāprabhu is the mercy incarnation, that "These people, so fallen, they cannot do anything." So

He has recommended a simple thing—chant Hare Kṛṣṇa, Hare Kṛṣṇa, Kṛṣṇa Kṛṣṇa, Hare Hare/ Hare Rāma, Hare Rāma, Rāma Rāma, Hare Hare.

(Lecture on *Śrīmad-Bhāgavatam* 7.9.46, Vṛndāvana, April 1, 1976)

This Is the Instruction by the Supreme Person, The Original Person, the Origin of Everything

So Kṛṣṇa is the Supreme Personality of Godhead, Īśvara. He's teaching us this *yajña*. He's giving us the hint. If you do not accept this movement, then you'll go on suffering, suffering, suffering, suffering. If you don't accept this principle, then your future is simply suffering. This is the symptom of Kali-yuga. *Manda-bhāgyāḥ,* all unfortunate. All unfortunate. Everyone must suffer. This is the position. But if you chant Hare Kṛṣṇa *mahā-mantra,* perform the *yajña* ... Because this is the instruction by the Supreme Person, the original person, the origin of everything, the Supreme Person from whom everything has come down. That is the order. So Caitanya Mahāprabhu taught us that *harer nāma harer nāma harer nāmaiva kevala*.... We are certainly in a difficult position. But the only remedy is that we must chant the holy name of the Lord repeatedly. And that will solve all the problems.

(Lecture on *Śrīmad-Bhāgavatam* 1.8.18, Māyāpur, September 28, 1974)

Painting by Rāmanātha Dāsa

4

AND THE TIGER BEGAN TO DANCE

Immediately Enthuse Your Ecstasy

This Kṛṣṇa consciousness movement is the greatest welfare activity in the human society. We are giving information to every man, without any discrimination of cast, creed, or color, that every human being especially, not only human beings, but all living entities, including the animals, beasts, birds, trees, aquatics—everyone—they can achieve to the highest perfection of life by this Kṛṣṇa consciousness. But especially the extra intelligence of the human being can be utilized to realize Kṛṣṇa. If we don't do that, we are missing a great opportunity. So our request to everyone is to understand this philosophy of Kṛṣṇa consciousness. If anyone wants to understand this philosophy through philosophical angle of vision or scientific angle of vision, we have got immense volumes of books. You can read and try to understand what is this great movement, Kṛṣṇa consciousness. But you can also, without reading books, without taking any trouble, if you simply agree to chant this *mahā-mantra,* Hare Kṛṣṇa, Hare Kṛṣṇa, Kṛṣṇa Kṛṣṇa, Hare Hare/ Hare Rāma, Hare Rāma, Rāma Rāma, Hare Hare, you get the same result. Even a child can join. Actually we have experienced that a child, a dog, an animal, everyone takes part in this movement. During the time of Lord Caitanya's movement, when He passed through a great forest known as Jhārikhaṇḍa in central India—there is a great forest—along with Him, the tigers, the elephants, the deers, everyone danced and chanted Hare Kṛṣṇa mantra. It is so nice and it is so spiritual, the very vibration will immediately enthuse your ecstasy in spiritual consciousness. Please, therefore, take to this chanting of the Hare Kṛṣṇa mantra.

(Ratha-yātrā festival, San Francisco, June 27, 1971)

Lord Caitanya's Chanting in Jhārikhaṇḍa Forest

Actually, when Caitanya Mahāprabhu passed through the forest known as Jhārikhaṇḍa in central India, He was only accompanied by His personal attendant, and when He was passing through the forest He touched one tiger. The tiger was sleeping, and the tiger answered roaring. So Caitanya Mahāprabhu's attendant, he thought, "Now we are gone." But actually, Caitanya Mahāprabhu asked the tiger, "Why you are sleeping? Just stand up. Chant Hare Kṛṣṇa.'" And the tiger began to dance. So actually, this happened. When Caitanya Mahāprabhu preached this Hare Kṛṣṇa movement, the tigers, the deers, everyone joined. So, of course, we are not so powerful, we may not attempt such great risk. Caitanya Mahāprabhu could induce tigers to dance, so we can at least induce every human being to dance. This is such a nice movement.

So even the stone-hearted man, he also melts by chanting Hare Kṛṣṇa. That we have experienced, seen. Simply by hearing the transcendental pastimes and characteristics of Lord

Caitanya, even hard-hearted men, they also melted. There were many instances such as Jagāi and Mādhāi. Many fallen souls, they became elevated to the highest spiritual platform. Actually, this Kṛṣṇa consciousness movement, *saṅkīrtana* movement, is so nice and attractive. That is the verdict of *Brahma-saṁhitā. Brahma-saṁhitā* says one who takes to this devotional life, his reactions of past deeds are adjusted immediately. So every one of us should take part in this movement of Kṛṣṇa consciousness by chanting Hare Kṛṣṇa, Hare Kṛṣṇa, Kṛṣṇa Kṛṣṇa, Hare Hare/ Hare Rāma, Hare Rāma, Rāma Rāma, Hare Hare.

(Lecture on "*Parama Karuṇa,*" Los Angeles, January 16, 1969)

The Elephants Began to Chant "Kṛṣṇa! Kṛṣṇa!" And Dance and Sing in Ecstasy

When the Lord passed through the solitary forest chanting the holy name of Kṛṣṇa, the tigers and elephants, seeing Him, gave way.

When the Lord passed through the jungle in great ecstasy, packs of tigers, elephants, rhinoceros, and boars came, and the Lord passed right through them.

Balabhadra Bhaṭṭācārya was very much afraid to see them, but by Śrī Caitanya Mahāprabhu's influence, all the animals stood to one side.

One day a tiger was lying on the path, and Śrī Caitanya Mahāprabhu, walking along the path in ecstatic love, touched the tiger with His feet.

The Lord said, "Chant the holy name of Kṛṣṇa!" The tiger immediately got up and began to dance and to chant "Kṛṣṇa! Kṛṣṇa!"

Another day, while Śrī Caitanya Mahāprabhu was bathing in a river, a herd of maddened elephants came there to drink water.

While the Lord was bathing and murmuring the Gāyatrī mantra, the elephants came before Him. The Lord immediately

splashed some water on the elephants and asked them to chant the name of Kṛṣṇa.

The elephants whose bodies were touched by the water splashed by the Lord began to chant "Kṛṣṇa! Kṛṣṇa!" and dance and sing in ecstasy.

Some of the elephants fell to the ground, and some screamed in ecstasy. Seeing this, Balabhadra Bhaṭṭācārya was completely astonished.

Sometimes Śrī Caitanya Mahāprabhu chanted very loudly while passing through the jungle. Hearing His sweet voice, all the does came near Him.

Hearing the Lord's great vibration, all the does followed Him left and right. While reciting a verse with great curiosity, the Lord patted them.

"Blessed are all these foolish deer because they have approached Mahārāja Nanda's son [Kṛṣṇa], who is gorgeously dressed and is playing on His flute. Indeed, both the does and the bucks worship the Lord with looks of love and affection."

While Śrī Caitanya Mahāprabhu was passing through the jungle, five or seven tigers came. Joining the deer, the tigers began to follow the Lord.

Seeing the tigers and deer following Him, Śrī Caitanya Mahāprabhu immediately remembered the land of Vṛndāvana. He then began to recite a verse describing the transcendental quality of Vṛndāvana.

"Vṛndāvana is the transcendental abode of the Lord. There is no hunger, anger, or thirst there. Though naturally inimical, human beings and fierce animals live together there in transcendental friendship."

When Śrī Caitanya Mahāprabhu said "Chant 'Kṛṣṇa! Kṛṣṇa!'" the tigers and deer began to chant "Kṛṣṇa!" and dance.

When all the tigers and does danced and jumped, Balabhadra Bhaṭṭācārya saw them and was struck with wonder.

Indeed, the tigers and deer began to embrace one another, and touching mouths, they began to kiss.

When Śrī Caitanya Mahāprabhu saw all this fun, He began to smile. Finally He left the animals and continued on His way.

Various birds, including the peacock, saw Śrī Caitanya Mahāprabhu and began to follow Him, chanting and dancing. They were all maddened by the holy name of Kṛṣṇa.

When the Lord loudly chanted "Haribol!" the trees and creepers became jubilant to hear Him.

PURPORT

The loud chanting of the Hare Kṛṣṇa mantra is so powerful that it can even penetrate the ears of trees and creepers, what to speak of those of animals and human beings. Śrī Caitanya Mahāprabhu once asked Haridāsa Ṭhākura how trees and plants could be delivered, and Haridāsa Ṭhākura replied that the loud chanting of the Hare Kṛṣṇa *mahā-mantra* would benefit not only trees and plants but insects and all other living beings. One should therefore not be disturbed by the loud chanting of Hare Kṛṣṇa, for it is beneficial not only to the chanter but to everyone who gets an opportunity to hear.

Thus all living entities in the forest of Jhārikhaṇḍa—some moving and some standing still—became maddened by hearing the holy name of Lord Kṛṣṇa vibrated by Śrī Caitanya Mahāprabhu.

In all the villages through which the Lord passed and in all the places He rested on His journey, everyone was purified and awakened to ecstatic love of God.

(*Śrī Caitanya-caritāmṛta, Madhya-līlā* 17.25–47)

Be Ready to Receive the Transcendental Gift

The understanding of Kṛṣṇa consciousness is innate in every living entity, and it is already developed to some extent when the living entity takes a human body. It is said in *Caitanya-caritāmṛita* (*Madhya-līlā* 22.107):

nitya-siddha kṛṣṇa-prema 'sādhya' kabhu naya
śravaṇādi-śuddha-citte karaye udaya

"Pure love for Kṛṣṇa is eternally established in the hearts of living entities. It is not something to be gained from another source. When the heart is purified by hearing and chanting, the living entity naturally awakens." Since Kṛṣṇa consciousness is inherent in every living entity, everyone should be given a chance to hear about Kṛṣṇa. Simply by hearing and chanting—*śravaṇaṁ kīrtanaṁ*—one's heart is directly purified, and one's original Kṛṣṇa consciousness is immediately awakened. Kṛṣṇa consciousness is not artificially imposed upon the heart; it is already there. When one chants the holy name of the Supreme Personality of Godhead, the heart is cleansed of all mundane contamination. In the first stanza of His *Śrī Śikṣāṣṭaka*, Lord Śrī Caitanya Mahāprabhu says:

"All glories to the Śrī Kṛṣṇa *saṅkīrtana*, which cleanses the heart of all the dust accumulated for years and extinguishes the fire of conditional life, of repeated birth and death. This *saṅkīrtana* movement is the prime benediction for humanity at large because it spreads the rays of the benediction moon. It is the life of all transcendental knowledge. It increases the ocean of transcendental bliss, and it enables us to fully taste the nectar for which we are always anxious."

Not only is the chanter of the *mahā-mantra* purified, but the heart of anyone who happens to hear the transcendental vibration of Hare Kṛṣṇa, Hare Kṛṣṇa, Kṛṣṇa Kṛṣṇa, Hare Hare/ Hare Rāma, Hare Rāma, Rāma Rāma, Hare Hare is also cleansed. Even the souls embodied in lower animals, insects, trees and other species of life also become purified and prepared to become fully Kṛṣṇa conscious simply by hearing the transcendental vibration. This was explained by Ṭhākura Haridāsa when Caitanya Mahāprabhu inquired from him how living entities lower than human beings can be delivered from material bondage. Haridāsa Ṭhākura said that the chanting of the holy names is so powerful that even if one chants in the remotest parts of the jungle, the trees and animals will advance in Kṛṣṇa consciousness simply by hearing the vibration. This was actually proved by Śrī Caitanya Mahāprabhu Himself when He passed through the forest of Jhārikhaṇḍa. At that time the tigers, snakes, deer, and all other animals abandoned their natural animosity and began chanting and dancing in *saṅkīrtana*. Of course, we cannot imitate the activities of Śrī Caitanya Mahāprabhu, but we should follow in His footsteps. We are not powerful enough to enchant the lower animals such as tigers, snakes, cats, and dogs or entice them to dance, but by chanting the holy names of the Lord we can actually convert many people throughout the world to Kṛṣṇa consciousness. Contributing or distributing the holy name of the Lord is a sublime example of contributing or giving charity (the *dadāti* principle). By the same token, one must also follow the *pratigṛhṇāti* principle and be willing and ready to receive the transcendental gift.

(*The Nectar of Instruction,* text 4, purport)

5

JAPA MEDITATION

HOW TO CHANT

We Capture Each Bead and Chant

Kṛṣṇa consciousness movement means we are teaching our disciples how to think of Kṛṣṇa twenty-four hours. This is Kṛṣṇa consciousness. And the simple method is to chant, Hare Kṛṣṇa, Hare Kṛṣṇa, Kṛṣṇa Kṛṣṇa, Hare Hare/ Hare Rāma, Hare Rāma, Rāma

Rāma, Hare Hare. So this is the process. We have got this bead bag and within this bag there are beads. We capture each bead and chant, Hare Kṛṣṇa, Hare Kṛṣṇa, Kṛṣṇa Kṛṣṇa, Hare Hare/ Hare Rāma, Hare Rāma, Rāma Rāma, Hare Hare. One bead equals sixteen times, so the whole bead chain there are one hundred and eight beads. So one round means about seventeen hundred. In this way, our disciples are advised to chant at least sixteen rounds. This is our daily duty. It takes about two hours.
(Lecture on *Śrīmad-Bhāgavatam* 1.7.2–4, Durban, October 14, 1975)

Kṛṣṇa Would Also Count on 108 Beads

Kṛṣṇa had many thousands of cows, and they were divided into groups according to their colors. They were also differently named according to color. When He would prepare to return from the pasturing ground, He would gather all the cows. As Vaiṣṇavas count 108 beads, which represent the 108 individual *gopīs,* so Kṛṣṇa would also count on 108 beads to count the different groups of cows.

(*Kṛṣṇa,* chapter 35, "The *Gopīs'* Feelings of Separation")

They Are Your Direct Link with Kṛṣṇa

I do not know just what has happened to your old beads, but you should keep your beads always very, very carefully, they are your direct link with Kṛṣṇa.

(Letter to Girirāja Dāsa, April 7, 1970)

Concentrate Fully on the Sound

Chanting *japa* should be done early in the morning with full concentration, preferably during the Brahma Muhurta time [one and a half hours before sunrise]. Concentrate fully on the sound vibration of the mantra, pronouncing each name distinctly, and gradually your speed in chanting will increase naturally. Do not worry so much about chanting fast. Most important is the hearing.

(Letter to Rādhāvallabha Dāsa, January 6, 1972)

One Must Practice It Seriously

"One who thinks himself lower than the grass, who is more tolerant than a tree, and who does not expect personal honor yet is always prepared to give all respect to others can very easily always chant the holy name of the Lord."

"Raising my hands, I declare, 'Everyone please hear me! String this verse on the thread of the holy name and wear it on your neck for continuous remembrance.'"

PURPORT

When chanting the Hare Kṛṣṇa *mahā-mantra,* in the beginning one may commit many offenses, which are called *nāmābhāsa* and *nāma-aparādha.* In this stage there is no possibility of achieving perfect love of Kṛṣṇa by chanting the Hare Kṛṣṇa *mahā-mantra.* Therefore one must chant the Hare Kṛṣṇa *mahā-mantra* according to the principles of the above verse, *tṛṇād api sunīcena taror iva sahiṣṇunā.* One should note in this connection that chanting involves the activities of the upper and lower lips as well as the tongue. All three must be engaged in chanting the Hare Kṛṣṇa *mahā-mantra.* The words "Hare Kṛṣṇa" should be very distinctly pronounced and heard. Sometimes one mechanically produces a hissing sound instead of chanting with the proper pronunciation with the help of the lips and tongue. Chanting is very simple, but one must practice it seriously. Therefore the author of *Śrī Caitanya-caritāmṛta,* Kṛṣṇadāsa Kavirāja Gosvāmī, advises everyone to keep this verse always strung about his neck.

(*Śrī Caitanya-caritāmṛta, Ādi-līlā* 17.31–32)

That Is Required—That Is Japa

Guest: May I sing one *bhajana?*
Prabhupāda: Hare Kṛṣṇa. We chant Hare Kṛṣṇa. We chant Hare Kṛṣṇa. It may not be melodious but we chant Hare Kṛṣṇa. There is no mention that it should be chanted lowly. So how you can say it is *gupta* [confidential]? It is not *gupta*. Especially it is *harer nām,* not *gupta*. That is, in the Kali-yuga it should be openly chanted, and we have to follow our predecessor, Haridāsa Ṭhākura, *nāmācārya*. When we chant, when we utter the *bīja* mantra, that we utter loudly. That is required. That is *japa*. So this mantra is *mahā-mantra,* and it should be chanted loudly, or as you like. There is no such restriction. And we have to follow the great personalities. Haridāsa Ṭhākura, he was chanting very loudly; Caitanya Mahāprabhu chanted very loudly. So what more evidence you want? My Guru Mahārāja chanted loudly, we are chanting loudly. Whole business finished. [*chuckles*] Is that all right?
(Lecture on *Śrīmad-Bhāgavatam* 6.1.14, Bombay, November 10, 1970)

Will This Aid Us in Our Concentrating?

Devotee: Prabhupāda? We know that His Divine Grace Bhaktisiddhānta Sarasvatī always sat very erect, and it is stated here in the *Bhagavad-gītā* that one should sit erect. Will this aid us in our concentrating on chanting our *japa,* if we try to concentrate, if we sit erect while chanting?
Prabhupāda: No, no, it doesn't require any sitting posture. But if you can sit, it helps you. It helps you. If you can sit straight like this, it will be very nice. It can help. Yes. You can concentrate in chanting and hearing. Therefore these things are required. But we are not very much particular about this. But he was *brahmacārī* [celibate student]. He could sit like that. That is the sign of *brahmacārī*. He was not false *brahmacārī,* but he was real *brahmacārī*.
(Lecture on *Bhagavad-gītā* 6.46–47, Los Angeles, February 21, 1969)

So Stress on This Point

As soon as we have got some time, chant Hare Kṛṣṇa. Either loudly or silent . . . As far as possible, loudly; if not possible, silently. But the tongue must go, Hare Kṛṣṇa, Hare Kṛṣṇa, Kṛṣṇa Kṛṣṇa, Hare Hare/ Hare Rāma, Hare Rāma, Rāma Rāma, Hare Hare. The tongue must work. And as far as possible, should be heard . . . And officially, *krkshaharamakrshkrshramram,* not like that. *Hare krishn krishnkrishnharhar"* Not like that. Every word should be distinctly chanted and heard, not official. So stress on this point.

(Room conversation, London, July 16, 1973)

Lord Kṛṣṇa Is Immediately Present

There is no difference between Kṛṣṇa's body and Himself or between His name and Himself. But as far as the conditioned soul is concerned, one's name is different from one's body, from one's original form, and so on.

PURPORT

. . . It is a fact, however, that the name of Kṛṣṇa and Kṛṣṇa the person are both spiritual. Everything about Kṛṣṇa is transcendental, blissful and objective. For a conditioned soul, the body is different from the soul, and the name given by the father is also different from the soul. The conditioned living entity's identification with material objects keeps him from attaining his actual position. Although he is an eternal servant of Kṛṣṇa, he acts differently. The *svarūpa,* or actual identification of the living entity, is described by Śrī Caitanya Mahāprabhu as *jīvera 'svarūpa' haya—kṛṣṇera 'nitya-dāsa'.* The conditioned soul has forgotten the real activities of his original position. However, this is not the case with Kṛṣṇa. Kṛṣṇa's name and His person are identical. There is no such thing as *māyā* Kṛṣṇa because Kṛṣṇa is not a product of the material creation. There is no difference between Kṛṣṇa's body and His soul. Kṛṣṇa is simultaneously both soul and body. The distinction between body and soul applies to conditioned souls. The body of the conditioned soul is different from the soul, and the conditioned soul's name is different from his body. One may be named Mr. John, but if we call for Mr. John, Mr. John may never actually appear. However, if we utter the holy name of Kṛṣṇa, Kṛṣṇa is immediately present on our tongue. In the *Padma Purāṇa*, Kṛṣṇa says, *mad-bhaktā yatra gāyanti tatra tiṣṭhāmi nārada:* "O Nārada, I am present wherever My devotees are chanting." When the devotees chant the holy name of Kṛṣṇa—Hare Kṛṣṇa, Hare Kṛṣṇa, Kṛṣṇa Kṛṣṇa, Hare Hare/ Hare Rāma, Hare Rāma, Rāma Rāma, Hare Hare—Lord Kṛṣṇa is immediately present.

(*Śrī Caitanya-caritāmṛta, Madhya-līlā* 17.132)

Chant Sincerely

It Depends on the Quality of Feeling

My Lord, Your Lordship can easily be approached, but only by those who are materially exhausted. One who is on the path of [material] progress, trying to improve himself with respectable parentage, great opulence, high education and bodily beauty, cannot approach You with sincere feeling.

PURPORT

Being materially advanced means taking birth in an aristocratic family and possessing great wealth, an education, and attractive personal beauty. All materialistic men are mad after possessing all these material opulences, and this is known as the advancement of material civilization. But the result is that by possessing all these material assets one becomes artificially puffed up, intoxicated by such temporary possessions. Consequently, such materially puffed up persons are incapable of uttering the holy name of the Lord by addressing Him feelingly, "O Govinda, O Kṛṣṇa." It is said in the *śāstras* that by once uttering the holy name of the Lord, the sinner gets rid of a quantity of sins that he is unable to commit. Such is the power of uttering the holy name of the Lord. There is not the least exaggeration in this statement. Actually the Lord's holy name has such powerful potency. But there is a quality to such utterances also. It depends on the quality of feeling. A helpless man can feelingly utter the holy name of the Lord, whereas a man who utters the same holy name in great material satisfaction cannot be so sincere. A materially puffed up person may utter the holy name of the Lord occasionally, but he is incapable of uttering the name in quality. Therefore, the four principles of material advancement, namely (1) high parentage, (2) good wealth, (3) high education, and (4) attractive beauty, are, so to speak, disqualifications for progress on the path of spiritual advancement. The material covering of the pure spirit soul is an external feature, as much as fever is an external feature of the unhealthy body. The general process is to decrease the degree of the fever and not to aggravate it by maltreatment. Sometimes it is seen that spiritually advanced persons become materially impoverished. This is no discouragement. On the other hand, such impoverishment is a good sign as much as the falling of temperature is a good sign. The principle of life should be to decrease the degree of material intoxication which leads one to be more and more illusioned about the aim of life. Grossly illusioned persons are quite unfit for entrance into the kingdom of God.

(*Śrīmad-Bhāgavatam* 1.8.26)

This World Is Full of Dangers

I was much aggrieved to hear the news of your accident and I was very anxious to learn that you are lying now in the hospital. I hope that you are progressing nicely, but in any condition I request that you continue to chant the Maha Mantra, Hare Krishna. Here is a chance for you to chant Hare Krishna exclusively in the hospital bed.

This world is full of dangers in every step. Just like in the ocean there is danger in every step but if we take shelter of boat which is known as the Lotus Feet of Lord Krishna, then this great ocean of danger becomes as harmless as a small pit. We shall be able to cross hundreds of such pits simply by chanting the Holy Names of the Lord, the Hare Krishna Mantra.

I am forwarding this letter through Rupanuga and I shall be glad to hear about your improved health from him. Praying to Krishna for your early recovery. Do not be worried. Krishna will save you from all dangers. Chant sincerely.

(Letter to Allen Ginsberg, December 21, 1968)

With Prīti, With Love

Kṛṣṇa is always ready to help us provided we are also ready to cooperate with Him. If we cooperate with Him, what Kṛṣṇa desires, if we want to do little, immediately Kṛṣṇa will help you. If you work one percent, Kṛṣṇa will help you ten percent. Again, if you work one percent, Kṛṣṇa will help you another ten percent. But the cent percent credit you get, by the help of Kṛṣṇa. Kṛṣṇa gives you intelligence if you are engaged twenty-four hours, without any other engagement, giving up all other nonsense business. Simply if you are engaged in Kṛṣṇa's business, *prīti-pūrvakam,* with love. Not as hackneyed: "Oh, here is the duty, chanting of Hare Kṛṣṇa. All right, *harekṛṣṇaharekṛṣṇahare* . . ." Not like that. With *prīti,* with love. Chant every name, "Hare Kṛṣṇa," and hear. Here is Kṛṣṇa; here is Rādhārāṇī. That kind of chanting, quality. Not "*harekṛṣṇaharekṛṣṇakṛṣṇakṛṣṇahare* . . ." Not like that. Not like that. *Prīti.* That *prīti* is required. That is the essential quality.

(Lecture on *Śrīmad-Bhāgavatam* 1.10.2,
Māyāpur, June 17, 1973)

Please Engage Me in Your Service

So our request is, everyone who is present here, today is Rādhā-ṣṭamī, so pray to Rādhārāṇī. And She is *hare,* Harā. This *hare,* this word, is Rādhārāṇī. Harā, Rādhārāṇī. Rādhā or Harā the same thing. So Hare Kṛṣṇa. So we are praying to Rādhārāṇī, "My Mother, Rādhārāṇī." And Kṛṣṇa, Hare Kṛṣṇa. "O Kṛṣṇa, O the Lord." Hare Kṛṣṇa, Hare Kṛṣṇa, the same thing, repetition. "O Rādhārāṇī, O Kṛṣṇa. O Rādhā-Kṛṣṇa. Rādhe-Kṛṣṇa," or "Hare Kṛṣṇa," the same thing. Hare Kṛṣṇa, Hare Kṛṣṇa, Kṛṣṇa Kṛṣṇa, Hare Hare. Again addressing, "O Kṛṣṇa, O Kṛṣṇa, O Rādhārāṇī." Hare Rāma. The same thing again, Hare Rāma. Rāma is also Kṛṣṇa. Rāma is Rāma. Rāma is Balarāma. They are all Kṛṣṇa. Hare Rāma, Hare Rāma, Rāma Rāma, Hare Hare. So this repetition of addressing Rādhā and Kṛṣṇa or Hare Kṛṣṇa is to pray, "My dear Lord and the energy, the spiritual energy of the Lord, kindly engage me in Your service." That's all. "I am now embarrassed with this material service. Please engage me in Your service."

(Lecture on *Bhagavad-gītā* 4.10,
Calcutta, September 23, 1974, Rādhāṣṭamī)

Kindly Pick Me Up

The king of the elephants, he was animal. You know the story, that he was attacked by a crocodile in the water. So there was a struggle for existence between the two, and after all, the crocodile is the animal in the water. He had great strength. And the elephant, although he's also very big, powerful animal, but he was not an animal of the water. So he was very helpless. So at last, he began to chant the holy name of the Lord and prayed, so he was saved. He was saved. And because the crocodile caught up the leg of the elephant, he was also saved because he was Vaiṣṇava. And this animal, crocodile, he was under the feet of a Vaiṣṇava, so he was also saved. This is the story. You know. So therefore, *chāḍiyā vaiṣṇava sevā.* He indirectly gave service to the Vaiṣṇava, and he also became delivered.

So *bhakti* is so nice thing that very easily you can get favor of the Supreme Personality. And if Kṛṣṇa is pleased upon you, then what remains? Everything you get. Everything you get. You don't require much money, much education, nothing of the sort. Simply you require your heart: "O Kṛṣṇa, You are my Lord. You are my master eternally. I am Your servant eternally. Let me be engaged in Your service." That is Hare Kṛṣṇa, Hare Kṛṣṇa, Kṛṣṇa Kṛṣṇa, Hare Hare/ Hare Rāma, Hare Rāma, Rāma Rāma, Hare Hare. This is the meaning of Hare Kṛṣṇa mantra: "O Kṛṣṇa, O energy of Kṛṣṇa, I am Your servant. Somehow or other I have now fallen in this material condition. Kindly pick me up and engage me in service." That is Caitanya Mahāprabhu's teaching to us. This material world is just like a great ocean, *bhava. Bhava* means repetition of birth and death, and *āmbu* means *āmbudhau,* means in the sea, in the ocean. So we are struggling hard for existence in this ocean. So Caitanya Mahāprabhu says, "I am Your servant eternal. Somehow or other I have fallen in this ocean and struggling. Pick me up." This is *bhakti-mārga,* devotional service, to become very humble, meek, always pray to Kṛṣṇa, "Kindly consider me as one of the particles of the dust of the lotus feet of Your Lordship."

(Lecture on *Śrīmad-Bhāgavatam* 7.9.9,
Mayapur, March 1, 1977)

6

TRANSCENDENTALLY SWEET LIKE SUGAR CANDY

That Sweet Nectar of Kṛṣṇa Nāma Saṅkīrtana

I am happy to hear that you continued to chant despite so many doubts and skepticism. That is the process. Even there may be doubts and skepticism, if one continues the chanting process, the doubts will all disappear, and real knowledge will be revealed by the Grace of Krishna. There is the example given of the jaundice patient. He is suffering from disease, and when given sugar-candy, which is the cure, he finds it very bitter and distasteful. But that does not mean the sugar-candy is not very sweet and delicious; it is simply due to his diseased condition that it seems bitter. In order to be cured from his disease, he must take the medicine of sugar-candy, despite the apparently bitter taste, and as he becomes cured, the real sweet taste of the candy is gradually revealed. Similarly, we are diseased, and only if we take to this chanting process may we be cured. Maya may put so many doubts and worthless arguments into our minds, but if we continue the chanting, the curing process will go on, never mind the doubts, and gradually we will get a taste of that sweet nectar of Krishna Nama Sankirtana.

(Letter to Terry and associates, March 22, 1968)

Transcendentally Sweet Like Sugar Candy

The holy name, character, pastimes, and activities of Kṛṣṇa are all transcendentally sweet like sugar candy. Although the tongue of one afflicted by the jaundice of *avidyā* [ignorance] cannot taste anything sweet, it is wonderful that simply by carefully chanting these sweet names every day, a natural relish awakens within his tongue, and his disease is gradually destroyed at the root.

PURPORT

The holy name of Lord Kṛṣṇa, His quality, pastimes, and so forth are all of the nature of absolute truth, beauty, and bliss. Naturally they are very sweet, like sugar candy, which appeals to everyone. Nescience, however, is compared to the disease called jaundice, which is caused by bilious secretions. Attacked by jaundice, the tongue of a diseased person cannot palatably relish sugar candy. Rather, a person with jaundice considers something sweet to taste very bitter. *Avidyā* (ignorance) similarly perverts the ability to relish the transcendentally palatable name, quality, form, and pastimes of Kṛṣṇa. Despite this disease, if one with great care and attention takes to Kṛṣṇa consciousness, chanting the holy name and hearing Kṛṣṇa's transcendental pastimes, his ignorance will be destroyed and his tongue enabled to taste the sweetness of the transcendental nature of Kṛṣṇa and His paraphernalia. Such a recovery of spiritual health is possible only by the regular cultivation of Kṛṣṇa consciousness.

When a man in the material world takes more interest in the materialistic way of life than in Kṛṣṇa consciousness, he is considered to be in a diseased condition. The normal condition is to remain an eternal servant of the Lord (*jīvera 'svarūpa' haya-kṛṣṇera 'nitya-dāsa'*). This healthy condition is lost when the living entity forgets Kṛṣṇa due to being attracted by the external features of Kṛṣṇa's *māyā* energy. This world of *māyā* is called *durāśraya,* which means "false or bad shelter." One who puts his faith in *durāśraya* becomes a candidate for hoping against hope. In the material world everyone is trying to become happy, and although their material attempts are baffled in every way, due to their nescience they cannot understand their mistakes. People try to rectify one mistake by making another mistake. This is the way of the struggle for existence in the material world. If one in this condition is advised to take to Kṛṣṇa consciousness and be happy, he does not accept such instructions.

This Kṛṣṇa consciousness movement is being spread all over the world just to remedy this gross ignorance. People in general are misled by blind leaders. The leaders of human society—the politicians, philosophers, and scientists—are blind because they are not Kṛṣṇa conscious. According to *Bhagavad-gītā,* because they are bereft of all factual knowledge due to their atheistic way of life, they are actually sinful rascals and are the lowest among men.

na māṁ duṣkṛtino mūḍhāḥ
prapadyante narādhamāḥ
māyayāpahṛta-jñānā
āsuraṁ bhāvam āśritāḥ

"Those miscreants who are grossly foolish, lowest among mankind, whose knowledge is stolen by illusion, and who partake of the atheistic nature of demons, do not surrender unto Me." (Bg. 7.15)

Such people never surrender to Kṛṣṇa, and they oppose the endeavor of those who wish to take Kṛṣṇa's shelter. When such atheists become leaders of society, the entire atmosphere is surcharged with nescience. In such a condition, people do not become very enthusiastic to receive this Kṛṣṇa consciousness movement, just as a diseased person suffering from jaundice does not relish the taste of sugar candy. However, one must know that for jaundice, sugar candy is the only specific medicine. Similarly, in the present confused state of humanity, Kṛṣṇa consciousness, the chanting of the holy name of the Lord—Hare Kṛṣṇa, Hare Kṛṣṇa, Kṛṣṇa Kṛṣṇa, Hare Hare/ Hare Rāma, Hare Rāma, Rāma Rāma, Hare Hare—is the only remedy for setting the world aright. Although Kṛṣṇa consciousness may not be very palatable for a diseased person, Śrīla Rūpa Gosvāmī nonetheless advises that if one wants to be cured of the material disease, he must take to it with great care and attention. One begins his treatment by chanting the Hare Kṛṣṇa *mahā-mantra* because by chanting this holy name of the Lord a person in the material condition will be relieved from all misconceptions (*ceto-darpaṇa-mārjanam*). *Avidyā,* a misconception about one's spiritual identity, provides the foundation for *ahaṅkāra,* or false ego within the heart.

The real disease is in the heart. If the mind is cleansed, however, if consciousness is cleansed, a person cannot be harmed by the material disease. To cleanse the mind and heart from all misconceptions, one should take to this chanting of the Hare Kṛṣṇa *mahā-mantra.* This is both easy and beneficial. By chanting the holy name of the Lord, one is immediately freed from the blazing fire of material existence.

There are three stages in chanting the holy name of the Lord—the offensive stage, the stage of lessening offenses, and the pure stage. When a neophyte takes to the chanting of the Hare Kṛṣṇa mantra, he generally commits many offenses. There are ten basic offenses, and if the devotee avoids these, he can glimpse the next stage, which is situated between offensive chanting and pure chanting. When one attains the pure stage, he is immediately liberated. This is called *bhava-mahā-dāvāgni-nirvāpaṇam*. As soon as one is liberated from the blazing fire of material existence, he can relish the taste of transcendental life.

The conclusion is that in order to get freed from the material disease, one must take to the chanting of the Hare Kṛṣṇa mantra. The Kṛṣṇa consciousness movement is especially meant for creating an atmosphere in which people can take to the chanting of the Hare Kṛṣṇa mantra. One must begin with faith, and when this faith is increased by chanting, a person can become a member of the Society. We are sending *saṅkīrtana* parties all over the world, and they are experiencing that even in the remotest part of the world, where there is no knowledge of Kṛṣṇa, the Hare Kṛṣṇa *mahā-mantra* attracts thousands of men to our camp. In some areas, people begin to imitate the devotees by shaving their heads and chanting the Hare Kṛṣṇa *mahā-mantra,* only a few days after hearing the mantra. This may be imitative, but imitation of a good thing is desired. Some imitators gradually become interested in being initiated by the spiritual master and offer themselves for initiation.

If one is sincere, he is initiated, and this stage is called *bhajana-kriyā.* One then actually engages in the service of the Lord by regularly chanting the Hare Kṛṣṇa *mahā-mantra,* sixteen rounds daily, and refraining from illicit sex, intoxicants, meat-eating, and gambling. By *bhajana-kriyā* one attains freedom from the contamination of materialistic life. He no longer goes to a restaurant or hotel to taste so-called palatable dishes made with meat and onions, nor does he care to smoke or drink tea or coffee. He not only refrains from illicit sex, but avoids sex life entirely. Nor is he interested in wasting his time in speculating or gambling. In this way it is to be understood that one is becoming cleansed of unwanted things (*anartha-nivṛtti*). The word *anartha* refers to unwanted things. *Anarthas* are vanquished when one becomes attached to the Kṛṣṇa consciousness movement.

When a person is relieved from unwanted things, he becomes fixed in executing his Kṛṣṇa activities. Indeed, he becomes attached to such activities and experiences ecstasy in executing devotional service. This is called *bhāva,* the preliminary awakening of dormant love of Godhead. Thus the conditioned soul becomes free from material existence and loses interest in the bodily conception of life, including material opulence, material knowledge and material attraction of all variety. At such a time one can understand who the Supreme Personality of Godhead is and what His *māyā* is.

Although *māyā* may be present, it cannot disturb a devotee once he attains the *bhāva* stage. This is because the devotee can see the real position of *māyā*. *Māyā* means forgetfulness of Kṛṣṇa, and forgetfulness of Kṛṣṇa and Kṛṣṇa consciousness stand side by side like light and shadow. If one remains in shadow, he cannot enjoy the facilities offered by light, and if one remains in light, he cannot be disturbed by the darkness of shadow. By taking to Kṛṣṇa consciousness, one gradually becomes liberated and remains in light. Indeed, he does not even touch the darkness. As confirmed in *Caitanya-caritāmṛta* (*Madhya* 22.31):

kṛṣṇa—sūrya-sama; māyā haya andhakāra
yāhāṅ kṛṣṇa, tāhāṅ nāhi māyāra adhikāra

"Kṛṣṇa is compared to sunshine, and *māyā* is compared to darkness. Wherever there is sunshine, there cannot be darkness. As soon as one takes to Kṛṣṇa consciousness, the darkness of illusion, the influence of the external energy, will immediately vanish."

(*The Nectar of Instruction,* text 7)

The Best Benediction

It is said that once a poor *brāhmaṇa* worshiped Lord Śiva for a benediction, and Lord Śiva advised the devotee to go to see Sanātana Gosvāmī. The devotee went to Sanātana Gosvāmī and informed him that Lord Śiva had advised him to seek out the best benediction from him (Sanātana). Sanātana had a touchstone with him, which he kept with the garbage. On the request of the poor *brāhmaṇa*, Sanātana Gosvāmī gave him the touchstone, and the *brāhmaṇa* was very happy to have it. He now could get as much gold as he desired simply by touching the touchstone to iron. But after he left Sanātana, he thought, "If a touchstone is the best benediction, why has Sanātana Gosvāmī kept it with the garbage?" He therefore returned and asked Sanātana Gosvāmī, "Sir, if this is the best benediction, why did you keep it with the garbage?" Sanātana Gosvāmī then informed him, "Actually, this is not the best benediction. But are you prepared to take the best benediction from me?" The *brāhmaṇa* said, "Yes, sir. Lord Śiva has sent me to you for the best benediction." Then Sanātana Gosvāmī asked him to throw the touchstone in the water nearby and then come back. The poor *brāhmaṇa* did so, and when he returned, Sanātana Gosvāmī initiated him with the Hare Kṛṣṇa mantra. Thus, by the benediction of Lord Śiva, the *brāhmaṇa* got the association of the best devotee of Lord Kṛṣṇa, and was thus initiated in the *mahā-mantra*, Hare Kṛṣṇa, Hare Kṛṣṇa, Kṛṣṇa Kṛṣṇa, Hare Hare/ Hare Rāma, Hare Rāma, Rāma Rāma, Hare Hare.

(*Śrīmad-Bhāgavatam* 4.7.6, purport)

Sowing of a Seed in the Heart

The thoughts of My pure devotees dwell in Me, their lives are fully devoted to My service, and they derive great satisfaction and bliss from always enlightening one another and conversing about Me.

PURPORT

. . . Lord Caitanya likens transcendental devotional service to the sowing of a seed in the heart of the living entity. There are innumerable living entities traveling throughout the different planets of the universe, and out of them there are a few who are fortunate enough to meet a pure devotee and get the chance to understand devotional service. This devotional service is just like a seed, and if it is sown in the heart of a living entity, and if he goes on hearing and chanting Hare Kṛṣṇa, Hare Kṛṣṇa, Kṛṣṇa Kṛṣṇa, Hare Hare/ Hare Rāma, Hare Rāma, Rāma Rāma, Hare Hare, that seed fructifies, just as the seed of a tree fructifies with regular watering. The spiritual plant of devotional service gradually grows and grows until it penetrates the covering of the material universe and enters into the *brahmajyoti* effulgence in the spiritual sky. In the spiritual sky also that plant grows more and more until it reaches the highest planet, which is called Goloka Vṛndāvana, the supreme planet of Kṛṣṇa. Ultimately, the plant takes shelter under the lotus feet of Kṛṣṇa and rests there. Gradually, as a plant grows fruits and flowers, that plant of devotional service also produces fruits, and the watering process in the form of chanting and hearing goes on.

(*Bhagavad-gītā* 10.9)

7

Initiation and The Ten Offenses

Chanting the Holy Name of the Lord

The importance of chanting Hare Kṛṣṇa, Hare Kṛṣṇa, Kṛṣṇa Kṛṣṇa, Hare Hare/ Hare Rāma, Hare Rāma, Rāma Rāma, Hare Hare is very strongly stressed in the Second Canto, first chapter, verse 11, of *Śrīmad-Bhāgavatam* in the following way. Śukadeva Gosvāmī tells Mahārāja Parīkṣit, "My dear King, if one is spontaneously attached to the chanting of the Hare Kṛṣṇa *mahā-mantra,* it is to be understood that he has attained the highest perfectional stage." It is specifically mentioned that the *karmīs* who are aspiring after the fruitive results of their activities, the salvationists who are aspiring to become one with the Supreme Person, and the *yogīs* who are aspiring after mystic perfections can achieve the results of all perfectional stages simply by chanting the *mahā-*

mantra. Śukadeva uses the word *nirṇītam,* which means "it has already been decided." He was a liberated soul and therefore could not accept anything which was not conclusive. So Śukadeva Gosvāmī especially stresses that it has already been concluded that one who has come to the stage of chanting the Hare Kṛṣṇa mantra with determination and steadiness must be considered to have already passed the trials of fruitive activities, mental speculation, and mystic yoga.

The same thing is confirmed in the *Ādi Purāṇa* by Kṛṣṇa. While addressing Arjuna He says, "Anyone who is engaged in chanting My transcendental name must be considered to be always associating with Me. And I may tell you frankly that for such a devotee I become easily purchased."

In the *Padma Purāṇa* also it is stated, "The chanting of the Hare Kṛṣṇa mantra is present only on the lips of a person who has for many births worshiped Vāsudeva." It is further said in the *Padma Purāṇa,* "There is no difference between the holy name of the Lord and the Lord Himself. As such, the holy name is as perfect as the Lord Himself in fullness, purity, and eternity. The holy name is not a material sound vibration, nor has it any material contamination." The holy name cannot, therefore, be chanted offenselessly by one who has failed to purify his senses. In other words, materialistic senses cannot properly chant the holy names of the Hare Kṛṣṇa *mahā-mantra.* But by adopting this chanting process, one is given a chance to actually purify himself, so that he may very soon chant offenselessly.

Caitanya Mahāprabhu has recommended that everyone chant the Hare Kṛṣṇa mantra just to cleanse the dust from the heart. If the dust of the heart is cleansed away, then one can actually understand the importance of the holy name. For persons who are not inclined to clean the dust from their hearts and who want to keep things as they are, it is not possible to derive the transcendental result of chanting the Hare Kṛṣṇa mantra. One should, therefore, be encouraged to develop his service attitude toward the Lord, because this will help him to chant without any offense. And so, under the guidance of a spiritual master, the disciple is trained to render service and at the same time chant the Hare Kṛṣṇa mantra. As soon as one develops his spontaneous service attitude, he can immediately understand the transcendental nature of the holy names of the *mahā-mantra.*

(*The Nectar of Devotion,* "Further Aspects of Transcendental Service")

The Lord Is So Kind to Us

Śrī Kṛṣṇa, the Personality of Godhead, who is the Paramātmā [Supersoul] in everyone's heart and the benefactor of the truthful devotee, cleanses desire for material enjoyment from the heart of the devotee who has developed the urge to hear His messages, which are in themselves virtuous when properly heard and chanted.

PURPORT

Messages of the Personality of Godhead Śrī Kṛṣṇa are nondifferent from Him. Whenever, therefore, offenseless hearing and glorification of God are undertaken, it is to be understood that Lord Kṛṣṇa is present there in the form of transcendental sound, which is as powerful as the Lord personally. Śrī Caitanya Mahāprabhu, in His *Śikṣāṣṭaka,* declares clearly that the holy name of the Lord has all the potencies of the Lord and that He has endowed His innumerable names with the same potency. There is no rigid fixture of time, and anyone can chant the holy name with attention and reverence at his convenience. The Lord is so kind to us that He can be present before us personally in the form of transcendental sound, but unfortunately we have no taste for hearing and glorifying the Lord's name and activities. We have already discussed developing a taste for hearing and chanting the holy sound. It is done through the medium of service to the pure devotee of the Lord.

(*Śrīmad-Bhāgavatam* 1.2.17)

The Spiritual Master Awakens the Sleeping Living Entity

It is the spiritual master who delivers the disciple from the clutches of *māyā* by initiating him into the chanting of the Hare Kṛṣṇa *mahā-mantra.* In this way a sleeping human being can revive his consciousness by chanting Hare Kṛṣṇa, Hare Kṛṣṇa, Kṛṣṇa Kṛṣṇa, Hare Hare/ Hare Rāma, Hare Rāma, Rāma Rāma, Hare Hare. In other words, the spiritual master awakens the sleeping living entity to his original consciousness so that he can worship Lord Viṣṇu. This is the purpose of *dīkṣā,* or initiation. Initiation means receiving the pure knowledge of spiritual consciousness.

(*Śrī Caitanya-caritāmṛta, Madhya-līlā* 9.61, urport)

When the Mantra Is Chanted By the Spiritual Master, It Becomes More Powerful

When a mantra is chanted by a great devotee, the mantra becomes more powerful. Although the Hare Kṛṣṇa *mahā-mantra* is powerful in itself, a disciple upon initiation receives the mantra from his spiritual master, for when the mantra is chanted by the spiritual master, it becomes more powerful.

(*Śrīmad-Bhāgavatam* 4.24.32, purport)

One Must Receive the Hare Kṛṣṇa Mantra From the Spiritual Master

One has to learn about the beauty and transcendental position of the holy name of the Lord by hearing the revealed scriptures from the mouths of devotees. Nowhere else can we hear of the sweetness of the Lord's holy name.

PURPORT

It is said in the *Padma Purāṇa, ataḥ śrī-kṛṣṇa-nāmādi, na bhaved grāhyam indriyaiḥ*. Chanting and hearing of the transcendental holy name of the Lord cannot be performed by the ordinary senses. The transcendental vibration of the Lord's holy name is completely spiritual. Thus it must be received from spiritual sources and must be chanted after having been heard from a spiritual master. One who hears the chanting of the Hare Kṛṣṇa mantra must receive it from the spiritual master by aural reception. Śrīla Sanātana Gosvāmī has forbidden us to hear the holy name of Kṛṣṇa chanted by non-Vaiṣṇavas, such as professional actors and singers, for it will have no effect. It is like milk touched by the lips of a serpent, as stated in the *Padma Purāṇa:*

avaiṣṇava-mukhodgīrṇaṁ pūtaṁ hari-kathāmṛtam
śravaṇaṁ naiva kartavyaṁ sarpocchiṣṭaṁ yathā payaḥ

As far as possible, therefore, the devotees in the Kṛṣṇa consciousness movement gather to chant the holy name of Kṛṣṇa in public so that both the chanters and the listeners may benefit.

(*Śrī Caitanya-caritāmṛta, Antya-līlā* 1.101)

You Kindly Associate With These Devotees

Hare Kṛṣṇa, Hare Kṛṣṇa, Kṛṣṇa Kṛṣṇa, Hare Hare/ Hare Rāma, Hare Rāma, Rāma Rāma, Hare Hare. If you chant these sixteen words, it is not very difficult. Anyone, there is no secrecy. There is no charge for it. We don't say that "I shall give you some secret mantra. You give me some money." No. We don't say. We openly chant this Hare Kṛṣṇa mantra. Anyone can chant also. But see the effect of chanting this mantra. That is up to you. If you begin chanting, you'll feel the effect very soon. So this is called *man-manāḥ,* always thinking of Kṛṣṇa. As soon as one chants Hare Kṛṣṇa, immediately he remembers Kṛṣṇa. He immediately remembers Kṛṣṇa's activities, Kṛṣṇa's pastimes, Kṛṣṇa's form, Kṛṣṇa's quality, Kṛṣṇa's attributes—everything. That is called to absorb the mind in Kṛṣṇa. That means you become immediately the first-class *yogī*. *Yogīnām api sarveṣāṁ mad-gatenāntar-ātmanā.* This is the process.

So these boys and girls who have taken to this Kṛṣṇa consciousness movement seriously, they are all first-class *yogīs* because they are always thinking of Kṛṣṇa. *Man-manā bhava mad-bhaktaḥ.* So if you want to develop Kṛṣṇa consciousness, then you kindly associate with these devotees. We are opening so many centers all over the world—we have already 102 centers—just to give opportunity to all classes of men to associate with devotees and develop your love for God. This is the purpose. And we have no other purpose, these centers are being opened. So I request you, those who are interested in loving God, in Kṛṣṇa consciousness, they will kindly associate with these devotees. This is our method. When a man, a gentleman or lady, comes to our association, he associates with us for three months, six months, then automatically he desires to be initiated. *Bhajana-kriyā* means one becomes anxious. The effect of *sādhu-saṅga* is to become anxious how to execute this devotional service properly. That is called initiation. So they come forward. The president recommends that "This boy or girl is now living with us for so many months, he's interested, he may be initiated." Then we initiate. But initiate with some condition. *Anartha-nivṛttiḥ syāt.* These are the different stages. Initiation means that he must be free from all kinds of sinful activities. These four principles, the pillars of sinful activities, are four in number: illicit sex life, meat-eating, intoxication, and gambling.

All these boys and girls who are sitting here, you know that they have given up automatically. They have been able, by association with Kṛṣṇa. It has become very practical and easy thing to give up all these four principles of sinful activities. Because without being pure, you cannot understand the Supreme Pure. God is the Supreme Pure.

Now, how is it possible? If one is simply engaged in pious activities. The most pious activity is to be engaged in this Kṛṣṇa consciousness movement. Then these are the different stages.

Artificially we are practiced to things. Just like meat-eating. Meat-eating, we do not practice it from the beginning of our birth. Just after birth the child, the baby, requires little honey or little milk, not the meat. But afterwards, the parents or the guardians are teaching how to eat meat. This is not our human business. Human teeth is meant for eating fruits and grains. That is scientific. Our teeth is made in that way. So anyway, meat-eating, intoxication, illicit sex, as soon as one takes to this Kṛṣṇa consciousness movement, these four pillars of sinful life are immediately broken. As soon as one becomes free from all sinful activities, he becomes firmly convinced of God consciousness. Then you taste, "Oh, it is so nice, Kṛṣṇa consciousness."

So because Lord Caitanya Mahāprabhu chanted these sixteen names—Hare Kṛṣṇa, Hare Kṛṣṇa, Kṛṣṇa Kṛṣṇa, Hare Hare/ Hare Rāma, Hare Rāma, Rāma Rāma, Hare Hare—therefore we also follow the footprints of Lord Caitanya Mahāprabhu. We are also chanting the same Hare Kṛṣṇa *mahā-mantra,* and we shall request you also. There is no expenditure, there is no loss on your part, but if there is any gain, why don't you try it? That is our request. Chant Hare Kṛṣṇa, Hare Kṛṣṇa, Kṛṣṇa Kṛṣṇa, Hare Hare/ Hare Rāma, Hare Rāma, Rāma Rāma, Hare Hare. This is the process for increasing your attachment for God, Kṛṣṇa. That is our real constitutional position, to love God. We are loving also, in this fallen state, but not God, all non-God or some pseudo God. But when we come to the real stage of loving God, then at that time our life becomes perfect, and it is said in the *Brahma-saṁhitā, premāñjana cchurita-bhakti-vilocanena santaḥ sadaiva hṛdayeśu vilokayanti.* When you develop your love of God, Kṛṣṇa, then you see God every moment, every step. *Santaḥ sadaiva. Sadaiva* means always. If you say, "Can you show me God?" there is no need of showing God. You qualify yourself, and God will be visible in every step of your life. Then your life will be successful.

Thank you very much. Hare Kṛṣṇa.

(Lecture on *Bhagavad-gītā* 7.1, Sydney, February 16, 1973)

So This Initiation Means . . .

This initiation ceremony is a Vedic principle to lead a conditioned soul to the higher level of transcendental life. In the Caitanya Caritamrta you will find the instruction as we have given it in our book, Teachings of Lord Caitanya, that after many, many births through approximately 8,400,000 species of life, a living entity gets this human form of life, which is a chance to get freedom from the material condition. When a child is born it is the responsibility of the state, of the father, of the mother, of the relatives, and of the teachers just to raise the child to the standard of Krishna Consciousness so that the child may not have any more to repeat the process of birth and death, but being fully situated in Krishna Consciousness he may be transferred to the spiritual world and situated in one of the Vaikuntha planets. The most important of the Vaikuntha planets is called Krishna Loka, or Goloka Vrindaban. In these days the propagation for landing on the moon planet is very encouraging to the common man, but so far as a Krishna Conscious person is concerned, he is not at all interested in any of the material planets. His target is to be transferred to the topmost spiritual planet, namely Krishna Loka.

So this initiation means the preliminary chance for preparing oneself to achieve this highest perfection. I am very glad that you are already interested in the Krishna Consciousness Movement, and you will please chant at least 16 rounds daily, observing the rules and regulations. The four principle rules is that you will refrain from 1) meat-eating or partaking of fish or eggs, 2) illicit sexual connections, 3) intoxication (including cigarettes, coffee and tea) and 4) gambling. In addition to these rules there are ten offenses to chanting the Maha Mantra which should be avoided. These rules are as follows: 1) Blaspheming the Lord's devotee. 2) Considering the Lord and the demi-gods on the same level. 3) Neglecting the orders of the spiritual master. 4) Minimizing the authority of the Scriptures. 5) Interpreting the Holy Name of God. 6) Committing sin on the strength of chanting. 7) Instructing the glories of the Lord's Name to the unfaithful. 8) Comparing the Holy Name with material piety. 9) Inattention while chanting the Holy Name. 10) Attachment to material things while engaged in the practice of chanting.

So follow faithfully the above rules and regulations, help your godbrothers and sister in London to propagate Krishna Consciousness, and there is no question that you will all come out successful.

(Letter to Kulaśekhara Dāsa and others, July 31, 1969)

There Are Ten Offenses We Should Avoid

Persons whose bodily features change in ecstasy and who breathe heavily and perspire due to hearing the glories of the Lord are promoted to the kingdom of God, even though they do not care for meditation and other austerities. The kingdom of God is above the material universes, and it is desired by Brahmā and other demigods.

PURPORT

...The *Śrīmad-Bhāgavatam,* Second Canto, third chapter, verse 24, also states that if a person does not cry or exhibit bodily changes after chanting the holy name of God without offense, it is to be understood that he is hard-hearted and that therefore his heart does not change even after he chants the holy name of God, Hare Kṛṣṇa. These bodily changes can take place due to ecstasy when we offenselessly chant the holy names of God: Hare Kṛṣṇa, Hare Kṛṣṇa, Kṛṣṇa Kṛṣṇa, Hare Hare/ Hare Rāma, Hare Rāma, Rāma Rāma, Hare Hare.

It may be noted that there are ten offenses we should avoid. The first offense is to decry persons who try in their lives to broadcast the glories of the Lord. People must be educated in understanding the glories of the Supreme; therefore the devotees who engage in preaching the glories of the Lord are never to be decried. It is the greatest offense. Furthermore, the holy name of Viṣṇu is the most auspicious name, and His pastimes are also nondifferent from the holy name of the Lord. There are many foolish persons who say that one can chant Hare Kṛṣṇa or chant the name of Kālī or Durgā or Śiva because they are all the same. If one thinks that the holy name of the Supreme Personality of Godhead and the names and activities of the demigods are on the same level, or if one accepts the holy name of Viṣṇu to be a material sound vibration, that is also an offense. The third offense is to think of the spiritual master who spreads the glories of the Lord as an ordinary human being. The fourth offense is to consider the Vedic literatures, such as the *Purāṇas* or other transcendentally revealed scriptures, to be ordinary books of knowledge. The fifth offense is to think that devotees have given artificial importance to the holy name of God. The actual fact is that the Lord is nondifferent from His name. The highest realization of spiritual value is to chant the holy name of God, as prescribed for the age—Hare Kṛṣṇa, Hare Kṛṣṇa, Kṛṣṇa Kṛṣṇa, Hare Hare/ Hare Rāma, Hare Rāma, Rāma Rāma, Hare Hare. The sixth offense is to give some interpretation on the holy name of God. The seventh offense is to act sinfully on the strength of chanting the holy name of God. It is understood that one can be freed from all sinful reaction simply by chanting the holy name of God, but if one thinks that he is therefore at liberty to commit all kinds of sinful acts, that is a symptom of offense. The eighth offense is to equate the chanting of Hare Kṛṣṇa with other spiritual activities, such as meditation, austerity, penance, or sacrifice. They cannot be equated at any level. The ninth offense is to specifically glorify the importance of the holy name before persons who have no interest. The tenth offense is to be attached to the misconception of possessing something, or to accept the body as one's self, while executing the process of spiritual cultivation.

When one is free from all ten of these offenses in chanting the holy name of God, he develops the ecstatic bodily features called *pulakāśru*. *Pulaka* means "symptoms of happiness," and *aśru* means "tears in the eyes." The symptoms of happiness and tears in the eyes must appear in a person who has chanted the holy name offenselessly. Here in this verse it is stated that those who have actually developed the symptoms of happiness and tears in the eyes by chanting the glories of the Lord are eligible to enter the kingdom of God. In the *Caitanya-caritāmṛta* it is said that if one does not develop these symptoms while chanting Hare Kṛṣṇa, it is to be understood that he is still offensive. *Caitanya-caritāmṛta* suggests a nice remedy in this connection. There it is said in verse 31, chapter eight, of *Ādi-līlā,* that if anyone takes shelter of Lord Caitanya and just chants the holy name of the Lord, Hare Kṛṣṇa, he becomes freed from all offenses.

(*Śrīmad-Bhāgavatam* 3.15.25)

Respectful Attitude to the Name

Kṛṣṇa becomes manifest to the devotee. *Ataḥ śrī-kṛṣṇa-nāmādi.* When one becomes a devotee, beginning from the tongue, *jihvādau,* by chanting Hare Kṛṣṇa mantra, He becomes revealed. That is the perfection of chanting without any offenses. Then you'll find the name is not different from Kṛṣṇa. When you are chanting, you'll find Kṛṣṇa is dancing on your tongue. This is the conclusion.

So we have to learn how to chant. Therefore in the *śāstras,* in the *Purāṇas,* the ten kinds of offenses are described. And Śrīla Jīva Gosvāmī has given very much stress to avoid these offenses. *Śuddha-nāma*. In the beginning we cannot chant pure form of the name, but still, by chanting process, then it becomes *nāmābhāsa,* almost pure. *Ābhāsa* means just like before sunrise you find the darkness is off, but it is not sunlight. It is different from sunlight, but still, there is the dawn, you can see everything distinctly. Similarly, first there is offensive name and, if you avoid, avoid the ten kinds of offenses, then gradually it becomes *nāmābhāsa*. And Śrīla Haridāsa Ṭhākura has said that by *nāmābhāsa,* one becomes liberated. There was some argument with Haridāsa Ṭhākura and one *brāhmaṇa* in the office of Raghunātha dāsa Gosvāmī's father and uncle. So there were some high level talks on this *nāmābhāsa*. So by *nāmābhāsa* one becomes liberated. By chanting Hare Kṛṣṇa mantra offensively, one becomes materially happy or distressed, but when one comes to the stage of *nāmābhāsa,* he becomes liberated. And when he chants pure name, there is *kṛṣṇa-prema*. Just like Rūpa Gosvāmī. He was chanting, we are also chanting. But we are not in the stage of Rūpa Gosvāmī or Sanātana Gosvāmī and Haridāsa Ṭhākura. Actually, if we come to that stage, then there will be *kṛṣṇa-prema,* love of Kṛṣṇa. Just like Rūpa Gosvāmī said that "What shall I chant with one tongue and two ears? If there were millions of tongues and trillions of ears, I could chant something." And we cannot finish even sixteen rounds, because we have not created our taste for chanting. Still we are in the *nāmāparādha* stage. But don't be disappointed. Go on chanting. You'll come to the right position, *nāmābhāsa,* then *śuddha-nāma.* Everything requires gradual development.

So this *nāma* is also another incarnation of Kṛṣṇa, because name and Kṛṣṇa is not different. *Abhinnatvād nāma-nāminoḥ.* There is no difference. Here, in the material world, there is difference between the name and the substance, but *advaya-jñāna,* in the Absolute world there is no such distinction. The name and the person, the same, identical. So actually, when we chant Hare Kṛṣṇa mantra, we directly associate with Kṛṣṇa, because name is the incarnation of Kṛṣṇa. *Nāma-rūpe kṛṣṇa-avatāra.* Therefore, if we are sensible, then we should take very much respectful attitude to the name, because name and Kṛṣṇa, the same. Suppose Kṛṣṇa comes here. How much respectful we shall be, immediately. So similarly, when we chant Hare Kṛṣṇa mantra, we should know Kṛṣṇa is there. Therefore we should be very much cautious and respectful, not neglectful. That is offense. That is offense. If you become inattentive, that is offense. You should know this. Try to avoid. Kṛṣṇa is giving us chance to meet Him in so many ways: *nāma, rūpa, līlā, parikara, vasiṣṭha.*

So *kṛṣṇa-nāma rūpe-avatāra.* So we should respect chanting

of Hare Kṛṣṇa mantra with very care, carefulness, cautious, so that we may not commit any offense. Then your business is successful. *Nāmnad balād yasya hi pāpa-buddhiḥ.* If somebody thinks that "I am living in Vṛndāvana. I am chanting Hare Kṛṣṇa mantra. So if I do something sinful, what it will do . . .? So what sinful I am doing? A little sinful . . ." Yes, little sinful will be excused if it is done not willingly. But if you commit sinful activities willingly, daily, then you'll be punished. That is laws of nature. Even if you are *bhakta*. You'll be given chance, but you'll have to be punished. So therefore we must be very careful. We are chanting Hare Kṛṣṇa mantra means dealing with Kṛṣṇa directly. Therefore we must be very careful, cautious, respectful. Then it is nice, it is success.

(Lecture on *The Nectar of Devotion*,
Vṛndāvana, October 30, 1972)

Once or Twice, You May Be Excused

So by chanting, we can come to the highest stage of perfection. In the beginning there may be offenses, but if we try to avoid the offenses, then it is *nāmābhāsa*. *Nāmābhāsa* means not actually pure name, but almost pure. *Nāmābhāsa* and *śuddha-nāma*. When one chants *śuddha-nāma,* name, holy name of God, then he is on the platform of loving platform with Kṛṣṇa. That is the perfectional stage. And in *nāmābhāsa* stage, not in pure, marginal, between pure and offensive, that is *mukti*. You become *mukta,* liberated from material bondage. And if we chant offensively, then we remain in the material world. Bhaktivinoda Ṭhākura has said it is mechanical, "Hare Kṛṣṇa, Hare Kṛṣṇa, Hare Kṛṣṇa," but still it is not Hare Kṛṣṇa.

So we must be purely chanting. But we should not be disappointed. Even impure . . . Therefore we must have fixed chanting process. Because we are not in the pure stage. Therefore, by force . . . Just like a boy in the school. We had this training in our childhood school. Our teacher would ask me, "You write ten pages, handwriting." So that means practicing ten pages, my handwriting will be set up. So if we do not follow sixteen rounds, where is the question of chanting Hare Kṛṣṇa? So don't be artificial; don't be, I mean to say, a showbottle. Be real thing. And that is wanted. If you want real benefit of spiritual life, don't be showbottle. Do you know showbottle? The medical shop, a big bottle. It is full of water only. And color is red or blue or something like. Real medicine does not require a showbottle. If one can chant purified, offenseless, once *kṛṣṇa-nāma,* he is free from all material bondage. Once only.

Devotee: Śrīla Prabhupāda, you spoke about the three stages of chanting. And you were speaking about the middle stage, the clearing stage. Is that . . . I didn't quite understand how that was explained. Is that like we're trying not to be offensive. It's offensive, but we're trying . . .

Prabhupāda: No, you do not try to be offensive, but because your past habit, you become offensive. Therefore ten kinds of offenses should be avoided. That we speak and give in list when initiation. Ten kinds of offenses should be avoided. The most offensive is that "By chanting Hare Kṛṣṇa mantra, I become sinless. So in the morning let me do, or in the night, let me do all sinful activities. In the morning I shall chant Hare Kṛṣṇa, and it will, everything will be nullified." This is the greatest offense. "Because I am chanting, therefore I can do anything sinful. It will be counteracted." This is the greatest rascaldom, sinful activities. Yes. By chanting Hare Kṛṣṇa mantra we become immediately sinless. That's a fact. But why shall we commit again? Just like the Christian people, they go to the church, confession: "Sir, I did this, all these sinful activities last week." "All right, pay me something." Again, from Monday, beginning sinful activities; come on Sunday. These are not allowed. You can be excused, but don't do again. If you continue to do it then you have to suffer. Once or twice, you may be excused. But if you continue to do that, you must be punished.

(Lecture on *Śrīmad-Bhāgavatam* 1.16.26–30, Hawaii, January 23, 1974)

Don't Make Farce

So you must have to follow these rules and regulation if you are serious. Then take initiation. Otherwise don't make farce. Don't make farce. That is my request. One has to be very determined. *Bhajante māṁ dṛḍha-vratāḥ.* This word is used in the *Bhāgavata, dṛḍha-vratāḥ,* strong determination: "Yes, in this life I shall go back to home, back to Godhead." This is determination. And what is the difficulty? No difficulty. Chant Hare Kṛṣṇa mantra. You are taking the beads, sixteen rounds. You can be finished, utmost two hours or three hours. So you have got twenty-four hours. If you want to sleep, of course, twenty-three hours, that is another thing. You have to minimize your sleeping. If you cannot finish sixteen rounds, then you must not sleep on that day, you must not eat. Why don't you forget to eat? Why do you forget chanting Hare Kṛṣṇa? This is negligence, *aparādha,* offense. Rather, you should forget your sleeping and eating and must finish sixteen rounds. This is called determination. This is called determined. So you are welcome to take initiation, but if you are neglectful, if you want to make it a farce, that is your business. I cannot give you any protection.

(Lecture on *Śrīmad-Bhāgavatam* 1.16.35,
Hawaii, January 28, 1974)

If In the Beginning One Chants With Offense

The chanting of the Hare Kṛṣṇa mantra is recommended even for persons who commit offenses, because if they continue chanting they will gradually chant offenselessly. By chanting the Hare Kṛṣṇa mantra without offenses, one increases his love for Kṛṣṇa. As stated by Śrī Caitanya Mahāprabhu, *premā pumartho mahān:* one's main concern should be to increase one's attachment to the Supreme Personality of Godhead and to increase one's love for Him.... Śrīla Viśvanātha Cakravartī Ṭhākura also quotes this verse from the *Padma Purāṇa:*

nāmāparādha-yuktānāṁ
nāmāny eva haranty agham
aviśrānti-prayuktāni
tāny evārtha-karāṇi ca

Even if in the beginning one chants the Hare Kṛṣṇa mantra with offenses, one will become free from such offenses by chanting again and again. *Pāpa-kṣayaś ca bhavati smaratāṁ tam aharniśam:* one becomes free from all sinful reactions if one chants day and night, following the recommendation of Śrī Caitanya Mahāprabhu. It was Śrī Caitanya Mahāprabhu who quoted the following verse:

harer nāma harer nāma
harer nāmaiva kevalam
kalau nāsty eva nāsty eva
nāsty eva gatir anyathā

"In this age of quarrel and hypocrisy the only means of deliverance is chanting the holy name of the Lord. There is no other way. There is no other way. There is no other way." If the members of the Kṛṣṇa consciousness movement strictly follow this recommendation of Śrī Caitanya Mahāprabhu, their position will always be secure.

(*Śrīmad-Bhāgavatam* 6.3.24, purport)

Whatever Our Condition May Be, We Should Begin

The Lord advised him, "Go to Vṛndāvana and chant the Hare Kṛṣṇa mantra constantly."

PURPORT

This is a solution to all sinful activities. In this Age of Kali everyone is perplexed by so many inconveniences—social, political, and religious—and naturally no one is happy. Due to the contamination of this age, everyone has a very short life. There are many fools and rascals who advise people to adopt this way of life or that way of life, but real liberation from life's perplexities means preparation for the next life. *Tathā dehāntara-prāptir dhīras tatra na muhyati.* One should be situated in his spiritual identity and return home, back to Godhead. The simplest method for this is recommended herein by Śrī Caitanya Mahāprabhu. We should constantly chant the holy names of the Lord, the Hare Kṛṣṇa *mahā-mantra.* Following in the footsteps of Śrī Caitanya Mahāprabhu, the Kṛṣṇa consciousness movement is recommending this process all over the world. We are saying, "Chant the Hare Kṛṣṇa *mahā-mantra,* be freed from all the complexities of life, and realize Kṛṣṇa, the Supreme Personality of Godhead. Engage in His devotional service and perfect your life so that you can return home, back to Godhead."

Śrī Caitanya Mahāprabhu further advised Subuddhi Rāya: "Begin chanting the Hare Kṛṣṇa mantra, and when your chanting is almost pure, all your sinful reactions will go away. After you chant perfectly, you will get shelter at the lotus feet of Kṛṣṇa."

PURPORT

The ten kinds of offenses should be considered. In the beginning, when one is initiated into the chanting of the Hare Kṛṣṇa *mahā-mantra,* there are naturally many offenses. Therefore the devotee should very carefully try to avoid these offenses and chant purely. This does not mean that the Hare Kṛṣṇa *mahā-mantra* is sometimes pure and sometimes impure. Rather, the chanter is impure due to material contamination. He has to purify himself so that the holy names will be perfectly effective. Chanting the holy name of the Lord inoffensively will help one get immediate shelter at Kṛṣṇa's lotus feet. This means that by chanting purely, one will immediately be situated on the transcendental platform. We should note, however, that according to Śrī Caitanya

Mahāprabhu's instructions, one should not wait to purify himself before chanting the Hare Kṛṣṇa mantra. Whatever our condition may be, we should begin chanting immediately. By the power of the Hare Kṛṣṇa mantra, we will gradually be relieved from all material contamination and will get shelter at the lotus feet of Kṛṣṇa, the ultimate goal of life.

(*Śrī Caitanya-caritāmṛta, Madhya-līlā* 25.198–199)

Receiving Spiritual Enlightenment

One should mentally honor the devotee who chants the holy name of Lord Kṛṣṇa, one should offer humble obeisances to the devotee who has undergone spiritual initiation [*dīkṣā*] and is engaged in worshiping the Deity, and one should associate with and faithfully serve that pure devotee who is advanced in undeviated devotional service and whose heart is completely devoid of the propensity to criticize others.

PURPORT

. . . In this Kṛṣṇa consciousness movement a chance is given to everyone without discrimination of caste, creed, or color. Everyone is invited to join this movement, sit with us, take *prasāda,* and hear about Kṛṣṇa. When we see that someone is actually interested in Kṛṣṇa consciousness and wants to be initiated, we accept him as a disciple for the chanting of the holy name of the Lord. When a neophyte devotee is actually initiated and engaged in devotional service by the orders of the spiritual master, he should be accepted immediately as a bona fide Vaiṣṇava, and obeisances should be offered unto him. Out of many such Vaiṣṇavas, one may be found to be very seriously engaged in the service of the Lord and strictly following all the regulative principles, chanting the prescribed number of rounds on *japa* beads and always thinking of how to expand the Kṛṣṇa consciousness movement. Such a Vaiṣṇava should be accepted as an *uttama-*

adhikārī, a highly advanced devotee, and his association should always be sought.

The process by which a devotee becomes attached to Kṛṣṇa is described in *Caitanya-caritāmṛta* (*Antya* 4.192): "At the time of initiation, when a devotee fully surrenders to the service of the Lord, Kṛṣṇa accepts him to be as good as He Himself."

Dīkṣā, or spiritual initiation, is explained in the *Bhakti-sandarbha* (868) by Śrīla Jīva Gosvāmī: "By *dīkṣā* one gradually becomes disinterested in material enjoyment and gradually becomes interested in spiritual life."

We have seen many practical examples of this, especially in Europe and America. Many students who come to us from rich and respectable families quickly lose all interest in material enjoyment and become very eager to enter into spiritual life. Although they come from very wealthy families, many of them accept living conditions that are not very comfortable. Indeed, for Kṛṣṇa's sake they are prepared to accept any living condition as long as they can live in the temple and associate with the Vaiṣṇavas. When one becomes so disinterested in material enjoyment, he becomes fit for initiation by the spiritual master. For the advancement of spiritual life *Śrīmad-Bhāgavatam* (6.1.13) prescribes: *tapasā brahmacaryeṇa śamena ca damena ca.* When a person is serious about accepting *dīkṣā,* he must be prepared to practice austerity, celibacy, and control of the mind and body. If one is so prepared and is desirous of receiving spiritual enlightenment (*divyaṁ jñānam*), he is fit for being initiated. *Divyaṁ jñānam* is technically called *tad-vijñāna,* or knowledge about the Supreme. *Tad-vijñānārthaṁ sa gurum evābhigacchet:* when one is interested in the transcendental subject matter of the Absolute Truth, he should be initiated. Such a person should approach a spiritual master in order to take *dīkṣā. Śrīmad-Bhāgavatam* (11.3.21) also prescribes: *tasmād guruṁ prapadyeta jijñāsuḥ śreya uttamam.* "When one is actually interested in the transcendental science of the Absolute Truth, he should approach a spiritual master."

...The chanting of the holy names of Kṛṣṇa is so sublime that if one chants the Hare Kṛṣṇa *mahā-mantra* offenselessly, carefully avoiding the ten offenses, he can certainly be gradually elevated to the point of understanding that there is no difference between the holy name of the Lord and the Lord Himself. One who has reached such an understanding should be very much respected by neophyte devotees. One should know for certain that without chanting the holy name of the Lord offenselessly, one cannot be a proper candidate for advancement in Kṛṣṇa consciousness. In *Śrī Caitanya-caritāmṛta* (*Madhya* 22.69) it is said: "One whose faith is soft and pliable is called a neophyte, but by gradually following the process, he will rise to the platform of a first-class devotee." Everyone begins his devotional life from the neophyte stage, but if one properly finishes chanting the prescribed number of rounds of *hari-nāma,* he is elevated step by step to the highest platform, *uttama-adhikārī.* The Kṛṣṇa consciousness movement prescribes sixteen rounds daily because people in the Western countries cannot concentrate for long periods while chanting on beads. Therefore the minimum number of rounds is prescribed. However, Śrīla Bhaktisiddhānta Sarasvatī Ṭhākura used to say that unless one chants at least sixty-four rounds (one hundred thousand names), he is considered fallen (*patita*). According to his calculation, practically every one of us is fallen, but because we are trying to serve the Supreme Lord with all seriousness and without duplicity, we can expect the mercy of Lord Śrī Caitanya Mahāprabhu, who is famous as *patita-pāvana,* the deliverer of the fallen.

...When one fully engages in chanting the Hare Kṛṣṇa *mahā-mantra,* he gradually realizes his own spiritual identity. Unless one faithfully chants the Hare Kṛṣṇa mantra, Kṛṣṇa does not reveal Himself: *sevonmukhe hi jihvādau svayam eva sphuraty adaḥ.* We cannot realize the Supreme Personality of Godhead by any artificial means. We must engage faithfully in the service of the Lord. Such service begins with the tongue (*sevonmukhe hi jihvādau*), which means that we should always chant the holy names of the Lord and accept *kṛṣṇa-prasāda*. We should not chant or accept anything else. When this process is faithfully followed, the Supreme Lord reveals Himself to the devotee.

(*The Nectar of Instruction,* text 5)

Don't Take This Movement As Something Cheap

If you want to stay in Krishna Consciousness you will have to develop firm faith in Guru and Sastra. Therefore, you must study my books very scrutinizingly, follow the four regulative principles very strictly and chant 16 rounds daily avoiding the ten offenses. Don't take this movement as something cheap.

(Letter to Śrutadeva Dāsa, October 30, 1976)

You Have Now Got the Golden Opportunity

My dear Sons and Daughters,

Please accept my blessings. Upon the recommendation of Bahudak I have gladly accepted all of you as my duly initiated disciples. . . .

Now my request to all of you is that you very seriously and sincerely stick to the principles of devotional service, and especially observe strictly the four prohibitions, and without fail always chant at least 16 rounds on your beads daily. In this way you will be always happy.

You have now got the golden opportunity of this human form of life, and it is not by accident that you have met your spiritual master, so if you are actually intelligent you will take advantage of Krishna's blessings upon you and go back to home, back to Godhead. The essential point to remember is that by your activity you will please always your spiritual master. That means following the orders and instructions of your spiritual master, and my first instruction to all of my disciples is that they become Kṛṣṇa conscious devotees themselves and help others to become devotees by spreading this Krishna Consciousness movement all over the world, utilizing their energy however they are best able to do it. In this way, if you keep yourselves always engaged in Krishna's business 24 hours, then you will be freed from all attachment to maya, by Krishna's grace. Just as when the darkness and the light come together, the darkness cannot stand before the light, so maya cannot remain in the presence of Krishna. Always remember therefore to chant Hare Krishna, and that will save you in all circumstances, without any doubt.

(Letter to Vancouver devotees, January 5, 1973)

8

The Greatest Meditator and the Greatest Yogī

Chant Sixteen Rounds

Accepting Only What Is Necessary

In the *Nāradīya Purāṇa* it is directed, "One should not accept more than necessary if he is serious about discharging devotional service." The purport is that one should not neglect following the principles of devotional service, nor should one accept the rulings of devotional service which are more than what he can easily perform. For example, it may be said that one should chant the Hare Kṛṣṇa mantra at least one hundred thousand times daily on his beads. But if this is not possible, then one must minimize his chanting according to his own capacity. Generally, we recommend our disciples to chant at least sixteen rounds on their *japa* beads daily, and this should be completed. But if one is not even able to chant sixteen rounds, then he must make it up the next day. He must be sure to keep his vow. If he does not strictly follow this out, then he is sure to be negligent. That is offensive in the service of the Lord. If we encourage offenses, we shall not be able to make progress in devotional service. It is better if one fixes up a regulative principle according to his own ability and then follows that vow without fail. That will make him advanced in spiritual life.

(*The Nectar of Devotion,*
"Evidence Regarding Devotional Principles")

A Fixed Number of Times Daily Is Essential

Since Your two hands will always be engaged in chanting and counting the holy names, how will You be able to carry the waterpot and external garments?

PURPORT

From this verse it is clear that Caitanya Mahāprabhu was chanting the holy names a fixed number of times daily. The Gosvāmīs used to follow in the footsteps of Śrī Caitanya Mahāprabhu, and Haridāsa Ṭhākura also followed this principle. Concerning the Gosvāmīs—Śrīla Rūpa Gosvāmī, Śrīla Sanātana Gosvāmī, Śrīla Raghunātha Bhaṭṭa Gosvāmī, Śrīla Jīva Gosvāmī, Śrīla Gopāla Bhaṭṭa Gosvāmī, and Śrīla Raghunātha dāsa Gosvāmī—Śrīnivāsa Ācārya confirms, *saṅkhyā-pūrvaka-nāma-gāna-natibhiḥ* (*Ṣaḍ-gosvāmy-aṣṭaka* 6). In addition to other duties, Śrī Caitanya Mahāprabhu introduced the system of chanting the holy name of the Lord a fixed number of times daily, as confirmed in this verse (*tomāra dui hasta baddha nāma-gaṇane*). Caitanya Mahāprabhu used to count on His fingers. While one hand was engaged in chanting, the other hand kept the number of rounds. This is corroborated in the *Caitanya-candrāmṛta* and also in Śrīla Rūpa Gosvāmī's *Stava-mālā*.

Therefore devotees in the line of Śrī Caitanya Mahāprabhu must chant at least sixteen rounds daily, and this is the number prescribed by the International Society for Krishna Consciousness. Haridāsa Ṭhākura daily chanted 300,000 names. Sixteen rounds is about 28,000 names. There is no need to imitate Haridāsa Ṭhākura or the other Gosvāmīs, but chanting the holy name a fixed number of times daily is essential for every devotee.

(*Śrī Caitanya-caritāmṛta, Madhya-līlā* 7.37)

Sixteen Rounds Is Absolutely Necessary

Kṛṣṇa is the origin of Lord Viṣṇu. He should always be remembered and never forgotten at any time. All the rules and prohibitions mentioned in the *śāstras* should be the servants of these two principles.

PURPORT

This verse is a quotation from the *Padma Purāṇa*. There are many regulative principles in the *śāstras* and directions given by the spiritual master. These regulative principles should act as servants of the basic principle—that is, one should always remember Kṛṣṇa and never forget Him. This is possible when one chants the Hare Kṛṣṇa mantra. Therefore one must strictly chant the Hare Kṛṣṇa *mahā-mantra* twenty-four hours daily. One may have other duties to perform under the direction of the spiritual master, but he must first abide by the spiritual master's order to chant a certain number of rounds. In our Kṛṣṇa consciousness movement, we have recommended that the neophyte chant at least sixteen rounds. This chanting of sixteen rounds is absolutely necessary if one wants to remember Kṛṣṇa and not forget Him. Of all the regulative principles, the spiritual master's order to chant at least sixteen rounds is most essential.

(*Śrī Caitanya-caritāmṛta, Madhya-līlā* 22.113)

In a Diseased Condition of Spiritual Life

Śrī Caitanya Mahāprabhu further inquired from Haridāsa, "Can you ascertain what your disease is?" Haridāsa Ṭhākura replied, "My disease is that I cannot complete my rounds."

PURPORT

If one cannot complete the fixed number of rounds he is assigned, he should be considered to be in a diseased condition of spiritual life. Śrīla Haridāsa Ṭhākura is called *nāmācārya*. Of course, we cannot imitate Haridāsa Ṭhākura, but everyone must chant a prescribed number of rounds. In our Kṛṣṇa consciousness movement we have fixed sixteen rounds as the minimum so that the Westerners will not feel burdened. These sixteen rounds must be chanted, and chanted loudly, so that one can hear himself and others.

(*Śrī Caitanya-caritāmṛta, Antya-līlā* 11.23)

Don't Make God Very Cheap Thing

Bhakti-yoga therefore requires a little *tapasya* [austerity], that, "We are addicted to so many sinful activities. We must give it up." That is *tapasya*. "We must observe fasting on *ekādaśī* day, on Lord's birthday." These are *tapasya*. "We must chant sixteen rounds. We must observe the rules and regulations." This is *tapasya*. Don't make God very cheap thing: "Oh, it is very cheap thing." No. It has been made very easy for the Kali-yuga people because they cannot undergo any kind of *tapasya*. There is simple *tapasya*. "Chant sixteen rounds. Don't take this. Don't do these four items. Take *prasādam*. Don't take just anything." So nothing is stopped. A little regulated, that this much, if we do not do, then how we can expect to see God and understand God? *Tapo divyam.* If simply we remain like hogs and cats and dogs, then how it is possible to realize God? *Paraṁ pavitram.* If I do not become *pavitra* myself, pure, how I can see the supreme pure? It is impossible. *Tapasya* must be there.

(Lecture on *Śrīmad-Bhāgavatam* 2.9.4, Japan, April 22, 1972)

That Is Our Spiritual Strength

The first management is that each and every member in the temple is chanting sixteen rounds regularly and following the regulations, that's all. That is our spiritual strength. That must be executed. Haridāsa Ṭhākura, such exalted personality, such advanced, still he is numerical counting even up to the point of his death. Therefore he was given the *nāmācārya,* because so rigid. Even at the time of his death, Lord Caitanya requested, "Now you can minimize." "No, Sir, I cannot minimize." And what is the number? Three hundred thousand. These are the examples. But the regulation is that if one day you cannot finish, you have to finish on the next day. But sixteen rounds is not very large number, the lowest. The lowest in India is twenty-five. Here sixteen rounds, twenty-five, not even twenty-five. So the president, local president, must see that the members are chanting. So in this way the institution will be managed, then it will make progress. That is our spiritual strength—to observe the regulative principles and at least chant sixteen rounds. Then you do other things.

(Room conversation with Governing Body members, Los Angeles, May 25, 1972)

The Ointment of Love

How to love Kṛṣṇa? Take it as ointment. As we apply some ointment to increase the sight of our eyes . . . doctor gives some prescription. So similarly, how to see God? You will see God with these eyes when it is clarified, *premāñjana-cchurita,* by the ointment of love of Godhead. So these are the function, how to love. One has to rise early in the morning. He doesn't like, but, "No. I will have to satisfy Kṛṣṇa." This is the beginning. "Oh, I have to chant sixteen rounds." He is lazy. He doesn't want to do it. But if he loves Kṛṣṇa, he must do it. He must do it.

(Initiation lecture, San Diego, June 30, 1972)

Sixteen Rounds Is Nothing

Just like we have asked our students to finish sixteen rounds chanting minimum. Sixteen rounds is nothing. In Vṛndāvana there are many devotees, they chant 120 rounds. Like that. So sixteen rounds is the minimum. Because I know in the Western countries it is difficult job to finish sixty-four rounds or 120 rounds, like that. Minimum sixteen rounds. That must be finished. *Tat-tat-karma-pravartanāt.* This is the direction. Observing the regulative principles. In this way, we must be abiding by the direction of the spiritual master and the *śāstra*. Then rest assured, success is guaranteed.

(Lecture on *The Nectar of Devotion*, Vṛndāvana, October 20, 1972)

"Chant Hare Kṛṣṇa Mantra Sixteen Times—Please !!"

So people are so rascal, they will not even chant Hare Kṛṣṇa mantra. So Kṛṣṇa is teaching. Kṛṣṇa is so kind. He's personally teaching. That is, perform *yajña*. He's personally chanting, dancing, Caitanya Mahāprabhu. Personally He's teaching us, "Perform this *yajña,* you rascal, and you'll get everything. You'll get everything." Now, where is the proof? The proof is this Kṛṣṇa consciousness movement. We are simply chanting Hare Kṛṣṇa *mahā-mantra* and spending millions of rupees. Simply. What we are doing? We are not doing any business. We have not many professional men. But why we are getting . . . ? We are spending eight hundred thousand rupees per month. And we have got food, we have got milk. We are feeding others also, bringing food. So why don't you see practically how these Kṛṣṇa conscious people are fabulously rich? This question was raised in Parliament also. So how we became fabulously rich? We do not do anything. I have not taught you anything magic. I simply request you, "Chant Hare Kṛṣṇa mantra sixteen times—please!!" But you are not even following that. This is the only remedy.

(Lecture on *Śrīmad-Bhāgavatam* 1.8.18,
Māyāpur, September 28, 1974)

To Gradually Become Attached to the Chanting

Simply by chanting the holy name of Kṛṣṇa one can obtain freedom from material existence. Indeed, simply by chanting the Hare Kṛṣṇa mantra one will be able to see the lotus feet of the Lord.

PURPORT

. . . Simply addressing the energy of the Supreme Lord as Hare and the Lord Himself as Kṛṣṇa very soon situates the Lord within the heart of the devotee. By thus addressing Rādhā and Kṛṣṇa, one directly engages in His Lordship's service. The essence of all revealed scriptures and all knowledge is present when one addresses the Lord and His energy by the Hare Kṛṣṇa mantra, for this transcendental vibration can completely liberate a conditioned soul and directly engage him in the service of the Lord.

Śrī Caitanya Mahāprabhu presented Himself as a grand fool, yet He maintained that all the words that He had heard from His spiritual master strictly followed the principles stated by Vyāsadeva in *Śrīmad-Bhāgavatam* (1.7.6).

anarthopaśamaṁ sākṣād
bhakti-yogam adhokṣaje
lokasyājānato vidvāṁś
cakre sātvata-saṁhitām

"The material miseries of a living entity, which are superfluous to him, can be directly mitigated by the linking process of devotional service. But the mass of people do not know this, and therefore the learned Vyāsadeva compiled this Vedic literature [*Śrīmad-Bhāgavatam*], which is in relation to the Supreme Truth." One can overcome all misconceptions and entanglement in the material world by practicing *bhakti-yoga,* and therefore Vyāsadeva, acting on the instruction of Śrī Nārada, has very kindly introduced *Śrīmad-Bhāgavatam* to relieve the conditioned souls from the clutches of *māyā.* Lord Caitanya's spiritual master instructed Him, therefore, that one must read *Śrīmad-Bhāgavatam* regularly and with scrutiny to gradually become attached to the chanting of the Hare Kṛṣṇa *mahā-mantra.*

(*Śrī Caitanya-caritāmṛta, Ādi-līlā* 7.73)

You Should Follow Rigidly

Prabhupāda: The spirit of service must be maintained. *Mukhe hi jihvadau svayam eva sphuraty adaḥ.* By service spirit beginning with tongue, Hare Kṛṣṇa. Then everything is revealed, Vaikuṇṭha atmosphere.

Akṣayānanda Swami: Of course when you tell us to chant sixteen rounds, we accept that figure in perfect faith, that you're the *ācārya*. But what of others we want to convince? Is there *śāstra,* any Vedic verse we can refer to, to corroborate that at least they must chant sixteen rounds? Or that many number of names?
Prabhupāda: No. In the *śāstra* it is not said like that.
Akṣayānanda Swami: I see.
Prabhupāda: It is said, *saṅkhyā-pūrvakaḥ.*
Akṣayānanda Swami: *Saṅkhyā-pūrvakaḥ.*
Prabhupāda: You must fix up.
Akṣayānanda Swami: Counting.
Prabhupāda: You must fix up in numerical strength.
Akṣayānanda Swami: I see.
Prabhupāda: Whatever you can.
Akṣayānanda Swami: Yes.
Prabhupāda: I have fixed up sixteen rounds, because you cannot do.
Akṣayānanda Swami: That's all we can do.
Prabhupāda: Yes. That also very difficult.
Akṣayānanda Swami: Yes.
Prabhupāda: Otherwise, Haridāsa Ṭhākura was chanting three hundred thousand.
Akṣayānanda Swami: Three lakhs of names.
Prabhupāda: That is not possible. You should not imitate, but whatever you fix up you must do.
Akṣayānanda Swami: Yes. Yes.
Prabhupāda: That is wanted.
Akṣayānanda Swami: I was told in the beginning that you asked the first disciples to chant sixty-four rounds?
Prabhupāda: Yes.
Akṣayānanda Swami: They were unable. Then you asked them to chant thirty-two?
Prabhupāda: *Saṅkhyā-pūrvaka nāma-gāna-natibhiḥ. saṅkhyā pūrva,* or numerical strength, must be there. And you should follow rigidly.

Akṣayānanda Swami: So if . . . if we are serious and sincere, it means that that sixteen will increase to continuously chanting.
Prabhupāda: Yes. You can do also now. It's not that because I've finished sixteen rounds . . .
Akṣayānanda Swami: No.
Prabhupāda: You can increase. But that sixteen must be finished.
(Morning walk, Vṛndāvana, December 11, 1975)

Increasing Your Rounds

Meditating on Kṛṣṇa Twenty-Four Hours a Day

Nowadays people are very much inclined to the meditational process, which is not practical in this age, but if anyone practices meditating on Kṛṣṇa twenty-four hours a day by chanting the Hare Kṛṣṇa mantra round his beads, he is surely the greatest meditator and the greatest *yogī,* as substantiated by the sixth chapter of *Bhagavad-gītā.*

(*Bhagavad-gītā* 9.27, purport)

Use Your Time in the Prison House To the Greatest Advantage

My advice to you is to continue your good attitude that you are keeping now and this alone will help you in advancing your cause of Krishna Consciousness. Yes, it will be great advantage if you can chant so much as one lac of Names daily [100,000 names—64 rounds], and also read scriptures. This is good opportunity for you to learn to sing all the verses in the Srimad-Bhagavatam as you began to do so nicely in San Francisco. That will be very nice.

Namacarya Haridasa Thakura was taken to the jail and he told the prisoners there, "Oh, you are so fortunate to have this opportunity to sit and chant the Holy Names without the Maya distractions of the outer world!" So you should think like that, and use your time in the prison house to the greatest advantage for spiritual advancement.

Please note that the other side of this page was appearing in the very popular magazine New Yorker, and even they are chanting Hare Krishna in mockery, still, it doesn't matter. Just so long they are chanting Hare Krishna, that is the success of our mission. The Kazi's men were breaking up the Kirtana parties of the Lord, and in mockery some of them chanted Hare Krishna, and thereafter, their tongues would not stop singing Hare Krishna. Our tongues should be like that, unable to ever stop singing the Glories of the Lord. We practice, and someday it will be like that.

Hope you are feeling well. And I hope you are receiving proper food there also.

(Letter to Upendra Dāsa, February 5, 1968)

Increase the Number and You Will Become More Strong

My Dear Mr. DDD,

It is very encouraging to me that you are regularly chanting your twenty rounds of beads daily. Be careful never to decrease but increase the number and you will become more strong in Krishna Consciousness. So continue to tend your Deities first-class and be happy in Krishna's service.

Always remember Krishna Who is your dearmost friend and always serve Him just to please Him, and He will give you all intelligence how to be a first-class devotee. Just try to learn all about Krishna, chant Hare Krishna, and you will be a great preacher of our Krishna Consciousness movement.

(Letter to Dvārakādhiśa Dāsa, March 3, 1970)

Why Just 25 Rounds?

Why just 25 rounds? You should chant as many as possible. Real Ekadasi means fasting and chanting and no other business. When one observes fasting, the chanting becomes easier. So on Ekadasi other business can be suspended as far as possible unless there is some urgent business.

(Letter to Jadurāṇī Devī Dāsī, July 9, 1971)

That Is the Only Remedy

Prabhupāda: They should be trained up. Sense enjoyment means not advanced in Kṛṣṇa consciousness. As soon as one is advancing in Kṛṣṇa consciousness, his sense enjoyment spirit will be reduced. That is the test. *Bhaktiḥ pareśānubhavo viraktir anyatra ca.* The test is, how you are advancing in Kṛṣṇa consciousness is the proportionate diminishing of sense enjoyment. That is the test. Just like cure of the disease means diminishing the fever, temperature. This is the test.

Devotee: What if that fever is not being diminished?

Prabhupāda: Then he should try to chant Hare Kṛṣṇa mantra, instead of sixteen rounds, sixty-four rounds. That is the way. Sixteen round is the minimum. Otherwise Haridāsa Ṭhākura was 300,000. So you have to increase. That is the only remedy. If one has got determination, he will make progress without any trouble. That determination is very difficult, that determination, "I must be Kṛṣṇa conscious fully." That determination. *Dṛḍha-vratāḥ.*

(Morning walk, Perth, May 14, 1975)

For a Sannyāsī, You Should Increase

So although you are young men—there are many difficulties to keep *sannyāsa*—but if you keep faith, full faith in Kṛṣṇa, the *māyā* will not be able to touch you. *Daivī hy eṣā guṇamayī mama māyā duratyayā. Māyā* is very strong, but if we keep ourself fully surrendered unto the Supreme Personality of Godhead, Kṛṣṇa, *māyā* will not be able to counteract this process. So you should always keep yourself fixed up in Kṛṣṇa consciousness. It is not very difficult. Strictly follow the rules and regulation and chant Hare Kṛṣṇa mantra as many times . . . for a *sannyāsī,* you should increase. Then you will be fixed up.

(*Sannyāsa* initiation lecture, Vṛndāvana, December 6, 1975)

If They Can Increase, It Is Better

And those who are being first initiated, they must chant at least sixteen rounds. *Saṅkhyā-pūrvaka-nāma-gāna-natibhiḥ.* The Gosvāmīs, they showed us the way. *Saṅkhyā-pūrvaka.* So many rounds we must chant, at least. Haridāsa Ṭhākura was chanting three hundred thousand times. We cannot do that. That is not possible. So we have made a minimum, sixteen rounds. So those who are being initiated, they must chant at least sixteen rounds. If they can increase, it is better. But not less than that. *Saṅkhyā-pūrvaka-nāma-gāna-natibhiḥ.*

(Initiation lecture, Hyderabad, August 22, 1976)

Why Not Sixteen Thousand Rounds?

Devotee: When chanting our sixteen rounds, we are not sure if these rounds are sincere . . .

Prabhupāda: You should be sure.

Devotee: How can we be sure?

Prabhupāda: There is beads.

Brahmānanda: No, he's saying that when we chant our rounds, how can we be sure that when we chant the round that the round is a perfect, attentive round, sincere?

Prabhupāda: Therefore it is *śāstra,* "You must." There is no question of understanding.
Brahmānanda: The quality of the chanting he's asking. How can we make the quality the best?
Prabhupāda: Quality you'll understand, first of all *come* to the quality. Without having quality, how he'll understand the quality? You follow the instruction of your spiritual master, of the *śāstra*. That is your duty. Quality, no quality—it is not your position to understand. When the quality comes there is no force. You will have a taste for chanting. You will desire at that time, "Why sixteen rounds? Why not sixteen thousand rounds?" That is quality. That is quality. It is by force. You'll not do it; therefore at least sixteen rounds. But when you come to the quality, you will feel yourself, "Why sixteen? Why not sixteen thousand?" That is quality, automatically. Just like Haridāsa Ṭhākura was doing. He was not forced to do. Even Caitanya Mahāprabhu, He requested, "Now you are old enough. You can reduce." So he refused, "No. Up to the end of my life I shall go on." That is quality. Have you got such tendency that you will go on chanting and nothing to do? That is quality. Now you are forced to do. Where is the question of quality? That is given a chance so that one day you may come to the quality, not that you have come to the quality. Quality is different. *Athāśaktiḥ. Aśakti,* attachment. Just like Rūpa Gosvāmī says that "How shall I chant with one tongue, and how shall I hear, two ears? Had it been millions of tongues and trillions of ears, then I could enjoy it." This is quality. Quality is not so cheap. Maybe after many births. For the time being you go on following the rules and regulations. It is being done by force. Where is the quality?

So you wanted to understand quality. This is the quality. You'll not be forced, but automatically you'll desire. That is quality. I am writing books. I am not being forced by anyone. Everyone can do that. Why one does not do it? Why I get up at night, one o'clock, and do this job? Because I cannot do without it. How one will do it artificially? This is quality. Therefore they like my purports. That quality is shown by Caitanya Mahāprabhu. *Śūnyāyitaṁ jagat sarvaṁ govinda viraheṇa me.* "Oh, I do not see Govinda. The whole world is vacant." *Śūnyāyitaṁ jagat sarvaṁ govinda viraheṇa me.* This is quality. Just like we have got practical example. One man's beloved has died, and he is seeing the whole universe vacant. Is it vacant? So that is quality of love. So there is no formula of quality. It is to be understood by himself. Just like if after eating something you feel refreshed and get strength, that is quality. You haven't got to take certificate: "Will you give me a certificate that I have eaten?" You'll understand whether eaten or not. That is quality. When you will feel so much ecstasy in chanting Hare Kṛṣṇa, that is quality. Not artificially—"Chant. Chant. Otherwise get out." This is not quality. This is in expectation that some day you may come to quality. That requires time. That requires sincerity. But quality is there. *Śravaṇādi-śuddha-citte-karaye* . . . It will be awakened. Not by force.

(Morning walk, Nairobi, November 2, 1975)

Chant Sixteen Thousand Rounds—That Is Welcome

Lokanātha: Prabhupāda, why we have chosen this sixteen as a number to chant the rounds?

Prabhupāda: Yes.

Lokanātha: Why not less or more?

Prabhupāda: We have fixed up sixteen.

Lokanātha: We are chanting sixteen.

Prabhupāda: No. We say "Minimum sixteen." Minimum.

Lokanātha: Why that sixteen minimum?

Prabhupāda: If you can, sixteen thousand you can go. Sixteen rounds is the minimum. But if you are able to chant sixteen thousand rounds, that is welcome. We have got so much engagement. Still, we say, "We don't find engagement." This is our misfortune. Hare Kṛṣṇa. *Jaya.* Haridāsa Ṭhākura was engaged in chanting and the prostitute came. She offered, "Let us enjoy." "Yes, let me finish. Let me finish this chanting." So much engagement, and still, we say, "No engagement." He refused to have sex with a beautiful young girl because he had engagement. "First of all let me finish my engagement." And we say we have no engagement. How unfortunate we are. Lord Caitanya says, *kīrtanīyaḥ sadā hariḥ*. Twenty-four-hours engagement He has given, and we see there is no engagement.

Lokanātha: Some devotees have fixed different number than sixteen. Some are chanting twenty minimum or twenty-five.

Prabhupāda: Yes. It should be increased.

Lokanātha: Is it recommended for our . . .?

Prabhupāda: But don't decrease. Don't decrease; increase. Therefore, one number is fixed. "At least this much I shall do." That is sixteen rounds.

Lokanātha: But you are recommending sixteen as a minimum, and some devotees are choosing twenty as a minimum.

Prabhupāda: So who forbids? Who says that "Don't do it"?

Lokanātha: They can chant?

Prabhupāda: Yes. That is wanted. But because you cannot do it, therefore we have fixed up this minimum. *Saṅkhyāta asaṅkhyāta. Saṅkhyāta* means with vow, numerical strength. And *asaṅkhyāta* means there is no limit.

(Morning walk, Bombay, November 10, 1975)

Painting by Yadurāṇī Devī Dāsī

9

Freedom From Offenses by The Mercy of Lord Caitanya

To Derive the Full Benefit of the Chanting

These five *tattvas* incarnate with Lord Caitanya Mahāprabhu, and thus the Lord executes His *saṅkīrtana* movement with great pleasure.

PURPORT

In *Śrīmad-Bhāgavatam* (11.5.32) there is the following statement regarding Śrī Caitanya Mahāprabhu:

kṛṣṇa-varṇaṁ tviṣākṛṣṇaṁ
sāṅgopāṅgāstra-pārṣadam
yajñaiḥ saṅkīrtana-prāyair
yajanti hi su-medhasaḥ

"In the Age of Kali, people who are endowed with sufficient intelligence will worship the Lord, who is accompanied by His associates, by performance of the *saṅkīrtana-yajña.*" Śrī Caitanya Mahāprabhu is always accompanied by His plenary expansion Śrī Nityānanda Prabhu, His incarnation Śrī Advaita Prabhu, His internal potency Śrī Gadādhara Prabhu, and His marginal potency Śrīvāsa Prabhu. He is in the midst of them as the Supreme Personality of Godhead. One should know that Śrī Caitanya Mahāprabhu is always accompanied by these other *tattvas.* Therefore our obeisances to Śrī Caitanya Mahāprabhu are complete when we say *śrī-kṛṣṇa-caitanya prabhu-nityānanda śrī-advaita gadādhara śrīvāsādi-gaura-bhakta-vṛnda.* As preachers of the Kṛṣṇa consciousness movement, we first offer our obeisances to Śrī Caitanya Mahāprabhu by chanting this Pañca-tattva mantra; then we say Hare Kṛṣṇa, Hare Kṛṣṇa, Kṛṣṇa Kṛṣṇa, Hare Hare/ Hare Rāma, Hare Rāma, Rāma Rāma, Hare Hare.

There are ten offenses in the chanting of the Hare Kṛṣṇa *mahā-mantra,* but these are not considered in the chanting of the Pañca-tattva mantra, namely, *śrī-kṛṣṇa-caitanya prabhu-nityānanda śrī-advaita gadādhara śrīvāsādi-gaura-bhakta-vṛnda.*

Śrī Caitanya Mahāprabhu is known as *mahā-vadānyāvatāra,* the most magnanimous incarnation, for He does not consider the offenses of the fallen souls. Thus to derive the full benefit of the chanting of the *mahā-mantra* (Hare Kṛṣṇa, Hare Kṛṣṇa, Kṛṣṇa Kṛṣṇa, Hare Hare/ Hare Rāma, Hare Rāma, Rāma Rāma, Hare Hare), we must first take shelter of Śrī Caitanya Mahāprabhu, learn the Pañca-tattva *mahā-mantra,* and then chant the Hare Kṛṣṇa *mahā-mantra.* That will be very effective.

(*Śrī Caitanya-caritāmṛta, Ādi-līlā* 7.4)

One Immediately Becomes Ecstatic

There are offenses to be considered while chanting the Hare Kṛṣṇa mantra. Therefore simply by chanting Hare Kṛṣṇa one does not become ecstatic.

PURPORT

It is very beneficial to chant the names *śrī-kṛṣṇa-caitanya prabhu-nityānanda* before chanting the Hare Kṛṣṇa *mahā-mantra* because by chanting these two holy names—*śrī-kṛṣṇa-caitanya prabhu-nityānanda*—one immediately becomes ecstatic, and if he then chants the Hare Kṛṣṇa *mahā-mantra* he becomes free of offenses. There are ten offenses to avoid in chanting the Hare Kṛṣṇa *mahā-mantra.* The first offense is to blaspheme great personalities who are engaged in distributing the holy name of the Lord. It is said in the *śāstra* (Cc., *Antya* 7.11), *kṛṣṇa-śakti vinā nahe tāra pravartana:* one cannot distribute the holy names of the Hare Kṛṣṇa *mahā-mantra* unless he is empowered by the Supreme Personality of Godhead. Therefore one should not criticize or blaspheme a devotee who is thus engaged.

Śrī Padma Purāṇa states:

satāṁ nindā nāmnaḥ paramam aparādhaṁ vitanute
yataḥ khyātiṁ yātaṁ katham u sahate tad-vigarhām

To blaspheme the great saintly persons who are engaged in preaching the glories of the Hare Kṛṣṇa *mahā-mantra* is the worst offense at the lotus feet of the holy name. One should not criticize a preacher of the glories of the Hare Kṛṣṇa *mahā-mantra*. If one does so, he is an offender. The *nāma-prabhu,* who is identical with Kṛṣṇa, will never tolerate such blasphemous activities, even from one who passes as a great devotee.

The second *nāmāparādha* is described as follows:

śivasya śrī-viṣṇor ya iha guṇa-nāmādi-sakalaṁ
dhiyā bhinnaṁ paśyet sa khalu hari-nāmāhita-karaḥ

In this material world, the holy name of Viṣṇu is all-auspicious. Viṣṇu's name, form, qualities, and pastimes are all transcendental, absolute knowledge. Therefore, if one tries to separate the Absolute Personality of Godhead from His holy name or His transcendental form, qualities, and pastimes, thinking them to be material, that is offensive. Similarly, to think that the names of demigods such as Lord Śiva are as good as the name of Lord Viṣṇu—or, in other words, to think that Lord Śiva and the other demigods are other forms of God and are therefore equal to Viṣṇu—is also blasphemous. This is the second offense at the lotus feet of the holy name of the Lord.

The third offense at the lotus feet of the holy name, which is called *guror avajñā,* is to consider the spiritual master to be material and therefore to envy his exalted position. The fourth offense (*śruti-śāstra-nindanam*) is to blaspheme Vedic literatures such as the four *Vedas* and the *Purāṇas*. The fifth offense (*artha-vādaḥ*) is to consider the glories of the holy name to be exaggerations. Similarly, the sixth offense (*hari-nāmni kalpanam*) is to consider the holy name of the Lord to be imaginary.

The seventh offense is described as follows:

nāmno balād yasya hi pāpa-buddhir
na vidyate tasya yamair hi śuddhiḥ

To think that since the Hare Kṛṣṇa mantra can counteract all sinful reactions one may therefore go on with his sinful activities and at the same time chant the Hare Kṛṣṇa mantra to neutralize them is the greatest offense at the lotus feet of *hari-nāma.*

The eighth offense is stated thus:

dharma-vrata-tyāga-hutādi-sarva-
śubha-kriyā-sāmyam api pramādaḥ

It is offensive to consider the chanting of the Hare Kṛṣṇa mantra to be a religious ritualistic ceremony. Performing religious ceremonies, following vows and practicing renunciation and sacrifice are all materialistic auspicious activities. The chanting of the Hare Kṛṣṇa *mahā-mantra* must not be compared to such materialistic religiosity. This is an offense at the lotus feet of the holy name of the Lord.

The ninth offense is described as follows:

aśraddadhāne vimukhe 'py aśṛṇvati
yaś copadeśaḥ śiva-nāmāparādhaḥ

It is an offense to preach the glories of the holy name among persons who have no intelligence or no faith in the subject matter. Such people should be given the chance to hear the chanting of the Hare Kṛṣṇa mantra, but in the beginning they should not be instructed about the glories or the spiritual significance of the holy name. By constant hearing of the holy name, their hearts will be purified, and then they will be able to understand the transcendental position of the holy name.

The tenth offense is as follows:

śrute 'pi nāma-māhātmye yaḥ prīti-rahito naraḥ
ahaṁ-mamādi-paramo nāmni so 'py aparādha-kṛt

If one has heard the glories of the transcendental holy name of the

Lord but nevertheless continues in a materialistic concept of life, thinking "I am this body and everything belonging to this body is mine," and does not show respect and love for the chanting of the Hare Kṛṣṇa *mahā-mantra,* that is an offense.

(*Śrī Caitanya-caritāmṛta, Ādi-līlā* 8.24)

This Is the Real Change

"If one's heart does not change, tears do not flow from his eyes, his body does not shiver, and his bodily hairs do not stand on end as he chants the Hare Kṛṣṇa *mahā-mantra,* it should be understood that his heart is as hard as iron. This is due to his offenses at the lotus feet of the Lord's holy name."

PURPORT

Śrīla Bhaktisiddhānta Sarasvatī Ṭhākura, commenting on this verse, which is a quotation from *Śrīmad-Bhāgavatam* (2.3.24), remarks that sometimes a *mahā-bhāgavata,* or very advanced devotee, does not manifest such transcendental symptoms as tears in the eyes, whereas sometimes a *kaniṣṭha-adhikārī,* a neophyte devotee, displays them artificially. This does not mean, however, that the neophyte is more advanced than the *mahā-bhāgavata* devotee. The test of the real change of heart that takes place when one chants the Hare Kṛṣṇa *mahā-mantra* is that one becomes detached from material enjoyment. This is the real change. *Bhaktiḥ pareśānubhavo viraktir anyatra ca.* If one is actually advancing in spiritual life, he must become very much detached from material enjoyment. If it is sometimes found that a *kaniṣṭha-adhikārī* (neophyte devotee) shows artificial tears in his eyes while chanting the Hare Kṛṣṇa mantra but is still completely attached to material things, his heart has not really changed. The change must be manifested in terms of one's real activities.

(*Śrī Caitanya-caritāmṛta, Ādi-līlā* 8.25)

If One Always Chants the Holy Name

Simply chanting the Hare Kṛṣṇa *mahā-mantra* without offenses vanquishes all sinful activities. Thus pure devotional service, which is the cause of love of Godhead, becomes manifest.

PURPORT

One cannot be situated in the devotional service of the Lord unless one is free from sinful life. This is confirmed in the *Bhagavad-gītā* (7.28):

yeṣāṁ tv anta-gataṁ pāpaṁ
janānāṁ puṇya-karmaṇām
te dvandva-moha-nirmuktā
bhajante māṁ dṛḍha-vratāḥ

"Persons who have acted piously in previous lives and in this life and whose sinful actions are completely eradicated are freed from the duality of delusion, and they engage themselves in My service with determination." A person who is already cleansed of all tinges of sinful life engages without deviation or duality of purpose in the transcendental loving service of the Lord. In this age, although people are greatly sinful, simply chanting the Hare Kṛṣṇa *mahā-mantra* can relieve them from the reactions of their sins. *Eka kṛṣṇa-nāme:* only by chanting Kṛṣṇa's name is this possible. This is confirmed in *Śrīmad-Bhāgavatam: kīrtanād eva kṛṣṇasya mukta-saṅgaḥ.* Caitanya Mahāprabhu has also taught us this. While passing on the road, He used to chant:

kṛṣṇa kṛṣṇa kṛṣṇa kṛṣṇa kṛṣṇa kṛṣṇa kṛṣṇa he
kṛṣṇa kṛṣṇa kṛṣṇa kṛṣṇa kṛṣṇa kṛṣṇa kṛṣṇa he
kṛṣṇa kṛṣṇa kṛṣṇa kṛṣṇa kṛṣṇa kṛṣṇa rakṣa mām
kṛṣṇa kṛṣṇa kṛṣṇa kṛṣṇa kṛṣṇa kṛṣṇa pāhi mām
rāma rāghava rāma rāghava rāma rāghava rakṣa mām
kṛṣṇa keśava kṛṣṇa keśava kṛṣṇa keśava pāhi mām

If one always chants the holy name of Kṛṣṇa, gradually one is freed from all reactions of sinful life, provided he chants offenselessly and does not commit more sinful activities on the strength of chanting the Hare Kṛṣṇa mantra. In this way one is purified, and his devotional service causes the arousal of his dormant love of God. If one simply chants the Hare Kṛṣṇa mantra and does not commit sinful activities and offenses, one's life is purified, and thus one comes to the fifth stage of perfection, or engagement in the loving service of the Lord (*premā pumārtho mahān*).

(*Śrī Caitanya-caritāmṛta, Ādi-līlā* 8.26)

One Must Be Freed from This Disease

When one's transcendental loving service to the Lord is actually awakened, it generates transformations in the body such as perspiration, trembling, throbbing of the heart, faltering of the voice, and tears in the eyes.

PURPORT

These bodily transformations are automatically manifested when one is actually situated in love of Godhead. One should not artificially imitate them. Our disease is desire for that which is material; even while advancing in spiritual life, we want material acclaim. One must be freed from this disease. Pure devotion must be *anyābhilāṣitā-śūnyam*, without desire for anything material. Advanced devotees manifest many bodily transformations, which are symptoms of ecstasy, but one should not imitate them to achieve cheap adoration from the public. When one actually attains the advanced stage, the ecstatic symptoms will appear automatically; one does not need to imitate them.

(*Śrī Caitanya-caritāmṛta, Ādi-līlā* 8.27)

The Holy Name of Kṛṣṇa Is So Powerful

As a result of chanting the Hare Kṛṣṇa *mahā-mantra,* one makes

such great advancement in spiritual life that simultaneously his material existence terminates and he receives love of Godhead. The holy name of Kṛṣṇa is so powerful that by chanting even one name, one very easily achieves these transcendental riches.

If one chants the exalted holy name of the Lord again and again and yet his love for the Supreme Lord does not develop and tears do not appear in his eyes, it is evident that because of his offenses in chanting, the seed of the holy name of Kṛṣṇa does not sprout.

PURPORT

If one chants the Hare Kṛṣṇa mantra offensively, one does not achieve the desired result. Therefore one should carefully avoid the offenses, which have already been described in connection with verse 24.

(*Śrī Caitanya-caritāmṛta, Ādi-līlā* 8.28–30)

Chant the Names of Nitāi-Gaura

But if one only chants, with some slight faith, the holy names of Lord Caitanya and Nityānanda, very quickly he is cleansed of all offenses. Thus as soon as he chants the Hare Kṛṣṇa *mahā-mantra,* he feels the ecstasy of love for God.

PURPORT

Śrīla Bhaktisiddhānta Sarasvatī Ṭhākura remarks in this connection that if one takes shelter of Lord Śrī Caitanya Mahāprabhu and Nityānanda, follows Their instructions to become more tolerant than the tree and humbler than the grass, and in this way chants the holy name of the Lord, very soon he achieves the platform of transcendental loving service to the Lord, and tears appear in his eyes. There are offenses to be considered in chanting the Hare Kṛṣṇa *mahā-mantra,* but there are no such considerations in chanting the names of Gaura-Nityānanda. Therefore, if one chants the Hare Kṛṣṇa *mahā-mantra* but his life is still full of sinful activities, it will be very difficult for him to achieve the platform of loving service to the Lord. But if in spite of being an offender one chants the holy names of Gaura-Nityānanda, he is very quickly freed from the reactions to his offenses. Therefore, one should first approach Lord Caitanya and Nityānanda, or worship Guru-Gaurāṅga, and then come to the stage of worshiping Rādhā-Kṛṣṇa. In our Kṛṣṇa consciousness movement, our students are first advised to worship Guru-Gaurāṅga, and then, when they are somewhat advanced, the Rādhā-Kṛṣṇa Deity is installed, and they are engaged in the worship of the Lord.

One should first take shelter of Gaura-Nityānanda in order to reach, ultimately, Rādhā-Kṛṣṇa. Śrīla Narottama dāsa Ṭhākura sings in this connection:

gaurāṅga balite ha'be pulaka śarīra
hari hari balite nayane ba'be nīra

āra kabe nitāi-cāṅdera karuṇā karibe
saṁsāra-vāsanā mora kabe tuccha habe

viṣaya chāḍiyā kabe śuddha habe mana
kabe hāma heraba śrī-vṛndāvana

In the beginning one should very regularly chant Śrī Gaurasundara's holy name and then chant the holy name of Lord Nityānanda. Thus one's heart will be cleansed of impure desires for material enjoyment. Then one can approach Vṛndāvana-dhāma to worship Lord Kṛṣṇa. Unless one is favored by Lord Caitanya and Nityānanda, there is no need to go to Vṛndāvana, for unless one's mind is purified, he cannot see Vṛndāvana, even if he goes there. Actually going to Vṛndāvana involves taking shelter of the six Gosvāmīs by reading the *Bhakti-rasāmṛta-sindhu, Vidagdha-mādhava, Lalita-mādhava,* and the other books that they have given. In this way one can understand the transcendental loving affairs between Rādhā and Kṛṣṇa. *Kabe hāma bujhaba śrī-yugala-pirīti.* The conjugal love between Rādhā and Kṛṣṇa is not an ordinary human affair; it is fully transcendental. In order to understand Rādhā and Kṛṣṇa, worship Them, and engage in Their loving service, one must be guided by Śrī Caitanya Mahāprabhu, Nityānanda Prabhu, and the six Gosvāmīs, Lord Caitanya's direct disciples.

For an ordinary man, worship of Śrī Caitanya and Nityānanda Prabhu or the Pañca-tattva is easier than worship of Rādhā and Kṛṣṇa. Unless one is very fortunate, he should not be induced to worship Rādhā-Kṛṣṇa directly. A neophyte student who is not sufficiently educated or enlightened should not indulge in the worship of Śrī Rādhā and Kṛṣṇa or the chanting of the Hare Kṛṣṇa mantra. Even if he does so, he cannot get the desired result. One should therefore chant the names of Nitāi-Gaura and worship Them without false prestige. Since everyone within this material world is more or less influenced by sinful activities, in the beginning it is essential that one take to the worship of Guru-Gaurāṅga and ask their favor, for thus despite all his disqualifications one will very soon become qualified to worship the Rādhā-Kṛṣṇa *vigraha.*

It should be noted in this connection that the holy names of Lord Kṛṣṇa and Gaurasundara are both identical with the Supreme Personality of Godhead. Therefore one should not consider one name to be more potent than the other. Considering the position of the people of this age, however, the chanting of Śrī Caitanya Mahāprabhu's name is more essential than the chanting of the Hare Kṛṣṇa *mahā-mantra* because Śrī Caitanya Mahāprabhu is the most magnanimous incarnation and His mercy is very easily achieved. Therefore one must first take shelter of Śrī Caitanya Mahāprabhu by chanting *śrī-kṛṣṇa-caitanya prabhu-nityānanda śrī-advaita gadādhara śrīvāsādi-gaura-bhakta-vṛnda.* By serving Gaura-Nityānanda one is freed from the entanglements of material existence and thus becomes qualified to worship the Rādhā-Kṛṣṇa Deity.

(*Śrī Caitanya-caritāmṛta, Ādi-līlā* 8.31)

"Give Us Strength to Receive Hare Krishna"

Devotee: Is it true that the Śrī Kṛṣṇa Caitanya mantra is more powerful than the *mahā-mantra*?

Prabhupāda: Śrī Kṛṣṇa Caitanya and *mahā-mantra,* the same. Kṛṣṇa and His name are the same. Śrī Kṛṣṇa Caitanya and Hare Kṛṣṇa are the same. *Śrī-kṛṣṇa-caitanya rādhā-kṛṣṇa nahe anya.* Śrī Kṛṣṇa Caitanya is combination of Hare and Kṛṣṇa. So there is no difference. They are all the same. But because we receive through the mercy of Śrī Kṛṣṇa Caitanya, Śrī Kṛṣṇa Caitanya has appeared to deliver us this *mahā-mantra;* therefore, we first of all pray to Śrī Kṛṣṇa Caitanya that "Give us strength to receive Hare Kṛṣṇa." Therefore we chant *śrī-kṛṣṇa-caitanya prabhu nityānanda śrī-advaita gadādhara śrīvāsādi-gaura-bhakta-vṛnda.*

(Lecture on *Bhagavad-gītā* 2.46–62,
Los Angeles, December 19, 1968)

To Become Immediately In Ecstasy of Transcendental Love

Because Śrī Caitanya Mahāprabhu appeared in His five different features, therefore the *ācāryas*, they worship all of them at a time. That is our prayer: *śrī-kṛṣṇa-caitanya prabhu nityānanda śrī-advaita gadādhara śrīvāsādi-gaura-bhakta-vṛnda.*

So to become immediately in ecstasy of transcendental love, if we chant this *śrī-kṛṣṇa-caitanya prabhu nityānanda,* it is easier. There is no offense in chanting this Pañca-tattva, but there is offense if you do not properly chant Hare Kṛṣṇa mantra. There are ten kinds of offenses. You know. But in chanting *śrī-kṛṣṇa-caitanya prabhu nityānanda,* there is no *aparādha*. You chant in any way, you'll get the result. This is the difference, taste. This is variety. Although there is no difference by chanting *śrī-kṛṣṇa-caitanya prabhu nityānanda* and Hare Kṛṣṇa mantra, *mahā-mantra*, but still by chanting this Pañca-tattva, you'll get immediately, quickly, result. Therefore our process is to chant the holy names of the Pañca-tattva and then we chant Hare Kṛṣṇa *mahā-mantra*. That is perfect.

(*Śrī Caitanya-caritāmṛta, Ādi-līlā* 7.5,
Māyāpur, March 7, 1974)

So Our Only Request Is That You Take Shelter of Śrī Caitanya Mahāprabhu

Śrī Kṛṣṇa Caitanya Mahāprabhu, has five features. What are those? Kṛṣṇa, Kṛṣṇa's manifestation, Kṛṣṇa's incarnation, Kṛṣṇa's different potencies, in this way. And Kṛṣṇa, the source of devotional service, He is Kṛṣṇa Caitanya, *bhakta-śaktikam*. To advance in devotional service requires spiritual strength. It is not so easy thing. That spiritual strength is also Kṛṣṇa, *bhakta-śaktikam*. Therefore we have to practice Hare Kṛṣṇa, Hare Kṛṣṇa, Kṛṣṇa Kṛṣṇa, Hare Hare/ Hare Rāma, Hare Rāma, Rāma Rāma, Hare Hare. Kṛṣṇa advises, "Always think of Me." Where is the difficulty? We have to think of something. We cannot keep our mind vacant. That is not possible. So make it a point, that think of Kṛṣṇa, that's all. Think of Kṛṣṇa, and if you chant, if you engage your tongue, "Hare Kṛṣṇa," and if you hear, then everything is compact in Kṛṣṇa consciousness.

So to achieve strength, Kṛṣṇa is prepared to help us in so many ways. He is coming as Lord Kṛṣṇa and ordering, *sarva-dharmān parityajya mām ekaṁ śaraṇaṁ vraja* [surrender unto Me]. Still we are making mistake; we don't accept Kṛṣṇa's word. Therefore Kṛṣṇa is coming as Caitanya Mahāprabhu, along with His associates Nityānanda Prabhu, Advaita Prabhu, Gadādhara Prabhu, just to teach us the same process: how to surrender to Kṛṣṇa. So our real business is that, how to surrender to Kṛṣṇa. And if we take shelter of Śrī Kṛṣṇa Caitanya Mahāprabhu, along with His associates, then the task becomes very easy. *Yajñaiḥ saṅkīrtana-prāyair yajanti hi su-medhasaḥ*. Very easy; not at all difficult. Caitanya Mahāprabhu's method for approaching Kṛṣṇa is very, very easy.

So our only request is that you take shelter of Śrī Caitanya Mahāprabhu, chant always *śrī-kṛṣṇa-caitanya prabhu-nityānanda śrī-advaita gadādhara śrīvāsādi-gaura-bhakta-vṛnda,* and Hare Kṛṣṇa, Hare Kṛṣṇa, Kṛṣṇa Kṛṣṇa, Hare Hare/ Hare Rāma, Hare Rāma, Rāma Rāma, Hare Hare. It is not very difficult task. So do not forget this principle, *pañca-tattvātmakaṁ kṛṣṇaṁ, bhakta-rūpa-svarūpakam/ bhaktāvatāraṁ bhaktākhyaṁ, namāmi bhakta-śaktikam. Bhakta-śakti,* everything requires strength, so we can derive strength by chanting Caitanya Mahāprabhu's name, and chanting Hare Kṛṣṇa. So chant Hare Kṛṣṇa mantra and be happy. That is the Kṛṣṇa consciousness movement. Thank you very much.

(Lecture on *Śrī Caitanya-caritāmṛta, Ādi-līlā* 1.14, Māyāpur, April 7, 1975)

10

Freedom from Offenses by Glorifying The Holy Name

In Glorification of the Holy Name

While chanting the holy name of the Lord, one should be careful to avoid ten offenses. From Sanat-kumāra it is understood that even if a person is a severe offender in many ways, he is freed from offensive life if he takes shelter of the Lord's holy name. Indeed, even if a human being is no better than a two-legged animal, he will be liberated if he takes shelter of the holy name of the Lord. One should therefore be very careful not to commit offenses at the lotus feet of the Lord's holy name. The offenses are described as follows: (a) to blaspheme a devotee, especially a devotee engaged in broadcasting the glories of the holy name, (b) to consider the name of Lord Śiva or any other demigod to be equally as powerful as the holy name of the Supreme Personality of Godhead (no one is equal to the Supreme Personality of Godhead, nor is anyone superior to Him), (c) to disobey the instructions of the spiritual master, (d) to blaspheme the Vedic literatures and literatures compiled in pursuance of the Vedic literatures, (e) to comment that the glories of the holy name of the Lord are exaggerated, (f) to interpret the holy name in a deviant way, (g) to commit sinful activities on the strength of chanting the holy name, (h) to compare the chanting of the holy name to pious activities, (i) to instruct the glories of the holy name to a person who has no understanding of the chanting of the holy name, (j) not to awaken in transcendental attachment for the chanting of the holy name, even after hearing all these scriptural injunctions.

It is recommended that even if one commits offenses, one should continue chanting the holy name. In other words, the chanting of the holy name makes one offenseless. In the book *Nāma-kaumudī* it is recommended that if one is an offender at the lotus feet of a Vaiṣṇava, he should submit to that Vaiṣṇava and be excused; similarly, if one is an offender in chanting the holy name, he should submit to the holy name and thus be freed from his offenses. One should be very humble and meek to offer one's desires and chant prayers composed in glorification of the holy name, such as *ayi mukta-kulair upāsya mānam* and *nivṛtta-tarṣair upagīyamānād.* One should chant such prayers to become free from offenses at the lotus feet of the holy name.

(*Śrīmad-Bhāgavatam* 7.5.23, purport)

O Hari-nāma!

nikhila-śruti-mauli-ratna-mālā-
dyuti-nīrājita-pāda-paṅkajānta

ayi mukta-kulair upāsyamānaṁ
paritas tvāṁ hari-nāma saṁśrayāmi

O Hari-nāma! The tips of the toes of Your lotus feet are constantly being worshiped by the glowing radiance emanating from the string of gems known as the *Upaniṣads,* the crown jewels of all the *Vedas*. You are eternally adored by liberated souls such as Nārada and Śukadeva. O Hari-nāma! I take complete shelter of You.

(Śrīla Rūpa Gosvāmī—*Nāmāṣṭaka,* verse 1)

The Right Medicine

nivṛtta-tarṣair upagīyamānād
bhavauṣadhāc chrotra-mano-'bhirāmāt
ka uttamaśloka-guṇānuvādāt
pumān virajyeta vinā paśughnāt

Descriptions of the Lord spoken by those who are free of material desires are the right medicine for the conditioned soul undergoing repeated birth and death, and they delight the ear and the mind. Therefore who will cease hearing such glorification of the Lord except a butcher or one who is killing his own self?

(*Śrīmad-Bhāgavatam* 10.1.4)

Kṛṣṇa Is Transcendentally Blissful

nāma cintāmaṇiḥ kṛṣṇaś
caitanya-rasa-vigrahaḥ
pūrṇaḥ śuddho nitya-mukto
'bhinnatvān nāma-nāminoḥ

The holy name of Kṛṣṇa is transcendentally blissful. It bestows all spiritual benedictions, for it is Kṛṣṇa Himself, the reservoir of all pleasure. Kṛṣṇa's name is complete, and it is the form of all transcendental mellows. It is not a material name under any condition, and it is no less powerful than Kṛṣṇa Himself. Since Kṛṣṇa's name is not contaminated by the material qualities, there is no question of its being involved with *māyā*. Kṛṣṇa's name is always liberated and spiritual; it is never conditioned by the laws of material nature. This is because the name of Kṛṣṇa and Kṛṣṇa Himself are identical.

(*Padma Purāṇa*)

There Is No Other Way

harer nāma harer nāma
harer nāmaiva kevalam
kalau nāsty eva nāsty eva
nāsty eva gatir anyathā

Chant the holy name, chant the holy name, chant the holy name. In this age of Kali, this age of quarrel and hypocrisy, the only means of deliverance is the chanting of the holy names of the Lord. There is no other way. There is no other way. There is no other way.

(*Bṛhan-nāradīya Purāṇa*)

The Highest Nectar

jayati jayati nāmānanda-rūpaṁ murārer
viramita-nija-dharma-dhyāna-pūjādi-yatnam
kathamapi sakṛd-āttaṁ muktidaṁ prāṇīnāṁ yat
paramam amṛtam ekaṁ jīvanaṁ bhūṣaṇaṁ me

All glories, all glories to the all-blissful holy name of Śrī Kṛṣṇa, which causes the devotee to give up all conventional religious duties, meditation, and worship. When somehow or other uttered even once by a living entity, the holy name awards him liberation. The holy name of Kṛṣṇa is the highest nectar. It is my very life and my only treasure.

(Śrīla Sanātana Gosvāmī, *Bṛhad-Bhāgavatāmṛta,* 1.1.9)

In the Courtyard of the Heart

tuṇḍe tāṇḍavinī ratiṁ vitanute tuṇḍāvalī-labdhaye
karṇa-kroḍa-kaḍambinī ghaṭayate karṇārbudebhyaḥ spṛhām
cetaḥ-prāṅgaṇa-saṅginī vijayate sarvendriyāṇāṁ kṛtiṁ
no jāne janitā kiyadbhir amṛtaiḥ kṛṣṇeti varṇa-dvayī

I do not know how much nectar the two syllables 'Kṛṣ-ṇa' have produced. When the holy name of Kṛṣṇa is chanted, it appears to dance within the mouth. We then desire many, many mouths. When that name enters the holes of the ears, we desire many millions of ears. And when the holy name dances in the courtyard of the heart, it conquers the activities of the mind, and therefore all the senses become inert.

(Śrīla Rūpa Gosvāmī, *Vidagdha-mādhava,* 1.15)

Constant Chanting

etan nirvidyamānānām
icchatām akuto-bhayam
yogināṁ nṛpa nirṇītaṁ
harer nāmānukīrtanam

O King, constant chanting of the holy name of the Lord after the ways of the great authorities is the doubtless and fearless way of success for all, including those who are free from all material desires, those who are desirous of all material enjoyment, and those who are self-satisfied by dint of transcendental knowledge.

(*Śrīmad-Bhāgavatam* 2.1.11)

How Glorious Are They

aho bata śva-paco 'to garīyān
yaj-jihvāgre vartate nāma tubhyam
tepus tapas te juhuvuḥ sasnur āryā
brahmānūcur nāma gṛṇanti ye te

Oh, how glorious are they whose tongues are chanting Your holy name! Even if born in the families of dog-eaters, such persons are worshipable. Persons who chant the holy name of Your Lordship must have executed all kinds of austerities and fire sacrifices and achieved all the good manners of the Āryans. To be chanting the holy name of Your Lordship, they must have bathed at holy places of pilgrimage, studied the *Vedas,* and fulfilled everything required.

(*Śrīmad-Bhāgavatam* 3.33.7)

The Living Entity's Only Business

etāvān eva loke 'smin
puṁsāṁ dharmaḥ paraḥ smṛtaḥ
bhakti-yogo bhagavati
tan-nāma-grahaṇādibhiḥ

In this material world the living entity's only business is to accept the path of *bhakti-yoga* and chant the holy name of the Lord. Devotional service, beginning with the chanting of the holy name of the Lord, is the ultimate religious principle for the living entity in human society.

(*Śrīmad-Bhāgavatam* 6.3.22)

The Most Auspicious Activity

tasmāt saṅkīrtanaṁ viṣṇor
jagan-maṅgalam aṁhasām
mahatām api kauravya
viddhy aikāntika-niṣkṛtam

Śukadeva Gosvāmī continued: "My dear King, the chanting of the holy name of the Lord is able to uproot even the reactions of the greatest sins. Therefore the chanting of the *saṅkīrtana* movement is the most auspicious activity in the entire universe. Please try to understand this so that others will take it seriously."

(*Śrīmad-Bhāgavatam* 6.3.31)

There Is One Chance

kaler doṣa-nidhe rājann
asti hy eko mahān guṇaḥ
kīrtanād eva kṛṣṇasya
mukta-saṅgaḥ paraṁ vrajet

This age of Kali is full of unlimited faults. Indeed, it is just like an ocean of faults. But there is one chance, one opportunity. Simply by chanting the Hare Kṛṣṇa mantra, one can be freed from the contamination of Kali-yuga and, in his original spiritual body, can return home, back to Godhead.

(*Śrīmad-Bhāgavatam* 12.3.51)

Please Constantly Chant the Mantra

śatru-cchedaika-mantraṁ sakalam
upaniṣad-vākya-sampūjya-mantraṁ
saṁsāroccheda-mantraṁ samucita-tamasaḥ

saṅgha-niryāṇa-mantram
sarvaiśvaryaika-mantraṁ
vyasana-bhujaga-sandaṣṭa-santrāṇa-mantraṁ
jihve śrī-kṛṣṇa-mantraṁ japa japa satataṁ
janma-sāphalya-mantram

O tongue, please constantly chant the mantra composed of Śrī Kṛṣṇa's names. This is the only mantra for destroying all enemies, the mantra worshiped by every word of the *Upaniṣads,* the mantra that uproots *saṁsāra,* the mantra that drives away all the darkness of ignorance, the mantra for attaining infinite opulence, the mantra for curing those bitten by the poisonous snake of worldly distress, and the mantra for making one's birth in this world successful.

(*Mukunda-mālā-stotra,* sūtra 31)

The Means of Awakening All Good Fortune

nāma-saṅkīrtana haite sarvānartha-nāśa
sarva-śubhodaya, kṛṣṇa-premera ullāsa

Simply by chanting the holy name of Lord Kṛṣṇa, one can be freed from all undesirable habits. This is the means of awakening all good fortune and initiating the flow of waves of love for Kṛṣṇa.

(*Śrī Caitanya-caritāmṛta, Antya-līlā* 20.11)

One Associates with the Lord Directly

kali-kāle nāma-rūpe kṛṣṇa-avatāra
nāma haite haya sarva-jagat-nistāra

In this Age of Kali, the holy name of the Lord, the Hare Kṛṣṇa *mahā-mantra,* is the incarnation of Lord Kṛṣṇa. Simply by chanting the holy name, one associates with the Lord directly. Anyone who does this is certainly delivered.

(*Śrī Caitanya-caritāmṛta, Ādi-līlā* 17.22)

I Reside in That Place

nāhaṁ tiṣṭhāmi vaikuṇṭhe
yogināṁ hṛdayeṣu vā
tatra tiṣṭhāmi nārada
yatra gāyanti mad-bhaktāḥ

My dear Nārada, actually I do not reside in My abode, Vaikuṇṭha, nor do I reside within the hearts of the *yogīs*, but I reside in that place where My pure devotees chant My holy name and discuss My form, pastimes and qualities.

(*Padma Purāṇa*)

I Become Easily Purchased

Anyone who is engaged in chanting My transcendental name must be considered to be always associating with Me. And I may tell you frankly that for such a devotee I become easily purchased.

(*Ādi Purāṇa,* quoted in *The Nectar of Devotion*)

One Cannot Find a Method of Religion More Sublime

hare kṛṣṇa hare kṛṣṇa kṛṣṇa kṛṣṇa hare hare
hare rāma hare rāma rāma rāma hare hare
iti ṣoḍaśakaṁ nāmnāṁ kali-kalmaṣa-nāśanaṁ
nātaḥ paratаropāyaḥ sarva-vedeṣu dṛśyate

The sixteen words—Hare Kṛṣṇa, Hare Kṛṣṇa, Kṛṣṇa Kṛṣṇa, Hare

Hare/ Hare Rāma, Hare Rāma, Rāma Rāma, Hare Hare—are especially meant for counteracting the contaminations of Kali (the present age of quarrel and hypocrisy). These sixteen names composed of thirty-two syllables are the only means to counteract the evil effects of Kali-yuga. After searching through all the Vedic literature, one cannot find a method of religion more sublime for this age than the chanting of Hare Kṛṣṇa.

(*Kali-santaraṇa Upaniṣad*)

* * *

Dear Nāma-prabhu, please forgive us for all our offenses. Please bless us with sincere devotion and genuine humility. We offer our most humble obeisances at Your lotus feet.

Hari-nāma prabhu ki jaya!

(The Editors)

Bhārgava Dāsa

11

In a Humble State of Mind

One Should Be Humbler than the Grass

To chant the holy name always, one should be humbler than the grass in the street and devoid of all desire for personal honor, but one should offer others all respectful obeisances.

A devotee engaged in chanting the holy name of the Lord should practice forbearance like that of a tree. Even if rebuked or chastised, he should not say anything to others to retaliate.

For even if one cuts a tree, it never protests, and even if it is drying up and dying, it does not ask anyone for water.

PURPORT

This practice of forbearance (*taror iva sahiṣṇunā*) is very difficult, but when one actually engages in chanting the Hare Kṛṣṇa mantra, the quality of forbearance automatically develops. A person advanced in spiritual consciousness through the chanting of the Hare Kṛṣṇa mantra need not practice to develop it separately, for a devotee develops all good qualities simply by chanting the Hare Kṛṣṇa mantra regularly.

(*Śrī Caitanya-caritāmṛta, Ādi-līlā* 17.26–28)

The Grass Never Protests

Thus a Vaiṣṇava should not ask anything from anyone else. If someone gives him something without being asked, he should accept it, but if nothing comes, a Vaiṣṇava should be satisfied to eat whatever vegetables and fruits are easily available.

One should strictly follow the principle of always chanting the holy name, and one should be satisfied with whatever he gets easily. Such devotional behavior solidly maintains one's devotional service.

One who thinks himself lower than the grass, who is more tolerant than a tree, and who does not expect personal honor yet is always prepared to give all respect to others can very easily always chant the holy name of the Lord.

PURPORT

The grass is specifically mentioned in this verse because everyone tramples upon it, yet the grass never protests. This example indicates that a spiritual master or leader should not be proud of his position; being always humbler than an ordinary common man, he should go on preaching the cult of Caitanya Mahāprabhu by chanting the Hare Kṛṣṇa mantra.

(*Śrī Caitanya-caritāmṛta, Ādi-līlā* 17.29–31)

String This Verse on the Thread of the Holy Name

Raising my hands, I declare, "Everyone please hear me! String this verse on the thread of the holy name and wear it on your neck for continuous remembrance."

One must strictly follow the principles given by Lord Caitanya Mahāprabhu in this verse. If one simply follows in the footsteps of Lord Caitanya and the Gosvāmīs, certainly he will achieve the ultimate goal of life, the lotus feet of Śrī Kṛṣṇa.

(*Śrī Caitanya-caritāmṛta, Ādi-līlā* 17.32–33)

A Pure Vaiṣṇava Never Takes Anyone's Insults Seriously

"All of you may now go to your homes. May Lord Kṛṣṇa bestow His blessings upon you all. Do not be sorry because of my being insulted."

PURPORT

From this statement by Haridāsa Ṭhākura, it is understood that a pure Vaiṣṇava never takes anyone's insults seriously. This is the teaching of Śrī Caitanya Mahāprabhu.

tṛṇād api sunicena
taror iva sahiṣṇunā
amāninā mānadena
kīrtanīyaḥ sadā hariḥ

"One should chant the holy name of the Lord in a humble state of mind, thinking oneself lower than the straw in the street. One should be more tolerant than a tree, devoid of all sense of false prestige, and ready to offer all respects to others. In such a state of mind one can chant the holy name of the Lord constantly."

A Vaiṣṇava is always tolerant and submissive like trees and grass. He tolerates insults offered by others, for he is simply interested in chanting the holy name of the Lord without being disturbed.

(*Śrī Caitanya-caritāmṛta, Antya-līlā* 3.207)

By Humility and Meekness One Attracts the Attention of Kṛṣṇa

Of the nine processes of devotional service, the most important is to always chant the holy name of the Lord. If one does so, avoiding the ten kinds of offenses, one very easily obtains the most valuable love of Godhead.

PURPORT

Śrīla Jīva Gosvāmī Prabhu gives the following directions in his *Bhakti-sandarbha* (270): "Chanting the holy name is the chief means of attaining love of Godhead. This chanting or devotional service does not depend on any paraphernalia, nor on one's having taken birth in a good family. By humility and meekness one attracts the attention of Kṛṣṇa. That is the verdict of all the *Vedas*. Therefore if one becomes very humble and meek, he can easily attain the lotus feet of Kṛṣṇa in this Age of Kali. That is the fulfillment of all great sacrifices, penances, and austerities because when one achieves ecstatic love of Godhead, he attains the complete perfection of life. Therefore whatever one does in executing devotional service must be accompanied by the chanting of the holy name of the Lord." The chanting of the holy name of Kṛṣṇa—Hare Kṛṣṇa, Hare Kṛṣṇa, Kṛṣṇa Kṛṣṇa, Hare Hare/ Hare Rāma,

Hare Rāma, Rāma Rāma, Hare Hare—has been praised by Śrīla Rūpa Gosvāmī in his *Nāmāṣṭaka* (verse 1):

nikhila-śruti-mauli-ratna-mālā-
dyuti-nīrājita-pāda-paṅkajānta
ayi mukta-kulair upāsyamānaṁ
paritas tvāṁ hari-nāma saṁśrayāmi

"O Hari-nāma! The tips of the toes of Your lotus feet are constantly being worshiped by the glowing radiance emanating from the string of gems known as the *Upaniṣads*, the crown jewels of all the *Vedas*. You are eternally adored by liberated souls such as Nārada and Śukadeva. O Hari-nāma! I take complete shelter of You."

Similarly, Śrīla Sanātana Gosvāmī has praised the chanting of the holy name as follows in his *Bṛhad-Bhāgavatāmṛta* (1.1.9):

jayati jayati nāmānanda-rūpaṁ murārer
viramita-nija-dharma-dhyāna-pūjādi-yatnam
katham api sakṛd āttaṁ mukti-daṁ prāṇināṁ yat
paramam amṛtam ekaṁ jīvanaṁ bhūṣaṇaṁ me

"All glories, all glories to the all-blissful holy name of Śrī Kṛṣṇa, which causes the devotee to give up all conventional religious duties, meditation, and worship. When somehow or other uttered even once by a living entity, the holy name awards him liberation. The holy name of Kṛṣṇa is the highest nectar. It is my very life and my only treasure."

In *Śrīmad-Bhāgavatam* (2.1.11) Śukadeva Gosvāmī says:

etan nirvidyamānānām
icchatām akuto-bhayam
yogināṁ nṛpa nirṇītaṁ
harer nāmānukīrtanam

"O King, constant chanting of the holy name of the Lord after the ways of the great authorities is the doubtless and fearless way of success for all, including those who are free from all material desires, those who are desirous of all material enjoyment, and those who are self-satisfied by dint of transcendental knowledge."

Similarly, Caitanya Mahāprabhu has said in His *Śikṣāṣṭaka* (3):

tṛṇād api sunīcena
taror iva sahiṣṇunā
amāninā mānadena
kīrtanīyaḥ sadā hariḥ

"One should chant the holy name of the Lord in a humble state of mind, thinking oneself lower than the straw in the street. One should be more tolerant than a tree, devoid of all sense of false prestige, and ready to offer all respect to others. In such a state of mind one can chant the holy name of the Lord constantly." Regarding the ten offenses in chanting the holy name, one may refer to *Ādi-līlā,* Chapter Eight, verse 24.

(*Śrī Caitanya-caritāmṛta, Antya-līlā* 4.71)

Always Appreciate This Opportunity

Ajāmila continued: I am a shameless cheater who has killed his brahminical culture. Indeed, I am sin personified. Where am I in comparison to the all-auspicious chanting of the holy name of Lord Nārāyaṇa?

PURPORT

Those engaged in broadcasting the holy name of Nārāyaṇa, Kṛṣṇa, through the Kṛṣṇa consciousness movement should always consider what our position was before we came and what it is now.

We had fallen into abominable lives as meat-eaters, drunkards, and woman hunters who performed all kinds of sinful activities, but now we have been given the opportunity to chant the Hare Kṛṣṇa mantra. Therefore we should always appreciate this opportunity. By the grace of the Lord we are opening many branches, and we should use this good fortune to chant the holy name of the Lord and serve the Supreme Personality of Godhead directly. We must be conscious of the difference between our present and past conditions and should always be very careful not to fall from the most exalted life.

(*Śrīmad-Bhāgavatam* 6.2.34)

Pray to Kṛṣṇa That We Will Not Fall Again

I am such a sinful person, but since I have now gotten this opportunity, I must completely control my mind, life, and senses and always engage in devotional service so that I may not fall again into the deep darkness and ignorance of material life.

PURPORT

Every one of us should have this determination. We have been elevated to an exalted position by the mercy of Kṛṣṇa and the spiritual master, and if we remember that this is a great opportunity and pray to Kṛṣṇa that we will not fall again, our lives will be successful.

(*Śrīmad-Bhāgavatam* 6.2.35)

Unless One Is Meek and Humble, Progress in Spiritual Life Is Very Difficult

Prahlāda Mahārāja prayed: How is it possible for me, who have been born in a family of asuras, to offer suitable prayers to satisfy the Supreme Personality of Godhead? Even until now, all the demigods, headed by Lord Brahmā, and all the saintly persons

could not satisfy the Lord by streams of excellent words, although such persons are very qualified, being in the mode of goodness. Then what is to be said of me? I am not at all qualified.

PURPORT

A Vaiṣṇava who is fully qualified to serve the Lord still thinks himself extremely low while offering prayers to the Lord. For example, Kṛṣṇadāsa Kavirāja Gosvāmī, the author of *Caitanya-caritāmṛta,* says:

jagāi mādhāi haite muñi se pāpiṣṭha
purīṣera kīṭa haite muñi se laghiṣṭha
(Cc., *Ādi* 5.205)

Thus he considers himself unqualified, lower than the worms in stool, and more sinful than Jagāi and Mādhāi. A pure Vaiṣṇava actually thinks of himself in this way. Similarly, although Prahlāda Mahārāja was a pure, exalted Vaiṣṇava, he thought himself most unqualified to offer prayers to the Supreme Lord. *Mahā-jano yena gataḥ sa panthāḥ.* Every pure Vaiṣṇava should think like this. One should not be falsely proud of his Vaiṣṇava qualifications. Śrī Caitanya Mahāprabhu has therefore instructed us:

tṛṇād api sunīcena
taror iva sahiṣṇunā
amāninā mānadena
kīrtanīyaḥ sadā hariḥ

"One should chant the holy name of the Lord in a humble state of mind, thinking oneself lower than the straw in the street; one should be more tolerant than a tree, devoid of all sense of false prestige and should be ready to offer all respect to others. In such a state of mind one can chant the holy name of the Lord constantly." Unless one is meek and humble, to make progress in spiritual life is very difficult.

(*Śrīmad-Bhāgavatam* 7.9.8)

"Every One of You Become Guru"

So this Hare Kṛṣṇa mantra is completely spiritual. If you chant it, spiritually enlightened, then surely it will act. *Paraṁ vijayate śrī-kṛṣṇa-saṅkīrtanam*. It will act. Therefore chanting is so important. Narottama dāsa Ṭhākura said this sound vibration is not this material sound. Kṛṣṇa is not material sound. It is Kṛṣṇa, spiritual. There is no difference between Kṛṣṇa, the Supreme Personality of Godhead, and His holy name, Kṛṣṇa. There is no difference. As Kṛṣṇa is *pūrṇa,* perfect, complete, *śuddha,* without any material contamination. *Pūrṇaḥ śuddho nitya,* eternal. *Pūrṇaḥ śuddho nitya-muktaḥ*. *Mukta* means not of this material world. *Mukti* means anything which does not belong to, in this material world. That is called *mukti*. So the holy name, chanting of holy name, if we act it properly, without any offense, then we are directly in connection with Kṛṣṇa. There is no doubt.

And Narottama dāsa Ṭhākura therefore says that this holy name of Kṛṣṇa is imported from Goloka Vṛndāvana. It is not material sound. *Golokera prema-dhana hari-nāma-saṅkīrtana*. It is not ordinary sound. Don't take it as ordinary. To think the holy name of the Lord as ordinary sound vibration, that is *nārakī* [hellish]. That is not considered by spiritually enlightened persons. But those who are rotting in hellish condition, for them these are the consideration. But it is not like that. It requires good brain to understand how Kṛṣṇa can appear in a form of sound which we can hear. It is for our benefit. Not that it is material. Therefore Narottama dāsa Ṭhākura says, *golokera prema-dhana hari-nāma saṅkīrtana. Hari-nāma-saṅkīrtana* is not ordinary sound. Don't treat it as ordinary sound. Just like by radio we can send message from Europe, it may come to India, such powerful machine and you can talk. That is possible. But that is not this sound. Don't think that this *hari-nāma-saṅkīrtana* is ordinary vibration of this material world. Never think so. You should immediately see that the *saṅkīrtana,* Hare Kṛṣṇa, is Kṛṣṇa and Rādhā. Harā and Kṛṣṇa. Rādhā-Kṛṣṇa or Sītā-Rāma or Lakṣmī-Nārāyaṇa. Any form of the

Lord Viṣṇu. Hare Kṛṣṇa means the Supreme Lord and His spiritual potency. So we address, Hare, "O, the energy, spiritual energy of the Lord," and Kṛṣṇa, "O the Supreme Lord," Hare Rāma, the same thing. Paraṁ Brahman. Rāma means Paraṁ Brahman, Kṛṣṇa means Paraṁ Brahman. So what is the meaning of addressing, "*He* Kṛṣṇa, *He* Rādhe, *He* Rāma." Why? Why you are asking? That "Just engage me in your service." That is taught by Śrī Caitanya Mahāprabhu:

ayi nanda-tanuja kiṅkaraṁ,
patitaṁ māṁ viṣame bhavāmbudhau
kṛpayā tava pāda-paṅkaja-
sthita-dhūlī-sadṛśaṁ vicintaya

This is our prayer. It is not our prayer that, "O Kṛṣṇa, O Rāma, give me some money, give me some woman." No. This is not the prayer. Of course, in the neophyte stage they can pray like that, but that is not, I mean to say, *śuddha-bhakti,* pure devotion.

Pure devotion means to pray to the Lord, begging some service. "My Lord, kindly engage me in Your service." That is the perfection of life, when one is engaged in the service of the Lord in love. You can become a very great saint and live in a secluded place and become puffed up that you have become very great personality, and people may come to see him, that "He's not to be seen, he's engaged in chanting." My Guru Mahārāja has condemned this. He said, *mana tumi kisera vaiṣṇava.* "My dear mind, your mental concoction, you are thinking that you have become a very big Vaiṣṇava. You do not do anything and sit down in a secluded place and imitating Haridāsa Ṭhākura, chanting. So you are a nonsense." Why? To get some cheap adoration as a great chanter. Because if one is actually chanting, why he should be attracted by woman and *biḍi* [cigarettes]? If he is actually in such position like Haridāsa Ṭhākura, then why he should be attracted by material things? That is a false show only. That is not possible for ordinary person. Therefore ordinary person must be physically engaged. That is not physical; that is also transcendental. Always busy in some business of Kṛṣṇa consciousness. That is wanted. So one who is living in Vṛndāvana, he must be very anxious how to spread the glories of Vṛndāvana-candra all over the world. That is wanted.

My Guru Mahārāja says, "What kind of Vaiṣṇava, rascal, you are? Simply for cheap adoration you are living in a secluded place. Your chanting of so-called Hare Kṛṣṇa mantra is simply cheating." He has said that. One must be ready very vigorously. And that is Caitanya Mahāprabhu's order. Caitanya Mahāprabhu never said that "You chant." He has given certainly the chanting. But so far His mission is concerned, He said that "Every one of you become guru. And deliver, preach, that people understand what is Kṛṣṇa."

yāre dekha, tāre kaha 'kṛṣṇa'-upadeśa
āmāra ājñāya guru hañā tāra' ei deśa

Pṛthivīte āche yata nagarādi. That is His mission. It is not that "Become a big Vaiṣṇava and sit down and imitate." This is all rascaldom. So don't follow this thing. So at least we cannot advise you in that way. We have learned from our Guru Mahārāja that preaching is very, very important thing, and when one is actually an experienced preacher, then he is able to chant Hare Kṛṣṇa mantra without any offense. Before that, this so-called chanting of Hare Kṛṣṇa mantra, you may practice and give up all other business to make a show of a big Vaiṣṇava. That is not required. Thank you very much.

(Lecture on *Śrīmad-Bhāgavatam* 1.7.19,
Vṛndāvana, September 17, 1976)

Chant Hare Kṛṣṇa Mahā-Mantra Without Any Disturbance

But our process is to submit. Unless we submit, there is no hope of advancing in Kṛṣṇa consciousness. That is Caitanya Mahāprabhu's teaching.

tṛṇād api sunīcena
taror api sahiṣṇunā
amāninā mānadena
kīrtanīyaḥ sadā hariḥ

If you want to chant Hare Kṛṣṇa mantra, then you have to take this principle, *tṛṇād api sunīcena.* You have to become humbler than the grass. Grass, it is lying on the street. Everyone is trampling down. Never protests. Everyone is trampling the grass. There is no protest. *Taror api sahiṣṇunā.* And tolerant than the tree. The tree is giving us so much help. It is giving us fruit, flower, leaves, and when there is scorching heat, shelter also. Sit down underneath. So beneficial, still, we cut. As soon as I like, I cut it down. But there is no protest. The tree does not say, "I have given you so much help, and you are cutting me?" No. Tolerant.

Yes. Therefore Caitanya Mahāprabhu has selected, *taror api sahiṣṇunā.* And *amāninā mānadena.* For oneself one should not expect any respectful position, but he, the devotee, should offer all respect to anyone. *Amāninā mānadena kīrtanīyaḥ sadā hariḥ.* If we acquire this qualification, then we can chant Hare Kṛṣṇa *mahā-mantra* without any disturbance. This is the qualification.

(Śrī Gaura-Pūrṇimā lecture on *Śrīmad-Bhāgavatam* 7.9.38, Māyāpur, March 16, 1976)

Never Become Unnecessarily Proud

There was also a *brāhmaṇa* named Vāsudeva, who was a great person but was suffering from leprosy. Indeed, his body was filled with living worms.

Although suffering from leprosy, the *brāhmaṇa* Vāsudeva was enlightened. As soon as one worm fell from his body, he would pick it up and place it back again in the same location.

Then one night Vāsudeva heard of Lord Caitanya Mahāprabhu's arrival, and in the morning he came to see the Lord at the house of Kūrma.

When the leper Vāsudeva came to Kūrma's house to see Caitanya Mahāprabhu, he was informed that the Lord had already left. The leper then fell to the ground unconscious.

When Vāsudeva, the leper *brāhmaṇa,* was lamenting due to not being able to see Caitanya Mahāprabhu, the Lord immediately returned to that spot and embraced him.

When Śrī Caitanya Mahāprabhu touched him, both the leprosy and his distress went to a distant place. Indeed, Vāsudeva's body became very beautiful, to his great happiness.

The *brāhmaṇa* Vāsudeva was astonished to behold the wonderful mercy of Śrī Caitanya Mahāprabhu, and he began to recite a verse from *Śrīmad-Bhāgavatam,* touching the Lord's lotus feet.

He said, "Who am I? A sinful, poor friend of a *brāhmaṇa.* And who is Kṛṣṇa? The Supreme Personality of Godhead, full in six opulences. Nonetheless, He has embraced me with His two arms."

The *brāhmaṇa* Vāsudeva continued, "O my merciful Lord, such mercy is not possible for ordinary living entities. Such mercy can be found only in You. Upon seeing me, even a sinful person goes away due to my bad bodily odor. Yet You have touched me. Such is the independent behavior of the Supreme Personality of Godhead."

Being meek and humble, the *brāhmaṇa* Vāsudeva worried that he would become proud after being cured by the grace of Śrī Caitanya Mahāprabhu.

To protect the *brāhmaṇa,* Śrī Caitanya Mahāprabhu advised him to chant the Hare Kṛṣṇa mantra incessantly. By doing so, he would never become unnecessarily proud.

(*Śrī Caitanya-caritāmṛta, Madhya-līlā* 7.136–147)

Painting by Muralidhara Dāsa

12

THE TRANSCENDENTAL GARDENER

The Gardener Smiled with Great Pleasure

The fruits ripened and became sweet and nectarean. The gardener, Śrī Caitanya Mahāprabhu, distributed them without asking any price.

All the wealth in the three worlds cannot equal the value of one such nectarean fruit of devotional service.

Not considering who asked for it and who did not, nor who was fit and who unfit to receive it, Caitanya Mahāprabhu distributed the fruit of devotional service.

PURPORT

This is the sum and substance of Lord Caitanya's *saṅkīrtana* movement. There is no distinction made between those who are fit and those who are not fit to hear or take part in the *saṅkīrtana* movement. It should therefore be preached without discrimination. The only purpose of the preachers of the *saṅkīrtana* movement must be to go on preaching without restriction. That is the way in which Śrī Caitanya Mahāprabhu introduced this *saṅkīrtana* movement to the world.

The transcendental gardener, Śrī Caitanya Mahāprabhu, distributed handful after handful of fruit in all directions, and when the poor, hungry people ate the fruit, the gardener smiled with great pleasure.

Lord Caitanya thus addressed the multifarious varieties of branches and subbranches of the tree of devotional service: "Since the tree of devotional service is transcendental, every one of its parts can perform the action of all the others. Although a tree is supposed to be immovable, this tree nevertheless moves.

"All the parts of this tree are spiritually cognizant, and thus as they grow they spread all over the world.

"I am the only gardener. How many places can I go? How many fruits can I pick and distribute?"

PURPORT

Here Śrī Caitanya Mahāprabhu indicates that the distribution of the Hare Kṛṣṇa *mahā-mantra* should be performed by combined forces. Although He is the Supreme Personality of Godhead, He laments, "How can I act alone? How can I alone pick the fruit and distribute it all over the world?" This indicates that all classes of devotees should combine to distribute the Hare Kṛṣṇa *mahā-mantra* without consideration of the time, place or situation.

Beg from Him the Hare Kṛṣṇa Mantra

"It would certainly be a very laborious task to pick the fruits and distribute them alone, and still I suspect that some would receive them and others would not.

"Therefore I order every man within this universe to accept this Kṛṣṇa consciousness movement and distribute it everywhere."

PURPORT

In this connection there is a song sung by Śrīla Bhaktivinoda Ṭhākura:

enechi auṣadhi māyā nāśibāra lāgi'
harināma-mahāmantra lao tumi māgi'
bhakativinoda prabhu-caraṇe paḍiyā
sei harināma-mantra la-ila māgiyā

The *saṅkīrtana* movement has been introduced by Lord Caitanya Mahāprabhu just to dispel the illusion of *māyā,* by which everyone in this material world thinks himself to be a product of matter and therefore to have many duties pertaining to the body. Actually, the living entity is not his material body: he is a spirit soul. He has a spiritual need to be eternally blissful and full of knowledge, but unfortunately he identifies himself with the body, sometimes as a human being, sometimes as an animal, sometimes a tree, sometimes an aquatic, sometimes a demigod, and so on. Thus with each change of body he develops a different type of consciousness with different types of activities and thus becomes increasingly entangled in material existence, transmigrating perpetually from one body to another. Under the spell of *māyā,* or illusion, he does not consider the past or future but is simply satisfied with the short life span that he has gotten for the present. To eradicate this illusion, Śrī Caitanya Mahāprabhu has brought the *saṅkīrtana* movement, and He requests everyone to accept and distribute it. A person who is actually a follower of Śrīla Bhaktivinoda Ṭhākura must immediately accept the request of Lord Caitanya Mahāprabhu by offering respectful obeisances unto His lotus feet and thus beg from Him the Hare Kṛṣṇa *mahā-mantra.* If one is fortunate enough to beg from the Lord this Hare Kṛṣṇa *mahā-mantra,* his life is successful.

"I am the only gardener. If I do not distribute these fruits, what shall I do with them? How many fruits can I alone eat?"

PURPORT

Lord Caitanya Mahāprabhu produced so many fruits of devotional service that they must be distributed all over the world; otherwise, how could He alone relish and taste each and every fruit? The original reason that Lord Śrī Kṛṣṇa descended as Śrī Caitanya Mahāprabhu was to understand Śrīmatī Rādhārāṇī's love for Kṛṣṇa and to taste that love. The fruits of the tree of devotional service were innumerable, and therefore He wanted to distribute them unrestrictedly to everyone. Śrīla Rūpa Gosvāmī therefore writes:

anarpita-carīṁ cirāt karuṇayāvatīrṇaḥ kalau
samarpayitum unnatojjvala-rasāṁ sva-bhakti-śriyam
hariḥ puraṭa-sundara-dyuti-kadamba-sandīpitaḥ
sadā hṛdaya-kandare sphuratu vaḥ śacī-nandanaḥ

There were many previous incarnations of the Supreme Personality of Godhead, but none were so generous, kind, and magnanimous as Śrī Caitanya Mahāprabhu, for He distributed the most confidential aspect of devotional service, namely, the conjugal love of Rādhā and Kṛṣṇa. Therefore Śrī Rūpa Gosvāmī Prabhupāda desires that Śrī Caitanya Mahāprabhu live perpetually in the hearts of all devotees, for thus they can understand and relish the loving affairs of Śrīmatī Rādhārāṇī and Kṛṣṇa.

"By the transcendental desire of the Supreme Personality of Godhead, water has been sprinkled all over the tree, and thus there are innumerable fruits of love of Godhead.

"Distribute this Kṛṣṇa consciousness movement all over the world. Let people eat these fruits and ultimately become free from old age and death."

PURPORT

The Kṛṣṇa consciousness movement introduced by Lord Caitanya is extremely important because one who takes to it becomes eternal, being freed from birth, death, and old age. People do not recognize that the real distresses in life are the four principles of birth, death, old age, and disease. They are so foolish that they resign themselves to these four miseries, not knowing the transcendental remedy of the Hare Kṛṣṇa *mahā-mantra*. Simply by chanting the Hare Kṛṣṇa *mahā-mantra,* one can become free from all misery, but because they are enchanted by the illusory energy, people do not take this movement seriously. Therefore those who are actually servants of Śrī Caitanya Mahāprabhu must seriously distribute this movement all over the world to render the greatest benefit to human society. Of course, animals and other lower species are not capable of understanding this movement, but if even a small number of human beings take it seriously, then by their chanting loudly, all living entities, including even trees, animals and other lower species, will be benefited. When Śrī Caitanya Mahāprabhu inquired from Haridāsa Ṭhākura how he was to benefit living entities other than humans, Śrīla Haridāsa Ṭhākura replied that the Hare Kṛṣṇa *mahā-mantra* is so potent that if it is chanted loudly, everyone will benefit, including the lower species of life.

Request Everyone to Chant the Hare Kṛṣṇa Mantra

"If the fruits are distributed all over the world, My reputation as a pious man will be known everywhere, and thus all people will glorify My name with great pleasure."

PURPORT

This prediction of Lord Caitanya Mahāprabhu's is now actually coming to pass. The Kṛṣṇa consciousness movement is being distributed all over the world through the chanting of the holy name of the Lord, the Hare Kṛṣṇa *mahā-mantra,* and people who were leading confused, chaotic lives are now feeling transcendental happiness. They are finding peace in *saṅkīrtana,* and therefore they are acknowledging the supreme benefit of this movement. This is the blessing of Lord Caitanya Mahāprabhu. His prediction is now factually being fulfilled, and those who are sober and conscientious are appreciating the value of this great movement.

"One who has taken his birth as a human being in the land of India [Bhārata-varṣa] should make his life successful and work for the benefit of all other people.

"'It is the duty of every living being to perform welfare activities for the benefit of others with his life, wealth, intelligence and words.'

"'By his work, thoughts and words, an intelligent man must perform actions which will be beneficial for all living entities in this life and the next.'

"I am merely a gardener. I have neither a kingdom nor very great riches. I simply have some fruits and flowers that I wish to utilize to achieve piety in My life."

PURPORT

. . . One cannot satisfy the Supreme Lord by his riches, wealth or opulent position, but anyone can collect a little fruit or a flower and offer it to the Lord. The Lord says that if one brings such an offering in devotion, He will accept it and eat it. When Kṛṣṇa eats, the entire world becomes satisfied. There is a story in the *Mahābhārata* illustrating how by Kṛṣṇa's eating, the sixty thousand disciples of Durvāsā Muni were all satisfied. Therefore it is a fact that if by our life (*prāṇaiḥ*), by our wealth (*arthaiḥ*), by our intelligence (*dhiyā*), or by our words (*vācā*) we can satisfy the Supreme Personality of Godhead, naturally the entire world will become happy. Therefore our main duty is to satisfy the Supreme Godhead by our actions, our money, and our words. This is very simple. Even if one does not have money, he can preach the Hare Kṛṣṇa mantra to everyone. One can go everywhere, to every home, and request everyone to chant the Hare Kṛṣṇa mantra. Thus the entire world situation will become very happy and peaceful.

"Although I am acting as a gardener, I also want to be the tree, for thus I can bestow benefit upon all.

" 'Just see how these trees are maintaining every living entity! Their birth is successful. Their behavior is just like that of great personalities, for anyone who asks anything from a tree never goes away disappointed.' "

The descendants of the tree [the devotees of Śrī Caitanya Mahāprabhu] were very glad to receive this order directly from the Lord.

The fruit of love of God is so delicious that wherever a devotee distributes it, those who relish the fruit, anywhere in the world, immediately become intoxicated.

PURPORT

Here the wonderful fruit of love of Godhead distributed by Lord Caitanya Mahāprabhu is described. We have practical experience that anyone who accepts this fruit and sincerely tastes it immediately becomes mad after it and gives up all his bad habits, being intoxicated by Caitanya Mahāprabhu's gift, the Hare Kṛṣṇa *mahā-mantra.* The statements of *Śrī Caitanya-caritāmṛta* are so practical that anyone can test them. As far as we are concerned, we are most confident of the success of the distribution of the great fruit of love of Godhead through the medium of chanting the *mahā-mantra*—Hare Kṛṣṇa, Hare Kṛṣṇa, Kṛṣṇa Kṛṣṇa, Hare Hare/ Hare Rāma, Hare Rāma, Rāma Rāma, Hare Hare.

Everyone Becomes Intoxicated

The fruit of love of Godhead distributed by Caitanya Mahāprabhu is such a great intoxicant that anyone who eats it, filling his belly, immediately becomes maddened by it, and automatically he chants, dances, laughs, and enjoys.

When Śrī Caitanya Mahāprabhu, the great gardener, sees that people are chanting, dancing, and laughing and that some of them are rolling on the floor and some are making loud humming sounds, He smiles with great pleasure.

PURPORT

This attitude of Śrī Caitanya Mahāprabhu is very important for persons engaged in the Hare Kṛṣṇa movement of Kṛṣṇa consciousness. In every center of our institution, ISKCON, we have arranged for a love feast every Sunday, and when we actually see people come to our center, chant, dance, take *prasādam*, become jubilant, and purchase books, we know that certainly Śrī Caitanya Mahāprabhu is always present in such transcendental activities, and He is very pleased and satisfied. Therefore the members of ISKCON must increase this movement more and more, according to the principles that we are presently trying to execute. Śrī Caitanya Mahāprabhu, thus being pleased, will smilingly glance upon them, bestowing His favor, and the movement will be successful.

The great gardener, Lord Caitanya, personally eats this fruit, and as a result He constantly remains mad, as if helpless and bewildered.

PURPORT

It is the mission of Śrī Caitanya Mahāprabhu to act Himself and teach the people. He says, *āpani ācari' bhakti karila pracāra* (Cc., *Ādi* 4.41). One must first act himself and then teach. This is the function of a real teacher. Unless one is able to understand the philosophy that he speaks, it will not be effective. Therefore one should not only understand the philosophy of the Caitanya cult but also implement it practically in one's life.

While chanting the Hare Kṛṣṇa *mahā-mantra,* Śrī Caitanya Mahāprabhu sometimes fainted and remained unconscious for many hours. He prays in His *Śikṣāṣṭaka* (7):

yugāyitaṁ nimeṣeṇa
cakṣuṣā prāvāṣāyitam
śūnyāyitaṁ jagat sarvaṁ
govinda-viraheṇa me

"O Govinda! Feeling Your separation, I am considering a moment to be like twelve years or more. Tears are flowing from My eyes like torrents of rain, and I am feeling all vacant in the world in Your absence." This is the perfectional stage of chanting the Hare Kṛṣṇa mantra and eating the fruit of love of Godhead, as exhibited by Śrī Caitanya Mahāprabhu. One should not artificially imitate this stage, but if one is serious and sincerely follows the regulative principles and chants the Hare Kṛṣṇa mantra, the time will come when these symptoms will appear. Tears will fill his eyes, he will be unable to chant the *mahā-mantra* distinctly, and his heart will throb in ecstasy. Śrī Caitanya Mahāprabhu says that one should not imitate this, but a devotee should long for the day to come when such symptoms of trance will automatically appear in his body.

With His *saṅkīrtana* movement the Lord made everyone mad like Himself. We do not find anyone who was not intoxicated by His *saṅkīrtana* movement.

(*Śrī Caitanya-caritāmṛta, Ādi-līlā* 9.27–52)

Rita Kaufman

13

THIS CHANTING IS OUR LIFE AND SOUL

Every City, Every Town, Every Village

Śrī Caitanya Mahāprabhu wanted that *pṛthivīte āche yata nagar-ādi grāma*. He wanted that everywhere in the nook and corner of this world, every city, every town, every village, there should be the chanting of Hare Kṛṣṇa *mahā-mantra.* Chanting should be preached. So by His grace it is going on.

(Public speech, Vṛndāvana, April 7, 1976)

Saṅkīrtana Will Knock at the Door of Their Hearts

KRISHNA CONSCIOUSNESS:
THE SANKIRTANA MOVEMENT

. . . Our basic Mission is to propagate the Sankirtana Movement (chanting of the Holy Names of God) all around the world as was recommended by the Incarnation of the Lord, Sri Caitanya Mahaprabhu. People in this age are reluctant very much to understand about God consciousness on account of their unfortunate condition of life. They are working hard day and night simply for sense gratification. But this transcendental vibration of Sankirtana will knock at the door of their hearts for spiritual awakening. Therefore, they should be given the chance for this opportunity.

It is not recommended that a Krishna Conscious devotee go into seclusion for chanting by himself and thereby gaining salvation for himself alone. Our duty and religious obligation is to go out into the streets where the people in general can hear the chanting and see the dancing. We have already seen practically how by this process many, many boys and girls of America and Europe have been saved from the immoral practices of this age and have now dedicated their lives to the service of Krishna.

The state laws are specifically meant for making citizens men of good character, and good character means avoiding the following sinful activities: intoxication, illicit sex life, gambling, and meat-eating. We are checking people from practicing these sinful activities. All of our students are applying these principles practically in their lives, and they are teaching others to follow the same principles. Therefore, it is the duty of the government to help us in our missionary work rather than to hinder us.

It is hoped that the government authorities will cooperate with our Sankirtana parties in enabling us to perform Sankirtana on the streets. To do this it is necessary that we be able to chant the Names of Krishna, dance, play the mrdanga drum, request donations, sell our society's journal, and on occasion, sit down with the mrdanga drum. As devotees of Lord Krishna it is our duty to teach the people how to love God and worship Him in their daily life. This is the aim and destination of human life.

A. C. Bhaktivedanta Swami

(Letter for the police sent to
Tamāl Krishna Dāsa, October 1, 1969)

Our Saṅkīrtana Movement Is Really Authorized

No one should perform *saṅkīrtana* on the streets of the city. Today I am excusing the offense and returning home.

PURPORT

Such orders stopping *saṅkīrtana* in the streets of the world's great cities have been imposed upon members of the Hare Kṛṣṇa movement. We have hundreds of centers all over the world, and we have been specifically persecuted in Australia. In most cities of the Western world we have been arrested many times by the police, but we are nevertheless executing the order of Śrī Caitanya Mahāprabhu by chanting on the streets of all the important cities, such as New York, London, Chicago, Sydney, Melbourne, Paris, and Hamburg. We must remember that such incidents took place in the past, five hundred years ago, and the fact that they are still going on indicates that our *saṅkīrtana* movement is really authorized, for if *saṅkīrtana* were an insignificant material affair, demons would not object to it. The demons of the time tried to obstruct the *saṅkīrtana* movement started by Śrī Caitanya Mahāprabhu. Similar demons are trying to obstruct the *saṅkīrtana* movement we are executing all over the world, and this proves that our *saṅkīrtana* movement is still pure and genuine, following in the footsteps of Śrī Caitanya Mahāprabhu.

(*Śrī Caitanya-caritāmṛta, Ādi-līlā* 17.127)

Our Process Will Remain the Same Eternally

Regarding kirtana party: My idea is that at least one dozen persons should form a Kirtana Party. Two persons play mrdangas, eight persons play karatalas, one person playing tamboura, and one person playing melodious harmonium. The person who will play on tamboura will be leader singer. You have just calculated what I want, when you suggest that the leader should sing as I do, and the others will respond. That will be very nice. But all the members of the party will be pure devotees. None of them should be outsiders. We do not want any outsiders as far as possible. Mrdanga playing as you are doing at present will make you more and more expert as you go on playing. Here also I see Gaurasundara simply by playing is improving. If all the members keep their faith in Krishna and tries to please Him, certainly everyone will be pleased by hearing our Kirtana. It is sure and certain. When such Kirtana will be demonstrated, only the harmonium player may sit, and all the others may stand up and join the Kirtana and dancing properly dressed. This is actual idea and I hope if such Kirtanas are performed even on public stage, we can sell tickets. That will be a source of earning to maintain our activities.

I am glad that Purusottama is trying to get our Society recognized in the U.N. as a non-government organization. And if it is successful, then we shall be able to perform Kirtana in the U.N. stage. And if we are recognized by the representatives for different nations, then we may be invited from different parts of the world, then our Sankirtana movement will be successful. Our process will remain the same eternally, namely, to begin with Sankirtana and prolong it at least for ½ hour, then speak something from Bhagavad-gita, Srimad-Bhagavatam, Brahma Samhita, etc. and invite questions and answer them. Then again concluded by chanting. This is my dream or idea, and I shall be glad if you, Brahmananda, Purusottama, Rayarama, and others can give this idea a practical shape and life, then I shall be very much thankful to you.

(Letter to Haṁsadūta Dāsa, February 4, 1968)

The Time Is Fast Approaching

I understand that Mukunda is leading now a nice Kirtan party in the streets, and there is good response. The time is fast approaching when we will have to perform such public Kirtan in all the important cities of the world. Here also, in the Expo, they have performed Kirtan for two days, and it is wonderfully successful.

(Letter to Yamunā Devī Dāsī, July 16, 1968)

Your Business Is to Satisfy Kṛṣṇa

Madhudviṣa: Prabhupāda, when we're out on *saṅkīrtana,* chanting, what would be the best way for us to engage the crowd to become participants in the chant with us?

Prabhupāda: Best way you go on chanting. Your business is not to, I mean to say, satisfy the crowd. Your business is to satisfy Kṛṣṇa, and then the crowd will be automatically satisfied. We are not going to please the crowd. We are going to give them something, Kṛṣṇa. So you should be very much careful whether you are delivering Kṛṣṇa in the right way. Then they'll be satisfied. Your only business should be to satisfy Kṛṣṇa. Then everything will be satisfied. *Tasmin tuṣṭe jagat tuṣṭa.* If Kṛṣṇa is satisfied, then whole world is satisfied. If you pour water on the root, then it is automatically distributed in every parts of the tree. So Kṛṣṇa is the big tree, root of the big tree, and you take to watering Kṛṣṇa, chant Hare Kṛṣṇa and follow the rules and regulation, everything will be all right.

(Lecture on *Bhagavad-gītā* 7.1, Los Angeles, December 2, 1968)

Their Performance of Saṅkīrtana Is Unparalleled

Indeed, their effulgence is like the brilliance of a million suns. Nor have I ever heard the Lord's names chanted so melodiously.

PURPORT

Such are the symptoms of pure devotees when they are chanting. All the pure devotees are as bright as sunshine, and their bodily luster is very effulgent. In addition, their performance of *saṅkīrtana* is unparalleled. There are many professional chanters who can perform congregational chanting with various musical instruments in an artistic and musical way, but their chanting cannot be as attractive as the congregational chanting of pure devotees. If a devotee sticks strictly to the principles governing Vaiṣṇava behavior, his bodily luster will naturally be attractive, and his singing and chanting of the holy names of the Lord will be effective. People will appreciate such *kīrtana* without hesitation. Even dramas about the pastimes of Lord Caitanya or Śrī Kṛṣṇa should be played by devotees. Such dramas will immediately interest an audience and be full of potency. The students of the International Society for Krishna Consciousness should note these two points and try to apply these principles in their spreading of the Lord's glories.

(*Śrī Caitanya-caritāmṛta, Madhya-līlā* 11.96)

As Much Chanting on the Streets As Possible

Regarding your questions about Sankirtana Party, I think you should try to always have Sankirtana going on. All other things are subsidiary. This chanting is our life and soul, so we must arrange our program now so that there will be as much chanting on the streets and at college engagements as possible. On May 12th, we had a very successful engagement at Ohio State University, and over one thousand boys and girls were chanting and dancing along with us. So this policy should be continued as far as possible.

(Letter to Satsvarūpa Dāsa, May 14, 1969)

If Need Be, the Whole Temple Can Be Locked

I have received a similar letter from Brahmananda also that you are finding some difficulty in keeping pace regularly with the routine work. My advice to you under the circumstances is that at least for one hour you must all go to have Sankirtana outside on the streets or in the park. That is your life and soul, first business. The next business is completing the chanting of 16 rounds every day. The next business is your editing, and if you find extra time, then you can attend the temple ceremonies. Otherwise you can stop these activities, but outdoor kirtana, your editing work and chanting of 16 rounds must be done. Outdoor kirtana must be done, even at the cost of suspending all editorial work. That is your first and foremost business. Temple worship is not so important. If need be, the whole temple can be locked, but the outdoor kirtana cannot be stopped.

(Letter to Rāyarāma Dāsa, May 17, 1969)

That Should Be Our Motto

Regarding your question about kirtana, practically we are not concerned with the instruments. They are used sometimes to make it sweeter, but if we divert our attention for using the instruments more, that is not good. Generally kirtana is performed with mrdanga and karatalas, but if somebody is expert instrument player, he can be admitted to join Sankirtana. We can accept everything for Krishna's service, but not taking the risk of diverting attention to any other thing which will hinder our Krishna Consciousness. That should be our motto, or principle.

(Letter to Jadurāṇī Devī Dāsī, May 26, 1969)

For Them Krishna Has Shown His Special Mercy

These concerts which you are attending will not go in vain, because all of these people who are now hearing these vibrations of Hare Krishna Mantra will be gradually coming to our camp of Krishna Consciousness. This is the Vedic process that simply by sound vibrations there will be the reaction of spiritual benefit. And for all of these people who are joining you in chanting and helping you in your various activities, for them Krishna has shown His Special Mercy, and it is to be understood that Krishna will guide them more and more to return to Him again in His Spiritual Abode, Goloka Vrindaban.

I am pleased to note that you have performed at certain "yoga" groups in the area, and already you are making a nice dent in their Maya, as they are now preferring the Maha Mantra to the chanting of Om. Actually, this chanting of Om is also a bona fide form of meditation, but as we learn from Vedic literature and from Caitanya Mahaprabhu, the chanting of Hare Krishna is the prime benediction for this age, and it is the authoritatively recommended means of God-realization. Also, I am very encouraged to learn that you have your own radio show for one hour every Sunday morning. Here in Los Angeles I have so many tapes of my singing prayers, chanting new tunes of Hare Krishna, playing mrdanga, and purports to prayers. So if you think that some of these tapes will be nice for your program, I will have copies made of some of them and have them sent to you.

(Letter to Gaurasundara Dāsa, August 2, 1969)

"Let Me Go to Hell—I Am Prepared"

Prabhupāda: There is a version by Rāmānujācārya. Rāmānujācārya, he was a great *ācārya* of this Vaiṣṇava *sampradāya.* His spiritual master gave him mantra: "My dear boy, you chant this mantra silently. Nobody can hear. It is very . . ." So then he asked, "What is the effect of this mantra?" He said, "By chanting this mantra, by meditation, you'll get liberation." So he immediately went out and in a public, big meeting he said that "You chant this mantra. You'll be all liberated." So he came back to his spiritual master, and his spiritual master was very angry that "I told you that you should chant silently." He said, "Yes, I have committed offense. So whatever punishment you like, you can give me. But because you told me that this mantra will liberate, I have given it publicly. Let everyone hear and be liberated. Let me go to hell. I don't mind. I have disobeyed your order. Let me go to hell. I am prepared. But by this chanting mantra, if anyone is liberated, let it be publicly distributed." His spiritual master embraced him: "You are greater than me." You see? So if a mantra has so power, why it should be secret? It should be distributed. People are suffering. So Caitanya Mahāprabhu said, "Chant this Hare Kṛṣṇa mantra. Anyone who will hear . . . Even the birds and beasts will hear and they will be liberated." That's all.

(Room conversation, London, September 11, 1969)

As Loud As Possible

Indian lady: Is it better to chant the Hare Kṛṣṇa mantra loud or is it better to hide the mantra?

Prabhupāda: As loud as possible.

Devotees: *Jaya*! *Haribol*!

Prabhupāda: So that others can hear and take benefit of it. There is no secret. It is not that secret mantra, that "I'll give you a special mantra, and you give me $35." It is open to everyone. Chant loudly, as loudly as possible. No question of payment.

(Lecture on *Śrīmad-Bhāgavatam* 6.1.15,
London, August 3, 1971)

What Is the Symptom of Love?

Who is bona fide representative? *Teṣāṁ satata-yuktānāṁ bhajatāṁ prīti-pūrvakam, buddhi-yogaṁ dadāmi tam*. Kṛṣṇa says that "I give him intelligence." To whom? *Satata-yuktānām,* those who are engaged twenty-four hours. In which way he is engaged? *Bhajatam, bhajana,* those who are engaged in devotional service. What kind of devotional service? *Prīti-pūrvakam,* with love and affection. One who is engaged in devotional service of the Lord in love and devotion. What is the symptom of love? The symptom, the prime symptom, most important symptom of love is that the devotee wants to see that his Lord's name, fame, etc., become widespread. He wants to see that "My Lord's name be known everywhere." This is love. If I love somebody, I want to see that his glories are spread all over the world. And Kṛṣṇa also says in the *Bhagavad-gītā, na ca tasmāt manuṣyeṣu kaścit me priya-kṛttamaḥ,* anyone who preaches His glory, nobody is dearer to Him than that person.

(Lecture on *Śrīmad-Bhāgavatam* 1.2.6,
New Vrindaban, September 5, 1972)

"Oh, You Are Going to Be Vaiṣṇava?"

Prabhupāda: Just like Jagāi-Mādhāi, in the beginning they were very much adverse to *saṅkīrtana, hari-saṅkīrtana.* But one day Mādhāi was telling to Jagāi, "My dear brother Jagāi, after all, these rascals sing very nicely, Hare Kṛṣṇa. They sing very . . ." "Oh, you are going to be Vaiṣṇava?" "No, no. I am not going to be Vaiṣṇava. I'm just appreciating. They sing very nicely." So you go like that. They will arrest you. You have got good experience. In London, they were arrested. You were in London. How many times you were arrested?

Gurudāsa: Three.

Prabhupāda: Three times. Our record is that our people were arrested thirty-six times. Now the police have become disgusted. They don't arrest. Yes. But this thing is going on in Australia, especially in Melbourne. So they asked me what to do. To do? Chant Hare Kṛṣṇa, and you'll get good opportunity. When you are put into jail, you'll be free to chant Hare Kṛṣṇa. So they are doing that.

(Lecture on *Śrīmad-Bhāgavatam* 1.2.5, Vṛndāvana, October 16, 1972)

The Four Walls Will Hear You

Pradyumna: Śrīla Rūpa Gosvāmī has given a definition of auspiciousness. He says that actual auspiciousness means welfare activities for all the people of the world.

Prabhupāda: Yes. Just like this Kṛṣṇa consciousness movement: it is welfare activities for all the people of the world. It is not a sectarian movement, not only for the human being, but also for the animals, birds, beasts, trees, everyone. This discussion was made by Haridāsa Ṭhākura with Lord Caitanya. In that statement, Haridāsa Ṭhākura affirmed it that by chanting Hare Kṛṣṇa mantra loudly, the trees, the birds, the beasts—everyone—will be benefited. This is the statement of Namācārya Haridāsa Ṭhākura. So when we chant Hare Kṛṣṇa mantra loudly, it is beneficial for everyone. This statement was put forward in Melbourne in the court. The court inquired that "Why do you chant Hare Kṛṣṇa mantra loudly in the street?" The reply we gave that "Just to benefit all the people." Actually, it is the fact. Of course, now there is no prosecution by the state. We are chanting very freely on the streets. That is the benefit. If we chant Hare Kṛṣṇa mantra, it benefits everyone, not only human beings. My Guru Mahārāja used to say if somebody complained that "We go and chant, but nobody attends our meeting," so Guru Mahārāja would reply that "Why? The four walls will hear you. That is sufficient. Don't be disappointed. Go on chanting. If there are four walls, they will hear. That's all."

(Lecture on *The Nectar of Devotion*, Vṛndāvana, November 7, 1972)

The Beginning Was Only Chanting—
There Was Nothing More

Prabhupāda: "My dear king, this question is all-auspicious for all the people of the world." If you simply inquire about Kṛṣṇa or hear about Kṛṣṇa, even though we do not understand, but that vibration of Kṛṣṇa.... Just like we are chanting "Hare Kṛṣṇa," we may not understand what is meaning of Hare Kṛṣṇa, but still, because it is transcendental sound, it is auspicious. Wherever you chant Hare Kṛṣṇa, they may hear or they may not hear, it is auspicious for them. So we are sending our men for street *saṅkīrtana*. It doesn't matter whether people are eager to hear it or not, but it is auspicious. It will create an atmosphere which is very, very congenial to the human society. That should be our principle. Not that because we are chanting, nobody is taking care, we shall not be disappointed. Our-this *saṅkīrtana* movement is so nice that simply by chanting, the vibration will create an auspicious atmosphere, *varīyān eṣa te praśnaḥ*. Now you can practically see, those who are old members, I began in this New York in that storefront simply by chanting. So I did not bribe you American boys and girls to come after me. The only asset was chanting. That was in Tompkins Square Park. This Brahmānanda Swami, he first came to dance in my chant. He and Acyutānanda, that was the first dancing of our Kṛṣṇa conscious movement. Yes. And I had no *mṛdaṅgas*. That was a, what is that?
Devotee: Bongo drum.
Prabhupāda: Drum, little drum. So I was chanting Hare Kṛṣṇa for from two to five, three hours, and so many boys and girls were coming and joining, and there was first photograph in the *Times, New York Times.* They appreciated and people also appreciated. So this chanting, the beginning was only chanting. There was nothing more. At that time there was no program of *prasāda* distribution. That, later on it came. So we should always be confident that this chanting is not a vibration of this

material world. This is not vibration of material world. Narottama dāsa Ṭhākura says, *golokera prema-dhana hari-nāma-saṅkīrtana*. It is imported from the spiritual world. It is completely spiritual.

(Lecture on *Śrīmad-Bhāgavatam* 2.1.1,
New York, April 19, 1973)

"Chant, Chant, Chant"—"Can't, Can't, Can't"

So this is your opportunity. Therefore Caitanya Mahāprabhu says: "My dear Lord, You are so kind upon Me that You are giving Your association always, constantly. You are prepared. You are giving. But I am so unfortunate. I am not taking advantage of it." *Durdaiva.* Misfortune. Our, this Kṛṣṇa consciousness movement is simply requesting people: "Chant Hare Kṛṣṇa."

There was a caricature-picture in some paper. Perhaps you remember. From Montreal or here, I don't remember. One old lady and her husband, sitting, face to face. The lady is requesting the husband: "Chant, chant, chant." And the husband is answering: "Can't, can't, can't." So this is going on. We are requesting everyone: "Please chant, chant, chant." And they are replying: "Can't, can't." This is their misfortune. This is their misfortune.

So still it is our duty to make all these misfortunate, unfortunate creatures fortunate. That is our mission. We therefore go in the street and chant. Although they say: "Can't," we go on chanting. That is our business. And, somehow or other, we push on some literature in his hand. He is becoming fortunate. He would have squandered his hard-earned money in so many nasty, sinful ways, and if he purchases one book, never mind what is the price, his money is properly utilized. The beginning of Kṛṣṇa consciousness is there. Because he is giving some money, hard-earned money, for this Kṛṣṇa consciousness movement, he is getting some spiritual profit. He's not losing. He's getting some spiritual profit. Therefore our business is, somehow or other, bring everyone in this Kṛṣṇa consciousness movement. He will be profited.

(Lecture on *Śrīmad-Bhāgavatam* 1.8.30,
Los Angeles, April 22, 1973)

"Go, Go, Go, Go!"

Prabhupāda: We should push Kṛṣṇa consciousness as disinfecting agent. They're all infected, the whole world. So by chanting you disinfect.
Umāpati: Just by our presence chanting, then?
Prabhupāda: Yes. Therefore chanting is so important. Philosophy later on. First of all, *ceto-darpaṇa-mārjanam,* cleansing the heart. Cleansing the heart. So by hearing this chanting their heart will be cleansed gradually. Then they will understand the real position. So we have to do this chanting, not sit down in a solitary place, chanting himself. No, not like that. You are to vibrate the sound for the benefit of others.
Umāpati: That is the mystical process of this movement.
Prabhupāda: Yes, yes. So that their heart may be cleansed and they can understand. And if I sit down in a solitary place, for my benefit, that may be his benefit, but it is not very high-class engagement. He must sacrifice for others. That is the Cāṇakya Paṇḍita's moral instruction, that "Everyone should sacrifice for the Supreme." Caitanya Mahāprabhu is God Himself. He comes down to preach, to become *sannyāsī,* and to take so much trouble all over India and everywhere, and giving instruction and sending men, "Go, go, go, go!" He's perfect. Why He's coming? He doesn't require. No. For the benefit of others. We must follow the footsteps of Caitanya Mahāprabhu.

(Morning walk, Los Angeles, December 5, 1973)

Simply with Mṛdaṅga and Karatāla

My opinion is that it is not necessary for us to utilize these different musical talents for spreading Krishna Consciousness. I would rather see people follow strictly the path of Lord Caitanya and His Sankirtana devotees. We are using mrdanga, karatala, that is enough. We are not musicians. We are Krishna bhaktas. Therefore we do not stress so much importance on these different musical talents. Sri Caitanya Mahaprabhu is God Himself. Had He thought it would have been better to spread Krishna Consciousness by another way He would have done so. But no, simply with mrdanga and karatala, traveling and chanting Hare Krishna, asking everyone to chant Hare Krishna, preaching simply Srimad-Bhagavatam philosophy, this is the process. There is no need for us to try and add anything to this simple method. It will only be a distraction. Therefore I request you to follow the simple path of Lord Caitanya Mahaprabhu and help me spread this wonderful mission all over the world. Keep yourself pure and fixed up in Krishna Consciousness by following the basic principles that I have given; chanting 16 rounds daily, following the four regulative principles, rising early, attending mangala arati and classes etc. This is of the utmost importance.

(Letter to Jagadīśa Paṇḍita Dāsa, December 28, 1974)

That Will Make You Triumphant

Prabhupāda: So there is agitation against chanting. That is also good. Yes, "Hare Kṛṣṇa is bad." [*laughs*]
Puṣṭa Kṛṣṇa: They don't want to be bothered with Hare Kṛṣṇa. Go on with their hellish life.
Prabhupāda: So we want that. Let them chant Hare Kṛṣṇa somehow or other. "We don't want to be bothered by Hare Kṛṣṇa." That means chanting Hare Kṛṣṇa.

Devotee: Because our *kīrtana* party now, we have, we go on *kīrtana,* eighty men. We go two nights a week with eighty men. Huge *kīrtana* with five *mṛdaṅgas* and guitars, and we get huge crowd from the whole street.

Prabhupāda: That will make you triumphant. Go on *kīrtana.*

(Room conversation, Auckland, April 27, 1976)

Painting by Yadurāṇī Devī Dāsī

14

THE GLORIES OF NĀMĀCĀRYA HARIDĀSA ṬHĀKURA

Haridāsa Ṭhākura Ki Jaya!

You'll be surprised to know that Haridāsa Ṭhākura, we always glorify him after our *kīrtana,* "Haridāsa Ṭhākura *ki jaya*!" This Haridāsa Ṭhākura, how he was undisturbed. There are many instances. Lord Jesus Christ, he was also undisturbed when he was being crucified. So similarly, this Haridāsa Ṭhākura, he happened to be a Mohammedan and he joined this Hare Kṛṣṇa movement. So the Mohammedan magistrate called him, "Oh, you are born in such a nice family and you are chanting Hare Kṛṣṇa? Hindu? You are chanting Hare Kṛṣṇa, Hindu's name? Then what is your explanation?" So Haridāsa Ṭhākura, he could understand that he is now in a dangerous position. So he replied, "Sir, many Hindus also have become Mohammedan. So if some Mohammedan becomes Hindu, what is the harm?" "Oh, you are arguing?" Means he was to be punished. Give the dog a bad name and hang it.

So it was ordered that this man should be caned. And at that time Navadvīpa had twenty-two marketplaces. So in each marketplace he should be taken and in the public he should be flogged. So that was done. And the idea was that by flogging he would die. The magistrate's idea was like that. But fortunately Haridāsa Ṭhākura did not die, neither he cried even. He was as good as silent. So these persons who were flogging, they fell at his feet. "Sir, the idea was that you would die. But now I see that you do not die. So now our punishment is awaiting. He will think that we have not flogged you sufficiently." Then Haridāsa Ṭhākura said, "What do you want?" "No, we want that you should die." Then he made himself into *samādhi* [trance] and the floggers took him to the magistrate, "Here is the condition." The magistrate thought, "He's now dead." So he told them, "Throw him in the water. Don't put him in the graveyard. He has become Hindu." So he was not disturbed, he was steady. So it is such a thing. He was chanting. The others were flogging him, and he was chanting Hare Kṛṣṇa, Hare Kṛṣṇa, Kṛṣṇa Kṛṣṇa, Hare Hare/ Hare Rāma, Hare Rāma, Rāma Rāma, Hare Hare.

(Lecture on *Bhagavad-gītā* 6.40–42,
New York, September 16, 1966)

This Is Tug of War

Viṣṇujana: How will it be possible, Prabhupāda, for a man whose mind is clouded to constantly chant Hare Kṛṣṇa? A man who's always thinking thoughts about family, friends, country, nation?

Prabhupāda: Yes. Think of. At the same time, chant. Two things will go on, and this will conquer. (*chuckles*) As *māyā* is forcing you to drag you from this Kṛṣṇa consciousness, you also force *māyā* by chanting Hare Kṛṣṇa. There is fight. And *māyā* will go away.

daivī hy eṣā guṇamayī, mama māyā duratyayā
mām eva ye prapadyante, māyām etāṁ taranti te

This *māyā* is very strong. She'll force you to entice you to other path. But if you do not stop, if you chant loudly ... Just like Haridāsa Ṭhākura was chanting and *māyā* could not victimize him. You know that? What was his stand? Simply chanting Hare Kṛṣṇa, Hare Kṛṣṇa, Kṛṣṇa Kṛṣṇa, Hare Hare/ Hare Rāma, Hare Rāma, Rāma Rāma, Hare Hare. *Māyā* could not entice. *Māyā* failed. *Māyā* became his disciple. He did not become *māyā's* disciple.

This is tug of war. So don't be afraid of *māyā*. Simply enhance chanting and you'll be conqueror. That's all. *Nārāyaṇa-parāḥ sarve na kutaścana bibhyati.* We are not afraid of *māyā* because Kṛṣṇa is there. Yes. Kṛṣṇa says, *kaunteya pratijānīhi na me bhaktaḥ praṇaśyati,* You just declare, "My devotee will never be vanquished by *māyā*." *Māyā* cannot do anything. Simply you have to become strong. And what is that strength? Chant Hare Kṛṣṇa, Hare Kṛṣṇa, Kṛṣṇa Kṛṣṇa, Hare Hare, loudly.

(Lecture on *Bhagavad-gītā* 3.6–10,
Los Angeles, December 23, 1968)

Please Sit and Listen to the Chanting of the Holy Name

O devotees of Śrī Caitanya Mahāprabhu, please hear something about the qualities of Haridāsa Ṭhākura that Śrīla Vṛndāvana dāsa Ṭhākura has not described in detail.

After leaving his home, Haridāsa Ṭhākura stayed for some time in the forest of Benāpola.

Haridāsa Ṭhākura constructed a cottage in a solitary forest. There he planted a *tulasī* plant, and in front of the *tulasī* he would chant the holy name of the Lord 300,000 times daily. He chanted throughout the entire day and night.

For his bodily maintenance he would go to a *brāhmaṇa's* house and beg some food. He was spiritually so influential that all the neighboring people worshiped him.

A landholder named Rāmacandra Khān was the zamindar of that district. He was envious of Vaiṣṇavas and was therefore a great atheist.

Unable to tolerate that such respect was being offered to Haridāsa Ṭhākura, Rāmacandra Khān planned in various ways to dishonor him. By no means could he find any fault in the character of Haridāsa Ṭhākura. Therefore he called for local prostitutes and began a plan to discredit His Holiness.

Rāmacandra Khān said to the prostitutes, "There is a mendicant named Haridāsa Ṭhākura. All of you devise a way to deviate him from his vows of austerity."

Among the prostitutes, one attractive young girl was selected. "I shall attract the mind of Haridāsa Ṭhākura," she promised, "within three days."

Rāmacandra Khān said to the prostitute, "My constable will go with you so that as soon as he sees you with Haridāsa Ṭhākura, immediately he will arrest him and bring both of you to me."

The prostitute replied, "First let me have union with him once; then the second time I shall take your constable with me to arrest him."

At night the prostitute, after dressing herself most attractively, went to the cottage of Haridāsa Ṭhākura with great jubilation.

After offering obeisances to the *tulasī* plant, she went to the door of Haridāsa Ṭhākura, offered him obeisances and stood there.

Exposing part of her body to his view, she sat down on the threshold of the door and spoke to him in very sweet words.

"My dear Ṭhākura, O great preacher, great devotee, you are so beautifully built, and your youth is just beginning. Who is the woman who could control her mind after seeing you?

"I am eager to be united with you. My mind is greedy for this. If I don't obtain you, I shall not be able to keep my body and soul together."

Haridāsa Ṭhākura replied, "I shall accept you without fail, but you will have to wait until I have finished chanting my regular rounds on my beads. Until that time, please sit and listen to the chanting of the holy name. As soon as I am finished, I shall fulfill your desire."

Hearing this, the prostitute remained sitting there while Haridāsa Ṭhākura chanted on his beads until the light of morning appeared.

When she saw that it was morning, the prostitute stood up and left. Coming before Rāmacandra Khān, she informed him of all the news.

"Today Haridāsa Ṭhākura has promised to enjoy with me. Tomorrow certainly I shall have union with him."

The next night, when the prostitute came again, Haridāsa Ṭhākura gave her many assurances.

"Last night you were disappointed. Please excuse my offense. I shall certainly accept you.

"Please sit down and hear the chanting of the Hare Kṛṣṇa *mahā-mantra* until my regular chanting is finished. Then your desire will surely be fulfilled."

After offering her obeisances to the *tulasī* plant and Haridāsa Ṭhākura, she sat down at the door. Hearing Haridāsa Ṭhākura chanting the Hare Kṛṣṇa mantra, she also chanted, "O my Lord Hari, O my Lord Hari."

PURPORT

Herein one can clearly see how a Vaiṣṇava delivers a fallen soul by a transcendental trick. The prostitute came to pollute Haridāsa Ṭhākura, but he took it as his duty to deliver the prostitute. As clearly demonstrated here, the process of deliverance is very simple. With faith and reverence the prostitute associated with Haridāsa Ṭhākura, who personally treated her material disease by chanting the Hare Kṛṣṇa *mahā-mantra*. Although the prostitute had an ulterior motive, somehow or other she got the association of a Vaiṣṇava and satisfied him by occasionally chanting in imitation, "O my Lord Hari, O my Lord Hari." The conclusion is that associating with a Vaiṣṇava, chanting the holy name of the Lord and offering obeisances to the *tulasī* plant or a Vaiṣṇava all lead one to become a transcendental devotee who is completely cleansed of all material contamination.

(*Śrī Caitanya-caritāmṛta, Antya-līlā* 3.98–122)

Simply by Hearing This Chanting

When the night came to an end, the prostitute was restless. Seeing this, Haridāsa Ṭhākura spoke to her as follows.

"I have vowed to chant ten million names in a month. I have taken this vow, but now it is nearing its end.

"I thought that today I would be able to finish my performance of *yajña,* my chanting of the Hare Kṛṣṇa mantra. I tried my best to chant the holy name all night, but I still did not finish.

"Tomorrow I will surely finish, and my vow will be fulfilled. Then it will be possible for me to enjoy with you in full freedom."

PURPORT

Haridāsa Ṭhākura never wanted to enjoy the prostitute, but he tricked her to deliver her by giving her a chance to hear the holy name of the Lord while he chanted. Pure devotees chant the Hare Kṛṣṇa mantra, and simply by hearing this chanting from a purified transcendental person, one is purified of all sinful activities, no matter how lowborn or fallen one may be. As soon as one is thus completely free from the reactions of sinful activities, he is eligible to render devotional service to the Lord. This is the process for engaging the fallen souls in devotional service. As Lord Kṛṣṇa says in the *Bhagavad-gītā* (7.28):

yeṣāṁ tv anta-gataṁ pāpaṁ
janānāṁ puṇya-karmaṇām
te dvandva-moha-nirmuktā
bhajante māṁ dṛḍha-vratāḥ

"Persons who have acted piously in previous lives and in this life and whose sinful actions are completely eradicated are freed from the duality of delusion, and they engage themselves in My service with determination."

(*Śrī Caitanya-caritāmṛta, Antya-līlā* 3.123–126)

Chant the Hare Kṛṣṇa Mantra Continuously

The prostitute returned to Rāmacandra Khān and informed him of what had happened. The next day she came earlier, at the beginning of the evening, and stayed with Haridāsa Ṭhākura.

After offering obeisances to the *tulasī* plant and Haridāsa Ṭhākura, she sat down on the threshold of the room. Thus she began to hear Haridāsa Ṭhākura's chanting, and she also personally chanted "Hari, Hari," the holy name of the Lord.

"Today it will be possible for me to finish my chanting," Haridāsa Ṭhākura informed her. "Then I shall satisfy all your desires."

The night ended while Haridāsa Ṭhākura was chanting, but by his association the mind of the prostitute had changed.

The prostitute, now purified, fell at the lotus feet of Haridāsa Ṭhākura and confessed that Rāmacandra Khān had appointed her to pollute him.

"Because I have taken the profession of a prostitute," she said, "I have performed unlimited sinful acts. My lord, be merciful to me. Deliver my fallen soul."

Haridāsa Ṭhākura replied, "I know everything about the conspiracy of Rāmacandra Khān. He is nothing but an ignorant fool. Therefore his activities do not make me feel unhappy.

"On the very day Rāmacandra Khān was planning his intrigue against me, I would have left this place immediately, but because you came to me I stayed here for three days to deliver you."

The prostitute said, "Kindly act as my spiritual master. Instruct me in my duty, by which I can get relief from material existence."

Haridāsa Ṭhākura replied, "Immediately go home and distribute to the *brāhmaṇas* whatever property you have. Then come back to this room and stay here forever in Kṛṣṇa consciousness.

"Chant the Hare Kṛṣṇa mantra continuously and render service to the *tulasī* plant by watering her and offering prayers to her. In this way you will very soon get the opportunity to be sheltered at the lotus feet of Kṛṣṇa."

PURPORT

At least five thousand years ago, Lord Śrī Kṛṣṇa expressed His desire that everyone surrender to Him (*sarva-dharmān parityajya mām ekaṁ śaraṇaṁ vraja*). Why is it that people cannot do this? Kṛṣṇa assures, *ahaṁ tvāṁ sarva-pāpebhyo mokṣayiṣyāmi mā śucaḥ:* "I shall deliver you from all sinful reactions. Do not fear." Everyone is suffering from the results of sinful activities, but Kṛṣṇa says that if one surrenders unto Him, He will protect one from sinful reactions. Modern civilization, however, is interested neither in Kṛṣṇa nor in getting relief from sinful acts. Therefore men are suffering. Surrender is the ultimate instruction of the *Bhagavad-gītā,* but for one who cannot surrender to the lotus feet of Kṛṣṇa, it is better to chant the Hare Kṛṣṇa mantra constantly, under the instruction of Haridāsa Ṭhākura.

In our Kṛṣṇa consciousness movement we are teaching our followers to chant the Hare Kṛṣṇa mantra continuously on beads. Even those who are not accustomed to this practice are advised to chant at least sixteen rounds on their beads so that they may be trained. Otherwise, Śrī Caitanya Mahāprabhu recommended:

tṛṇād api sunīcena
taror iva sahiṣṇunā
amāninā mānadena
kīrtanīyaḥ sadā hariḥ

"One should chant the holy name of the Lord in a humble state of mind, thinking oneself lower than the straw in the street. One should be more tolerant than a tree, devoid of all sense of false prestige, and ready to offer all respect to others. In such a state of mind one can chant the holy name of the Lord constantly." *Sadā* means "always." Haridāsa Ṭhākura says, *nirantara nāma lao:* "Chant the Hare Kṛṣṇa mantra without stopping."

Although Kṛṣṇa wants everyone to surrender to His lotus feet, because of people's sinful activities they cannot do this. *Na māṁ duṣkṛtino mūḍhāḥ prapadyante narādhamāḥ:* rascals and fools, the lowest of men, who engage in sinful activities, cannot suddenly surrender to the lotus feet of Kṛṣṇa. Nevertheless, if they begin chanting the Hare Kṛṣṇa mantra and rendering service unto the *tulasī* plant, they will very soon be able to surrender. One's real duty is to surrender to the lotus feet of Kṛṣṇa, but if one is unable to do so, he should adopt this process, as introduced by Śrī Caitanya Mahāprabhu and His most confidential servant, Nāmācārya Śrīla Haridāsa Ṭhākura. This is the way to achieve success in Kṛṣṇa consciousness.

(*Śrī Caitanya-caritāmṛta, Antya-līlā* 3.127–137)

The Prostitute Became a Celebrated Devotee

After thus instructing the prostitute about the process of chanting the Hare Kṛṣṇa mantra, Haridāsa Ṭhākura stood up and left, continuously chanting "Hari, Hari."

Thereafter, the prostitute distributed to the *brāhmaṇas* whatever household possessions she had, following the order of her spiritual master.

The prostitute shaved her head clean in accordance with Vaiṣṇava principles and stayed in that room wearing only one cloth. Following in the footsteps of her spiritual master, she began chanting the holy name of Kṛṣṇa 300,000 times a day. She chanted throughout the entire day and night.

She worshiped the *tulasī* plant, following in the footsteps of her spiritual master. Instead of eating regularly, she chewed whatever food she received as alms, and if nothing was supplied she would fast. Thus by eating frugally and fasting she conquered her senses, and as soon as her senses were controlled, symptoms of love of Godhead appeared in her person.

Thus the prostitute became a celebrated devotee. She became very advanced in spiritual life, and many stalwart Vaiṣṇavas would come to see her.

Seeing the sublime character of the prostitute, everyone was astonished. Everyone glorified the influence of Haridāsa Ṭhākura and offered him obeisances.

(*Śrī Caitanya-caritāmṛta, Antya-līlā* 3.138–143)

Māyā Enchants the Entire World

There is another incident concerning Haridāsa Ṭhākura's uncommon behavior. One will be astonished to hear about it.

Hear about such incidents without putting forth dry arguments, for these incidents are beyond our material reasoning. One must believe in them with faith.

One day Haridāsa Ṭhākura was sitting in his cave, reciting the holy name of the Lord very loudly.

The night was full of moonlight, which made the waves of the Ganges look dazzling. All directions were clear and bright.

Thus everyone who saw the beauty of the cave, with the *tulasī* plant on a clean altar, was astonished and satisfied at heart.

At that time, in that beautiful scene, a woman appeared in the courtyard. The beauty of her body was so bright that it tinged the entire place with a yellow hue.

The scent of her body perfumed all directions, and the tinkling of her ornaments startled the ear.

After coming there, the woman offered obeisances to the *tulasī* plant, and after circumambulating the *tulasī* plant she came to the door of the cave where Haridāsa Ṭhākura was sitting.

With folded hands she offered obeisances at the lotus feet of Haridāsa Ṭhākura. Sitting at the door, she then spoke in a very sweet voice.

"My dear friend," she said, "you are the friend of the entire world. You are so beautiful and qualified. I have come here only for union with you.

"My dear sir, kindly accept me and be merciful toward me, for it is a characteristic of all saintly persons to be kind toward the poor and fallen."

After saying this, she began to manifest various postures, which even the greatest philosopher would lose his patience upon seeing.

Haridāsa Ṭhākura was immovable, for he was deeply determined. He began to speak to her, being very merciful toward her.

"I have been initiated into a vow to perform a great sacrifice by chanting the holy name a certain number of times every day.

"As long as the vow to chant is unfulfilled, I do not desire anything else. When I finish my chanting, then I have an opportunity to do anything.

"Sit down at the door and hear the chanting of the Hare Kṛṣṇa *mahā-mantra*. As soon as the chanting is finished, I shall satisfy you as you desire."

After saying this, Haridāsa Ṭhākura continued to chant the holy name of the Lord. Thus the woman sitting before him began to hear the chanting of the holy name.

In this way, as he chanted and chanted, the morning approached, and when the woman saw that it was morning, she got up and left.

For three days she approached Haridāsa Ṭhākura in this way, exhibiting various feminine postures that would bewilder the mind of even Lord Brahmā.

Haridāsa Ṭhākura was always absorbed in thoughts of Kṛṣṇa and the holy name of Kṛṣṇa. Therefore the feminine poses the woman exhibited were just like crying in the forest.

At the end of the night of the third day, the woman spoke to Haridāsa Ṭhākura as follows.

"My dear sir, for three days you have cheated me by giving me false assurances, for I see that throughout the entire day and night your chanting of the holy name is never finished."

Haridāsa Ṭhākura said, "My dear friend, what can I do? I have made a vow. How, then, can I give it up?"

After offering obeisances to Haridāsa Ṭhākura, the woman said, "I am the illusory energy of the Supreme Personality of Godhead. I came here to test you."

PURPORT

In the *Bhagavad-gītā* (7.14) Lord Kṛṣṇa says:

daivī hy eṣā guṇa-mayī
mama māyā duratyayā
mām eva ye prapadyante
māyām etāṁ taranti te

"This divine energy of Mine, consisting of the three modes of material nature, is difficult to overcome. But those who have surrendered unto Me can easily cross beyond it." This was actually proved by the behavior of Haridāsa Ṭhākura. *Māyā* enchants the entire world. Indeed, people have forgotten the ultimate goal of life because of the dazzling attractions of the material world. But this dazzling attraction, especially the attractive beauty of a woman, is meant for persons who are not surrendered to the Supreme Personality of Godhead. The Lord says, *mām eva ye prapadyante māyām etāṁ taranti te:* "One who is surrendered unto Me cannot be conquered by the illusory energy." The illusory energy personally came to test Haridāsa Ṭhākura, but herein she admits her defeat, for she was unable to captivate him. How is this possible? It was because Haridāsa Ṭhākura, fully surrendered to the lotus feet of Kṛṣṇa, was always absorbed in thoughts of Kṛṣṇa by chanting the holy names of the Lord 300,000 times daily as a vow.

(*Śrī Caitanya-caritāmṛta, Antya-līlā* 3.227–250)

This Process Alone Saved Him

"I have previously captivated the mind of even Brahmā, what to speak of others. Your mind alone have I failed to attract.

PURPORT

Beginning from Lord Brahmā down to the insignificant ant, everyone, without exception, is attracted by the illusory energy of the Supreme Personality of Godhead. The demigods, human beings, animals, birds, beasts, trees, and plants are all attracted by sexual desire. That is the illusion of *māyā*. Everyone, whether man or woman, thinks that he is the enjoyer of the illusory energy. In this way, everyone is captivated and engaged in material activities. However, because Haridāsa Ṭhākura was always thinking of the Supreme Personality of Godhead and was always busy satisfying the senses of the Lord, this process alone saved him from the captivation of *māyā*. This is practical proof of the strength of devotional service. Because of his full engagement in the service of the Lord, he could not be induced to enjoy *māyā*. The verdict of the *śāstras* is that a pure Vaiṣṇava, or devotee of the Lord, never thinks of enjoying the material world, which culminates in sex life. He never thinks himself an enjoyer; instead, he always wants to be enjoyed by the Supreme Personality of Godhead. Therefore the conclusion is that the Supreme Personality of Godhead is eternal, transcendental, beyond the perception of sense gratification, and beyond the material qualities. Only if a living entity gives up the false conception that the body is the self and always thinks himself an eternal servant of Kṛṣṇa and the Vaiṣṇavas can he surpass the influence of *māyā* (*mām eva ye prapadyante māyām etāṁ taranti te*). A pure living entity who thus attains the stage of *anartha-nivṛtti,* cessation of everything unwanted, has nothing to enjoy in the material world. One attains this stage only by properly performing the functions of devotional service. Śrīla Rūpa Gosvāmī has written:

ādau śraddhā tataḥ sādhu-saṅgo 'tha bhajana-kriyā
tato 'nartha-nivṛttiḥ syāt tato niṣṭhā rucis tataḥ

"In the beginning one must have a preliminary desire for self-realization. This will bring one to the stage of trying to associate with persons who are spiritually elevated. In the next stage, one becomes initiated by an elevated spiritual master, and under his instruction the neophyte devotee begins the process of devotional service. By execution of devotional service under the guidance of the spiritual master, one becomes freed from all material attachments, attains steadiness in self-realization, and acquires a taste for hearing about the Absolute Personality of Godhead, Śrī Kṛṣṇa." (*Bhakti-rasāmṛta-sindhu* 1.4.15) If one is actually executing devotional service, then *anarthas,* the unwanted things associated with material enjoyment, will automatically disappear.

(*Śrī Caitanya-caritāmṛta, Antya-līlā* 3.251)

Now I Want to Chant the Holy Name

"My dear sir, you are the foremost devotee. Simply seeing you and hearing you chant the holy name of Kṛṣṇa has purified my consciousness. Now I want to chant the holy name of the Lord. Please

be kind to me by instructing me about the ecstasy of chanting the Hare Kṛṣṇa *mahā-mantra.*

"There is now a flood of the eternal nectar of love of Godhead due to the incarnation of Lord Caitanya. All living entities are floating in that flood. The entire world is now thankful to the Lord.

"Anyone who does not float in this inundation is most condemned. Such a person cannot be delivered for millions of *kalpas.*

"Formerly I received the holy name of Lord Rāma from Lord Śiva, but now, due to your association, I am greatly eager to chant the holy name of Lord Kṛṣṇa.

"The holy name of Lord Rāma certainly gives liberation, but the holy name of Kṛṣṇa transports one to the other side of the ocean of nescience and at last gives one ecstatic love of Kṛṣṇa."

PURPORT

In an indirect way, this verse explains the chanting of the Hare Kṛṣṇa *mahā-mantra.* The Hare Kṛṣṇa *mahā-mantra*—Hare Kṛṣṇa, Hare Kṛṣṇa, Kṛṣṇa Kṛṣṇa, Hare Hare/ Hare Rāma, Hare Rāma, Rāma Rāma, Hare Hare—includes both the holy name of Lord Kṛṣṇa and the name of Lord Rāma. Lord Rāma gives one the opportunity to be liberated, but simply by liberation one does not get actual spiritual benefit. Sometimes if one is liberated from the material world but has no shelter at the lotus feet of Kṛṣṇa, one falls down to the material world again. Liberation is like a state of convalescence, in which one is free from a fever but is still not healthy. Even in the stage of convalescence, if one is not very careful, one may have a relapse. Similarly, liberation does not offer as much security as the shelter of the lotus feet of Kṛṣṇa. It is stated in the *śāstra:*

ye 'nye 'ravindākṣa vimukta-māninas
tvayy asta-bhāvād aviśuddha-buddhayaḥ
āruhya kṛcchreṇa paraṁ padaṁ tataḥ
patanty adho 'nādṛta-yuṣmad-aṅghrayaḥ

"O Lord, the intelligence of those who think themselves liberated but who have no devotion is impure. Even though they rise to the highest point of liberation by dint of severe penances and austerities, they are sure to fall down again into material existence, for they do not take shelter at Your lotus feet." (*Śrīmad-Bhāgavatam* 10.2.32) *Yuṣmad-aṅghrayaḥ* refers to the lotus feet of Kṛṣṇa. If one does not take shelter of Kṛṣṇa's lotus feet, he falls down (*patanty adhaḥ*), even from liberation. The Hare Kṛṣṇa *mahā-mantra,* however, gives liberation and at the same time offers shelter at the lotus feet of Kṛṣṇa. If one takes shelter at the lotus feet of Kṛṣṇa after liberation, he develops his dormant ecstatic love for Kṛṣṇa. That is the highest perfection of life.

(*Śrī Caitanya-caritāmṛta, Antya-līlā* 3.252–257)

Haridāsa Ṭhākura Formally Initiated Her

"Please give me the holy name of Kṛṣṇa and thus make me fortunate, so that I also may float in the flood of love of Godhead inaugurated by Śrī Caitanya Mahāprabhu."

After speaking in this way, Māyā worshiped the lotus feet of Haridāsa Ṭhākura, who initiated her by saying, "Just perform chanting of the Hare Kṛṣṇa *mahā-mantra*."

PURPORT

Now even Māyā wanted to be favored by Haridāsa Ṭhākura. Therefore Haridāsa Ṭhākura formally initiated her by asking her to chant the Hare Kṛṣṇa *mahā-mantra.*

(*Śrī Caitanya-caritāmṛta, Antya-līlā* 3.258–259)

Allured By Ecstatic Love of Lord Kṛṣṇa

After thus being instructed by Haridāsa Ṭhākura, Māyā left with great pleasure. Unfortunately, some people have no faith in these

narrations. Therefore I shall explain the reasons why people should have faith. Everyone who hears this will be faithful.

During the incarnation of Lord Caitanya to inaugurate the Kṛṣṇa consciousness movement, even such personalities as Lord Brahmā, Lord Śiva, and the four Kumāras took birth upon this earth, being allured by ecstatic love of Lord Kṛṣṇa.

All of them, including the great sage Nārada and devotees like Prahlāda, came here in the guise of human beings, chanting the holy names of Lord Kṛṣṇa together and dancing and floating in the inundation of love of Godhead.

The goddess of fortune and others, allured by love of Kṛṣṇa, also came down in the form of human beings and tasted the holy name of the Lord in love.

What to speak of others, even Kṛṣṇa, the son of Nanda Mahārāja, personally descends to taste the nectar of love of Godhead in the form of the chanting of Hare Kṛṣṇa.

What is the wonder if the maidservant of Kṛṣṇa, His external energy, begs for love of Godhead? Without the mercy of a devotee and without the chanting of the holy name of the Lord, love of Godhead cannot be possible.

In the activities of Lord Śrī Caitanya Mahāprabhu, the three worlds dance and chant, having come in touch with love of Godhead. This is the characteristic of His pastimes.

The holy name of Kṛṣṇa is so attractive that anyone who chants it—including all living entities, moving and nonmoving, and even Lord Kṛṣṇa Himself—becomes imbued with love of Kṛṣṇa. This is the effect of chanting the Hare Kṛṣṇa *mahā-mantra*.

I have heard from the mouth of Raghunātha dāsa Gosvāmī all that Svarūpa Dāmodara Gosvāmī recorded in his notes about the pastimes of Śrī Caitanya Mahāprabhu.

I have briefly described those pastimes. Whatever I have written is by the mercy of Śrī Caitanya Mahāprabhu, since I am an insignificant living being. I have described but a fragment of the glories of Haridāsa Ṭhākura. Hearing this satisfies the aural reception of every devotee.

Praying at the lotus feet of Śrī Rūpa and Śrī Raghunātha, always desiring their mercy, I, Kṛṣṇadāsa, narrate *Śrī Caitanya-caritāmṛta,* following in their footsteps.

(*Śrī Caitanya-caritāmṛta, Antya-līlā* 3.260–272)

15

The Perfection Of Chanting

Develop to the Stage of Ecstatic Love

This ecstatic love is prior to the pure love of Kṛṣṇa, because in the next verse Nārada confirms that by the gradual process of hearing from the great sages he developed love of Godhead. In that connection, Nārada continues to say in the First Canto, fifth chapter, verse 28, of the *Bhāgavatam,* "First I passed my days in the association of the great sages during the rainy autumn season. Every morning and evening I heard them while they were singing and chanting the Hare Kṛṣṇa mantra, and thus my heart gradually became purified. As soon as I heard them with great attention, the influence of the modes of material ignorance and passion disappeared, and I became firmly fixed in devotional service to the Lord."

These are practical examples of how one can develop to the stage of ecstatic love simply by the association of pure devotees. It is essential, therefore, that one constantly associate with pure devotees who are engaged morning and evening in chanting the Hare Kṛṣṇa mantra. In this way one will get the chance to purify his heart and develop this ecstatic pure love for Kṛṣṇa.

(*The Nectar of Devotion,* "Ecstatic Love")

You Are Touching Kṛṣṇa

So as Nṛsiṁhadeva touched the head of Prahlāda Mahārāja, immediately you can have that same facility. "What is that facility? How? Nṛsiṁhadeva is not here. Kṛṣṇa is not here." No. He is here. "What is that?" *Nama rūpe kali kale kṛṣṇa avatāra.* Kṛṣṇa is present by His name, Kṛṣṇa. Don't think this Kṛṣṇa, Hare Kṛṣṇa, this name, is different from Kṛṣṇa. Absolute. Kṛṣṇa, the Deity Kṛṣṇa, the name Kṛṣṇa, the person Kṛṣṇa—everything, the same Absolute Truth. There is no differentiation. So in this age simply by chanting *kīrtanād eva kṛṣṇasya mukta-saṅgaḥ paraṁ vrajet.* Simply by chanting the holy name of Kṛṣṇa ... *nama-cintāmaṇi kṛṣṇaḥ caitanya-rasa-vigrahaḥ, pūrṇaḥ śuddho nitya-muktaḥ.* Don't think the holy name of Kṛṣṇa is different from Kṛṣṇa. It is *pūrṇam. Pūrṇaḥ pūrṇam adaḥ pūrṇam idam.* Everything *pūrṇa. Pūrṇa* means complete. We have tried to explain this completeness in our *Īśopaniṣad.* You have read. So stick to the holy name of Kṛṣṇa. You'll get the same benefit as Prahlāda Mahārāja got by direct touch of the lotus palm of Nṛsiṁhadeva. There is no difference. Always think like that, that as soon as you are chanting Hare Kṛṣṇa, you must know that you are touching Kṛṣṇa with your tongue. Then you get the same benefit as Prahlāda Mahārāja.

(Lecture on *Śrīmad-Bhāgavatam* 7.9.6, Māyāpur, February 26, 1977)

That Is Factual Perfection of Chanting

So this is the superexcellence of chanting the holy name of Kṛṣṇa or God. Here it is said that "Such description or prescription for performing ritualistic ceremony, they are not sufficient to purify a man." But if one chants the holy name of God, Hare Kṛṣṇa mantra, *yathā harer nāma-padair udāhātaiḥ, padaiḥ,* once, once only, Kṛṣṇa, Rāma, Nārāyaṇa . . . So *harer nāma,* not other name, only *harer nāma. Yathā harer nāma-padair udāhātaiḥ.* Simply once chanting. *Uttamaśloka-guṇopalambhakam.* The purification of chanting *harer nāma* means as soon as you chant the holy name of Kṛṣṇa immediately you will see the form of Kṛṣṇa, you will realize the qualities of Kṛṣṇa, you will immediately remember the pastimes of Kṛṣṇa. That is pure chanting of Hare Kṛṣṇa mantra. That is commented by Śrīla Jīva Gosvāmī, that a pure devotee who chants Hare Kṛṣṇa mantra, immediately all these—*nāma, rūpa, guṇa, līlā, parikara, vasiṣṭha* . . . Simply by chanting name you will feel the form of Kṛṣṇa: "Here is Kṛṣṇa." *Nāma, rūpa, guṇa.* "Here are the qualities. Oh, Kṛṣṇa is so qualified. He is so kind. He is so magnanimous." So many qualities you will remember. *Nāma, rūpa, guṇa, līlā.* Then His pastimes. "Oh, Kṛṣṇa instructed Arjuna. Kṛṣṇa played with His cowherd boys. Kṛṣṇa had very nice talks with the *gopīs,* with His mother Yaśodā." These things will be remembered. That is factual perfection of chanting.

(Lecture on *Śrīmad-Bhāgavatam* 6.2.11, Allahabad, January 16, 1971)

Constantly Chanting the Hare Kṛṣṇa Mantra

Such descriptions of Kṛṣṇa's transcendental pastimes and activities were remembered by the *gopīs* during His absence from Vṛndāvana. They give us some idea of how attractive Kṛṣṇa is, not only to human beings but to all animate and inanimate objects. In Vṛndāvana, everyone and everything is attracted to Kṛṣṇa, including the trees, the plants, the water, and animals like the deer and cows. That is the perfect description of Kṛṣṇa's all-attractiveness. The example of the *gopīs* is very instructive to persons who are trying to be absorbed in Kṛṣṇa consciousness. One can very easily associate with Kṛṣṇa simply by remembering His transcendental pastimes. Everyone has a tendency to love someone. That Kṛṣṇa should be the object of love is the central point of Kṛṣṇa consciousness. By constantly chanting the Hare Kṛṣṇa mantra and remembering the transcendental pastimes of Kṛṣṇa, one can be fully in Kṛṣṇa consciousness and thus make his life sublime and fruitful.

(*Kṛṣṇa,* "The *Gopīs'* Feelings of Separation")

They Simply Engaged in Chanting
The Glories of Śrī Kṛṣṇa

When they saw that it was getting gradually darker, they stopped. Their mind and intelligence became absorbed in thoughts of Kṛṣṇa; they all imitated the activities of Kṛṣṇa and His speeches. Due to their heart and soul being completely given to Kṛṣṇa, they began to chant His glories, completely forgetting their family interests. In this way, all the *gopīs* returned to the bank of the Yamunā and assembled there, and expecting that Kṛṣṇa must return to them, they simply engaged in chanting the glories of Śrī Kṛṣṇa—Hare Kṛṣṇa, Hare Kṛṣṇa, Kṛṣṇa Kṛṣṇa, Hare Hare/ Hare Rāma, Hare Rāma, Rāma Rāma, Hare Hare.

(*Kṛṣṇa,* "Kṛṣṇa's Hiding from the *Gopīs*")

Attain Perfection In Chanting the Holy Name

"After describing the potency of the Hare Kṛṣṇa mahā-mantra, My spiritual master taught Me another verse, advising Me to always keep the name within My throat.

"'In this age of Kali there is no alternative, there is no alternative, there is no alternative for spiritual progress than the holy name, the holy name, the holy name of the Lord.'

"Since I received this order from My spiritual master, I always chant the holy name, but I thought that by chanting and chanting the holy name I had been bewildered.

"While chanting the holy name of the Lord in pure ecstasy, I lose Myself, and thus I laugh, cry, dance, and sing just like a madman.

"Collecting My patience, therefore, I began to consider that chanting the holy name of Kṛṣṇa had covered all My spiritual knowledge.

PURPORT

Śrī Caitanya Mahāprabhu hints in this verse that to chant the holy name of Kṛṣṇa one does not need to speculate on the philosophical aspects of the science of God, for one automatically becomes ecstatic and without consideration immediately chants, dances, laughs, cries, and sings just like a madman.

"I saw that I had become mad by chanting the holy name, and I immediately submitted this at the lotus feet of My spiritual master.

PURPORT

Śrī Caitanya Mahāprabhu, as an ideal teacher, shows us how a disciple should deal with his spiritual master. Whenever there is doubt regarding any point, he should refer the matter to his spiritual master for clarification. Śrī Caitanya Mahāprabhu said that while chanting and dancing He had developed the kind of mad ecstasy that is possible only for a liberated soul. Yet even in His liberated position, He referred everything to His spiritual master whenever there were doubts. Thus in any condition, even when liberated, we should never think ourselves independent of the spiritual master, but must refer to him as soon as there is some doubt regarding our progressive spiritual life.

"My dear lord, what kind of mantra have you given Me? I have become mad simply by chanting this *mahā-mantra*!

PURPORT

Śrī Caitanya Mahāprabhu prays in His *Śikṣāṣṭaka:*

yugāyitaṁ nimeṣeṇa
cakṣuṣā prāvṛṣāyitam
śūnyāyitaṁ jagat sarvaṁ
govinda-viraheṇa me

"O Govinda! Feeling Your separation, I am considering a moment to be like twelve years or more. Tears are flowing from my eyes like torrents of rain, and I am feeling all vacant in the world in Your absence." It is the aspiration of a devotee that while he chants the Hare Kṛṣṇa *mahā-mantra* his eyes will fill with tears, his voice falter, and his heart throb. These are good signs in chanting the holy name of the Lord. In ecstasy, one should feel the entire world to be vacant without the presence of Govinda. This is a sign of separation from Govinda. In material life we are all separated from Govinda and are absorbed in material sense gratification. Therefore, when one comes to his senses on the spiritual platform he becomes so eager to meet Govinda that without Govinda the entire world becomes a vacant place.

"Chanting the holy name in ecstasy causes Me to dance, laugh, and cry. When My spiritual master heard all this, he smiled and then began to speak.

PURPORT

When a disciple very perfectly makes progress in spiritual life, this gladdens the spiritual master, who then also smiles in ecstasy, thinking, "How successful my disciple has become!" He feels so glad that he smiles as he enjoys the progress of the disciple, just as a smiling parent enjoys the activities of a child who is trying to stand up or crawl perfectly.

"'It is the nature of the Hare Kṛṣṇa *mahā-mantra* that anyone who chants it immediately develops his loving ecstasy for Kṛṣṇa.

PURPORT

In this verse it is explained that one who chants the Hare Kṛṣṇa mantra develops *bhāva,* ecstasy, which is the point at which revelation begins. It is the preliminary stage in developing one's original love for God. Lord Kṛṣṇa mentions this *bhāva* stage in the *Bhagavad-gītā* (10.8):

ahaṁ sarvasya prabhavo
mattaḥ sarvaṁ pravartate
iti matvā bhajante māṁ
budhā bhāva-samanvitāḥ

"I am the source of all spiritual and material worlds. Everything emanates from Me. The wise who know this perfectly engage in My devotional service and worship Me with all their hearts." A neophyte disciple begins by hearing and chanting, associating with devotees and practicing the regulative principles, and thus he vanquishes all of his unwanted bad habits. In this way he develops attachment for Kṛṣṇa and cannot forget Kṛṣṇa even for a moment. *Bhāva* is almost the successful stage of spiritual life.

A sincere student aurally receives the holy name from the spiritual master, and after being initiated he follows the regulative principles given by the spiritual master. When the holy name is properly served in this way, automatically the spiritual nature of the holy name spreads; in other words, the devotee becomes qualified in offenselessly chanting the holy name. When one is completely fit to chant the holy name in this way, he is eligible to make disciples all over the world, and he actually becomes *jagad-guru*. Then the entire world, under his influence, begins to chant the holy names of the Hare Kṛṣṇa *mahā-mantra*. Thus all the disciples of such a spiritual master increase in attachment for Kṛṣṇa, and therefore he sometimes cries, sometimes laughs, sometimes dances, and sometimes chants. These symptoms are very prominently manifest in the body of a pure devotee. Sometimes when our students of the Kṛṣṇa consciousness movement chant and dance, even in India people are astonished to see how these foreigners have learned to chant and dance in this ecstatic fashion. As explained by Caitanya Mahāprabhu, however, actually this is not due to practice, for without extra endeavor these symptoms become manifest in anyone who sincerely chants the Hare Kṛṣṇa *mahā-mantra*.

Many fools, not knowing the transcendental nature of the Hare Kṛṣṇa *mahā-mantra*, sometimes impede our loudly chanting this mantra, yet one who is actually advanced in the fulfillment of chanting the Hare Kṛṣṇa *mahā-mantra* induces others to chant also. Kṛṣṇadāsa Kavirāja Gosvāmī explains, *kṛṣṇa-śakti vinā nahe tāra pravartana:* unless one receives special power of attorney from the Supreme Personality of Godhead, he cannot preach the glories of the Hare Kṛṣṇa *mahā-mantra*. As devotees propagate the Hare Kṛṣṇa *mahā-mantra*, the general population of the entire world gets the opportunity to understand the glories of the holy name. While chanting and dancing or hearing the holy name of the Lord, one automatically remembers the Supreme Personality of Godhead, and because there is no difference between the holy name and Kṛṣṇa, the chanter is immediately linked with Kṛṣṇa. Thus connected, a devotee develops his original attitude of service to the Lord. In this attitude of constantly serving Kṛṣṇa, which is called *bhāva*, he always thinks of Kṛṣṇa in many different ways. One who has attained this *bhāva* stage is no longer under the clutches of the illusory energy. When other spiritual ingredients, such as trembling, perspiration, and tears, are added to this *bhāva* stage, the devotee gradually attains love of Kṛṣṇa.

The holy name of Kṛṣṇa is called the *mahā-mantra.* Other mantras mentioned in the *Nārada Pañcarātra* are known simply as mantras, but the chanting of the holy name of the Lord is called the *mahā-mantra.*

I Only Lament to See Others Bereft of Your Love

"'Religiosity, economic development, sense gratification and liberation are known as the four goals of life, but before love of Godhead, the fifth and highest goal, these appear as insignificant as straw in the street.

"'For a devotee who has actually developed *bhāva,* the pleasure derived from *dharma, artha, kāma,* and *mokṣa* appears like a drop in the presence of the sea.

"'The conclusion of all revealed scriptures is that one should awaken his dormant love of Godhead. You are greatly fortunate to have already done so.

"'It is a characteristic of love of Godhead that by nature it induces transcendental symptoms in one's body and makes one more and more greedy to achieve the shelter of the lotus feet of the Lord.

"'When one actually develops love of Godhead, he naturally sometimes cries, sometimes laughs, sometimes chants, and sometimes runs here and there just like a madman.

PURPORT

In this connection Bhaktisiddhānta Sarasvatī Gosvāmī says that sometimes persons who have no love of Godhead at all display ecstatic bodily symptoms. Artificially they sometimes laugh, cry. and dance just like madmen, but this cannot help one progress in

Kṛṣṇa consciousness. Rather, such artificial agitation of the body is to be given up when one naturally develops the necessary bodily symptoms. Actual blissful life, manifested in genuine spiritual laughing, crying, and dancing, is the symptom of real advancement in Kṛṣṇa consciousness, which can be achieved by a person who always voluntarily engages in the transcendental loving service of the Lord. If one who is not yet developed imitates such symptoms artificially, he creates chaos in the spiritual life of human society.

"'Perspiration, trembling, standing on end of one's bodily hairs, tears, faltering voice, fading complexion, madness, melancholy, patience, pride, joy, and humility—these are various natural symptoms of ecstatic love of Godhead, which causes a devotee to dance and float in an ocean of transcendental bliss while chanting the Hare Kṛṣṇa mantra.

PURPORT

Transcendental love of Godhead is not under the jurisdiction of the material energy, for it is the transcendental bliss and pleasure potency of the Supreme Personality of Godhead. Since the Supreme Lord is also under the influence of transcendental bliss, when one comes in touch with such bliss in love of Godhead, one's heart melts, and the symptoms of this are standing of the hairs on end, etc. Sometimes a person thus melts and manifests these transcendental symptoms yet at the same time is not well behaved in his personal transactions. This indicates that he has not yet reached complete perfection in devotional life. In other words, a devotee who dances in ecstasy but after dancing and crying appears to be attracted to material affairs has not yet reached the perfection of devotional service, which is called *āśaya-śuddhi,* or the perfection of existence. One who attains the perfection of existence is completely averse to material enjoyment and engrossed in transcendental love of Godhead. It is therefore to be concluded that the ecstatic symptoms of *āśaya-śuddhi* are visible when a devotee's service has no material cause and is purely spiritual in nature. These are characteristics of transcendental love of Godhead, as stated in *Śrīmad-Bhāgavatam* (1.2.6):

sa vai puṁsāṁ paro dharmo
yato bhaktir adhokṣaje
ahaituky apratihatā
yayātmā suprasīdati

"That religion is best which causes its followers to become ecstatic in love of God that is unmotivated and free from material impediments, for this alone can completely satisfy the self."

"'It is very good, my dear child, that You have attained the supreme goal of life by developing love of Godhead. Thus You have pleased me very much, and I am very much obliged to You.

PURPORT

According to the revealed scriptures, if a spiritual master can convert even one soul into a perfectly pure devotee, his mission in life is fulfilled. Śrīla Bhaktisiddhānta Sarasvatī Ṭhākura always used to say, "Even at the expense of all the properties, temples, and *maṭhas* that I have, if I could convert even one person into a pure devotee, my mission would be fulfilled." It is very difficult, however, to understand the science of Kṛṣṇa, what to speak of developing love of Godhead. Therefore if by the grace of Lord Caitanya and the spiritual master a disciple attains the standard of pure devotional service, the spiritual master is very happy. The spiritual master is not actually happy if the disciple brings him money, but when he sees that a disciple is following the regulative principles and advancing in spiritual life, he is very glad and feels obliged to such an advanced disciple.

"'My dear child, continue dancing, chanting and performing *saṅkīrtana* in association with devotees. Furthermore, go out and

preach the value of chanting *kṛṣṇa-nāma,* for by this process You will be able to deliver all fallen souls.'

PURPORT

It is another ambition of the spiritual master to see his disciples not only chant, dance, and follow the regulative principles but also preach the *saṅkīrtana* movement to others in order to deliver them, for the Kṛṣṇa consciousness movement is based on the principle that one should become as perfect as possible in devotional service oneself and also preach the cult for others' benefit. There are two classes of unalloyed devotees—namely, *goṣṭhyānandīs* and *bhajanānandīs. Bhajanānandī* refers to one who is satisfied to cultivate devotional service for himself, and *goṣṭhyānandī* is one who is not satisfied simply to become perfect himself but wants to see others also take advantage of the holy name of the Lord and advance in spiritual life. The outstanding example is Prahlāda Mahārāja. When he was offered a benediction by Lord Nṛsiṁhadeva, Prahlāda Mahārāja said:

naivodvije para duratyaya-vaitaraṇyās,
tvad-vīrya-gāyana-mahāmṛta-magna-cittaḥ
śoce tato vimukha-cetasa indriyārtha-
māyā-sukhāya bharam udvahato vimūḍhān

"My dear Lord, I have no problems and want no benediction from You because I am quite satisfied to chant Your holy name. This is sufficient for me because whenever I chant I immediately merge in an ocean of transcendental bliss. I only lament to see others bereft of Your love. They are rotting in material activities for transient material pleasure and spoiling their lives toiling all day and night simply for sense gratification, with no attachment for love of Godhead. I am simply lamenting for them and devising various plans to deliver them from the clutches of *māyā*." (*Bhāg.* 7.9.43)

Śrīla Bhaktisiddhānta Sarasvatī Ṭhākura explains in his *Anubhāṣya,* "A person who has attracted the attention of the spiritual master by his sincere service likes to dance and chant with similarly developed Kṛṣṇa conscious devotees. The spiritual master authorizes such a devotee to deliver fallen souls in all parts of the world. Those who are not advanced prefer to chant the Hare Kṛṣṇa mantra in a solitary place." Such activities constitute, in the language of Śrīla Bhaktisiddhānta Sarasvatī Ṭhākura, a type of cheating process in the sense that they imitate the activities of exalted personalities like Haridāsa Ṭhākura. One should not attempt to imitate such exalted devotees. Rather, everyone should endeavor to preach the cult of Śrī Caitanya Mahāprabhu in all parts of the world and thus become successful in spiritual life. One who is not very expert in preaching may chant in a secluded place, avoiding bad association, but for one who is actually advanced, preaching and meeting people who are not engaged in devotional service are not disadvantages. A devotee gives the nondevotees his association but is not affected by their misbehavior. Thus by the activities of a pure devotee even those who are bereft of love of Godhead get a chance to become devotees of the Lord one day. In this connection Śrīla Bhaktisiddhānta Sarasvatī Ṭhākura advises that one discuss the verse in *Śrīmad-Bhāgavatam* beginning *naitat samācarej jātu manasāpi hy anīśvaraḥ* (10.33.30), and the following verse in *Bhakti-rasāmṛta-sindhu* (1.2.255):

anāsaktasya viṣayān
yathārham upayuñjataḥ
nirbandhaḥ kṛṣṇa-sambandhe
yuktaṁ vairāgyam ucyate

One should not imitate the activities of great personalities. One should be detached from material enjoyment and should accept everything in connection with Kṛṣṇa's service.

We Believed In His Words

"Saying this, My spiritual master taught Me a verse from *Śrīmad-Bhāgavatam*. It is the essence of all the *Bhāgavatam's* instructions; therefore he recited this verse again and again.

PURPORT

This verse from *Śrīmad-Bhāgavatam* (11.2.40) was spoken by Śrī Nārada Muni to Vasudeva to teach him about *bhāgavata-dharma*. Vasudeva had already achieved the result of *bhāgavata-dharma* because Lord Kṛṣṇa appeared in his house as his son, yet in order to teach others, he desired to hear from Śrī Nārada Muni to be enlightened in the process of *bhāgavata-dharma*. This is the humbleness of a great devotee.

"'When a person is actually advanced and takes pleasure in chanting the holy name of the Lord, who is very dear to him, he is agitated and loudly chants the holy name. He also laughs, cries, becomes agitated, and chants just like a madman, not caring for outsiders.'

"I firmly believe in these words of My spiritual master, and therefore I always chant the holy name of the Lord, alone and in the association of devotees. That holy name of Lord Kṛṣṇa sometimes causes Me to chant and dance, and therefore I chant and dance. Please do not think that I intentionally do it. I do it automatically."

PURPORT

A person who cannot keep his faith in the words of his spiritual master but acts independently never receives the authority to chant the holy name of the Lord. It is said in the *Vedas* (*Śvetāśvatara Upaniṣad* 6.23):

yasya deve parā bhaktir
yathā deve tathā gurau

tasyaite kathitā hy arthāḥ
prakāśante mahātmanaḥ

"Only unto those great souls who have implicit faith in both the Lord and the spiritual master are all the imports of Vedic knowledge automatically revealed." This Vedic injunction is very important, and Śrī Caitanya Mahāprabhu supported it by His personal behavior. Believing in the words of His spiritual master, He introduced the *saṅkīrtana* movement, just as the present Kṛṣṇa consciousness movement was started with belief in the words of our spiritual master. He wanted to preach, we believed in his words and tried somehow or other to fulfill them, and now this movement has become successful all over the world. Therefore faith in the words of the spiritual master and in the Supreme Personality of Godhead is the secret of success. Śrī Caitanya Mahāprabhu never disobeyed the orders of His spiritual master and stopped propagating the *saṅkīrtana* movement. Śrī Bhaktisiddhānta Sarasvatī Gosvāmī, at the time of his passing away, ordered all his disciples to work conjointly to preach the mission of Caitanya Mahāprabhu all over the world. Later, however, some self-interested, foolish disciples disobeyed his orders. Each one of them wanted to become head of the mission, and they fought in the courts, neglecting the order of the spiritual master, and the entire mission was defeated. We are not proud of this; however, the truth must be explained. We believed in the words of our spiritual master and started in a humble way—in a helpless way—but due to the spiritual force of the order of the supreme authority, this movement has become successful.

It is to be understood that when Śrī Caitanya Mahāprabhu chanted and danced, He did so by the influence of the pleasure potency of the spiritual world. Śrī Caitanya Mahāprabhu never considered the holy name of the Lord to be a material vibration, nor does any pure devotee mistake the chanting of the Hare Kṛṣṇa mantra to be a material musical manifestation. Lord Caitanya never tried to be the master of the holy name; rather He taught us how to be servants of the holy name. If one chants the holy name of the Lord just to make a show, not knowing the secret of success, he may increase his bile secretion, but he will never attain perfection in chanting the holy name. Śrī Caitanya Mahāprabhu presented Himself in this way: "I am a great fool and do not have knowledge of right and wrong. In order to understand the real meaning of the *Vedānta-sūtra,* I never followed the explanation of the *śaṅkara-sampradāya* or Māyāvādī *sannyāsīs*. I'm very much afraid of the illogical arguments of the Māyāvādī philosophers. Therefore I think I have no authority regarding their explanations of the *Vedānta-sūtra.* I firmly believe that simply chanting the holy name of the Lord can remove all misconceptions of the material world. I believe that simply by chanting the holy name of the Lord one can attain the shelter of the lotus feet of the Lord. In this age of quarrel and disagreement, the chanting of the holy names is the only way to liberation from the material clutches.

"By chanting the holy name," Lord Caitanya continued, "I became almost mad. However, after inquiring from My spiritual master I have come to the conclusion that instead of striving for achievement in the four principles of religiosity [*dharma*], economic development [*artha*], sense gratification [*kāma*], and liberation [*mokṣa*], it is better if somehow or other one develops transcendental love of Godhead. That is the greatest success in life. One who has attained love of Godhead chants and dances by his nature, not caring for the public." This stage of life is known as *bhāgavata-jīvana,* or the life of a devotee.

Śrī Caitanya Mahāprabhu continued, "I never chanted and danced to make an artificial show. I dance and chant because I firmly believe in the words of My spiritual master. Although the Māyāvādī philosophers do not like this chanting and dancing, I nevertheless perform it on the strength of his words. Therefore it is to be concluded that I deserve very little credit for these activities of chanting and dancing, for they are being done automatically by the grace of the Supreme Personality of Godhead."

(*Śrī Caitanya-caritāmṛta, Ādi-līlā* 7.75–96)

16

CHANTING AT THE TIME OF DEATH

Therefore One Should Constantly, Incessantly Chant the Mahā-Mantra

And whoever, at the end of his life, quits his body remembering Me alone at once attains My nature. Of this there is no doubt.

PURPORT

In this verse the importance of Kṛṣṇa consciousness is stressed. Anyone who quits his body in Kṛṣṇa consciousness is at once transferred to the transcendental nature of the Supreme Lord. The Supreme Lord is the purest of the pure. Therefore anyone who is constantly Kṛṣṇa conscious is also the purest of the pure. The word *smaran* ("remembering") is important. Remembrance of Kṛṣṇa is not possible for the impure soul who has not practiced Kṛṣṇa consciousness in devotional service. Therefore one should practice Kṛṣṇa consciousness from the very beginning of life. If one wants to achieve success at the end of his life, the process of remembering Kṛṣṇa is essential. Therefore one should constantly, incessantly chant the *mahā-mantra*—Hare Kṛṣṇa, Hare Kṛṣṇa, Kṛṣṇa Kṛṣṇa, Hare Hare/ Hare Rāma, Hare Rāma, Rāma Rāma, Hare Hare. Lord Caitanya has advised that one be as tolerant as a tree (*taror iva sahiṣṇunā*). There may be so many impediments for a person who is chanting Hare Kṛṣṇa. Nonetheless, tolerating all these impediments, one should continue to chant Hare Kṛṣṇa, Hare Kṛṣṇa, Kṛṣṇa Kṛṣṇa, Hare Hare/ Hare Rāma, Hare Rāma, Rāma Rāma, Hare Hare, so that at the end of one's life one can have the full benefit of Kṛṣṇa consciousness.

(*Bhagavad-gītā* 8.5)

Always Think of Kṛṣṇa

Whatever state of being one remembers when he quits his body, O son of Kuntī, that state he will attain without fail.

PURPORT

The process of changing one's nature at the critical moment of death is here explained. A person who at the end of his life quits his body thinking of Kṛṣṇa attains the transcendental nature of the Supreme Lord, but it is not true that a person who thinks of something other than Kṛṣṇa attains the same transcendental state. This is a point we should note very carefully. How can one die in the proper state of mind? Mahārāja Bharata, although a great personality, thought of a deer at the end of his life, and so in his next life he was transferred into the body of a deer. Although as a deer he remembered his past activities, he had to accept that animal body. Of course, one's thoughts during the course of one's life accumulate to influence one's thoughts at the moment of death, so this life creates one's next life. If in one's present life one lives in the mode of goodness and always thinks of Kṛṣṇa, it is possible for one to remember Kṛṣṇa at the end of one's life. That will help one be transferred to the transcendental nature of Kṛṣṇa. If one is transcendentally absorbed in Kṛṣṇa's service, then his next body will be transcendental (spiritual), not material. Therefore the chanting of Hare Kṛṣṇa, Hare Kṛṣṇa, Kṛṣṇa Kṛṣṇa, Hare Hare/ Hare Rāma, Hare Rāma, Rāma Rāma, Hare Hare is the best process for successfully changing one's state of being at the end of one's life.

(*Bhagavad-gītā* 8.6)

Perseverance

When a person is undisturbed even in the presence of various causes of disturbance, he is called reserved and perseverant. An example of this perseverance and reservation is found in the behavior of King Parīkṣit, as described in the First Canto, nineteenth chapter, verse 15, of *Śrīmad-Bhāgavatam*. The King says there to all the sages present before him at the time of his death, "My dear *brāhmaṇas,* you should always accept me as your surrendered servant. I have come to the bank of the Ganges just to devote my heart and soul unto the lotus feet of Lord Kṛṣṇa. So please bless me, that Mother Ganges may also be pleased with me. Let the curse of the *brāhmaṇa's* son fall upon me—I do not mind. I only request that at the last moment of my life all of you will kindly chant the holy name of Viṣṇu, so that I may realize His transcendental qualities."

(*The Nectar of Devotion,* "Character of One in Ecstatic Love")

He Will Be Saved from Hellish Life After Death

If one chants the holy name of Hari and then dies because of an accidental misfortune, such as falling from the top of a house,

slipping and suffering broken bones while traveling on the road, being bitten by a serpent, being afflicted with pain and high fever, or being injured by a weapon, one is immediately absolved from having to enter hellish life, even though he is sinful.

PURPORT

As stated in *Bhagavad-gītā* (8.6):

yaṁ yaṁ vāpi smaran bhāvaṁ
tyajaty ante kalevaram
taṁ tam evaiti kaunteya
sadā tad-bhāva-bhāvitaḥ

"Whatever state of being one remembers when he quits his body, that state he will attain without fail." If one practices chanting the Hare Kṛṣṇa mantra, he is naturally expected to chant Hare Kṛṣṇa when he meets with some accident. Even without such practice, however, if one somehow or other chants the holy name of the Lord (Hare Kṛṣṇa) when he meets with an accident and dies, he will be saved from hellish life after death.

(*Śrīmad-Bhāgavatam* 6.2.15)

Chant the Holy Name of the Lord with Love and Faith

While suffering at the time of death, Ajāmila chanted the holy name of the Lord, and although the chanting was directed toward his son, he nevertheless returned home, back to Godhead. Therefore if one faithfully and inoffensively chants the holy name of the Lord, where is the doubt that he will return to Godhead?

PURPORT

At the time of death one is certainly bewildered because his bodily functions are in disorder. At that time, even one who throughout his life has practiced chanting the holy name of the Lord may not be able to chant the Hare Kṛṣṇa mantra very distinctly. Nevertheless, such a person receives all the benefits of chanting the holy name. While the body is fit, therefore, why should we not chant the holy name of the Lord loudly and distinctly? If one does so, it is quite possible that even at the time of death he will be properly able to chant the holy name of the Lord with love and faith. In conclusion, one who chants the holy name of the Lord constantly is guaranteed to return home, back to Godhead, without a doubt.

(*Śrīmad-Bhāgavatam* 6.2.49)

Even You Send Me into the Hell

Simply our prayer should be, 'My dear Krishna, please remind me to always chant Your Holy Name, please do not put me into forgetfulness. You are sitting within me as Supersoul, so you can put me into forgetfulness or into remembering You. So please do not put me into forgetfulness. Please always remind me to chant, even You send me into the hell, it doesn't matter, just so long as I can always chant Hare Krishna.'

(Letter to Devananda, November 23, 1968)

You Cannot Escape—Death Is Waiting Behind You

Now, here is the solution of the problem. As Kṛṣṇa says in the fourteenth verse, seventh chapter, of *Bhagavad-gītā:* "It is very difficult to surmount the problems offered by the laws of material nature, but one who surrenders unto Me, he overcomes." Therefore we are teaching this Kṛṣṇa consciousness to solve the problems of life. It is not sentiment or fanaticism or any sectarian religion. It is a fact that if you want to solve the problems of life, you have to become Kṛṣṇa conscious. There is no other alternative. *Kṛṣṇa-nāma karo bhāi āra saba mithyā.* You understand

Bengali? It says that, "Just chant Hare Kṛṣṇa. Everything else is false. All other means of making some solution, false." Why? *Palaiba patha nāi yama āche piche*. "You cannot escape. Death is waiting behind you." So before death overcomes you, you make a solution of the problem. That is intelligence, that "The greatest danger is awaiting me—death." That is sure. "As sure as death." Everyone knows.

(Lecture on *Bhagavad-gītā* 7.14, Hamburg, September 8, 1969)

We Do Not Know When We Shall Meet Our Next Death

If you have got some time, the best thing would be to chant Hare Krishna more and more. Because our life is very short, and we have to finish our Krishna Consciousness this life very quickly. We do not know when we shall meet our next death, our next exit from this platform. But before going out of this platform, we may try to finish Krishna Consciousness. That is our main business.

(Letter to Jayapatāka Swami, October 6, 1968)

Death May Come At Any Moment

Devotee: [*reading*] "Mahārāja Parīkṣit met Śukadeva Gosvāmī just a week before his death, and the King was perplexed as to what should be done before he was to pass on. Many other sages also arrived there, but no one could give him the proper direction. Śukadeva Gosvāmī, however, gave this direction to him as follows: 'My dear King, if you want to be fearless in meeting your death next week (for actually everyone is afraid at the point of death), then you must immediately begin the process of hearing and chanting and remembering God.' If one can chant and hear Hare Kṛṣṇa and always remember Lord Kṛṣṇa, then he is sure to become fearless at death, which may come at any moment."

Prabhupāda: Yes. This is our prescription, that "Chant Hare Kṛṣṇa mantra without any stop." And even death comes, death may come at any moment, but if at the time of death, somehow or other you can utter "Kṛṣṇa" or remember Kṛṣṇa, and as soon as you utter the name of Kṛṣṇa you remember Kṛṣṇa's form, Kṛṣṇa's pastimes, everything. So let us chant Hare Kṛṣṇa mantra twenty-four hours. There is no impediment. Nobody can check it. If you are determined that "I shall always chant Hare Kṛṣṇa mantra," nobody can check. But we do not feel so much attached to the chanting. Therefore it is checked. So therefore we have fixed up a certain amount of rounds. Just like we have given to you sixteen rounds. At least as a regulative principle you must chant. Then gradually we may increase and automatically chant Hare Kṛṣṇa mantra. That will be very good approach.

(Lecture on *The Nectar of Devotion*,
Calcutta, January 25, 1973)

So Kṛṣṇa Is Very Kind

So here it is said, because at the time of death he has uttered "Nārāyaṇa," so now there is no question of offense. There is no question of. It is said in the *Bhagavad-gītā* that *yeṣāṁ tv anta-gataṁ pāpam:* by chanting Hare Kṛṣṇa mantra, one gradually becomes free from all sinful reaction. If at the time of death one can chant Hare Kṛṣṇa, then he is glorious. I have several times said, the test will be examined at the time of death. Your austerity, penances, chanting of the holy name, all these things. Just like there is examination. Before promotion to the higher class one is examined in the school, and if the marks are sufficient, then he is promoted. So our promotion will depend at the time of death, where we are going. *Tathā dehāntara-prāptiḥ.* Death means we are going to change our body. So this change of body will be decided at the time of death. It is already decided what kind of body we are going to get, but the final decision will be taken at the time of death.

That is said by Kṛṣṇa. Everyone can understand. If at the time of death one chants Hare Kṛṣṇa, then you know certainly that he has gone to Vaikuṇṭha. There is no doubt about it. And even there is *aparādha,* that is not taken into consideration because at the time of death he has uttered. This is special consideration. Here it is said, "Now he is quite fit for going back to home, back to Godhead. So you do not touch him. He is completely free."

So in Kali-yuga, therefore, name is so important. This formula should be seriously taken. *Aśeṣa.* Unlimited amount or unlimited number of sinful activities are already finished. So the Viṣṇudūtas forbade them, that "Don't touch him. He is not fit for going to Yamaloka, but he is fit for going to Viṣṇuloka." The most important thing is how to become successful at the time of death. Chant Hare Kṛṣṇa. This should be there. That will be the perfection of life.

Then they explain, *sāṅketya.* Just like sometimes on the street some outsider, seeing you, they chant Hare Kṛṣṇa only by the symbolic, *sāṅketya.* Because they see: "They have got *tilaka, kanthi.*" Therefore these things are required. Don't become immediately *paramahaṁsa*—no *tilaka,* no *kanthi* and no bead bag. This is not good. *Sāṅketya.* So that others may understand, "Here is a Vaiṣṇava. Here is a Kṛṣṇa devotee . . ." And if he is simple, he'll chant, "Hare Kṛṣṇa." This chance should be given. Therefore it is necessary, how people can utter. That chanting may save him from the greatest danger. Therefore it is said, *sāṅketyaṁ pārihāsyam.* If somebody jokes . . . Sometimes they do that. "Hare Kṛṣṇa" means he is not seriously chanting, but he is trying to joke the other party who is engaged in chanting. And that is also good, *pārihāsya.* During Caitanya Mahāprabhu's time, the Muslims, they used to joke the Hindus, "Hare Kṛṣṇa, Hare Kṛṣṇa." So the practice made them chanting Hare Kṛṣṇa. And the police officer was informed by the constables that "These Hindus are chanting 'Hare Kṛṣṇa, Hare Kṛṣṇa.'" The police officer asked him, "Then why you are chanting Hare Kṛṣṇa?" By imitating, they became practiced to chant

Hare Kṛṣṇa. It is so nice, even joking, symbolic. Without any care, "Hare Kṛṣṇa." In any way, if you chant Hare Kṛṣṇa.

So nice thing, this Hare Kṛṣṇa movement. Some way or other, if we can take it very seriously, then our life will be succesful at the end of life, if we can chant. Therefore Kulaśekhara Mahārāja says, he was emperor, he is praying, "My Lord, now I am healthy. I am quite conscious. So this time, if I absorb my mind in Your lotus feet and die, it is very good. It is very good because in the natural time of death, the three elements—*kapha, vāta, pitaiḥ*—they'll be dismantled, and there will be different sounds, and mind will be distracted. Brain will be falling. So hardly there is possibility of chanting Your holy name. The best thing is, now I am feeling healthy, my whole system, physical system, is quite fit. Let me chant and die immediately." This is desire of the devotee.

So Kṛṣṇa is very kind. If you chant seriously, without offense, even the mental condition at the time of death is disordered, Kṛṣṇa will help you how to chant without any offense. The only qualification is that we must be very sincere. Even by symbolic chanting, by joking, if one can get the benefit, why not do it carefully? Why not do it carefully? What is the wrong there? Be serious and chant Hare Kṛṣṇa very carefully in order to get success of life at the time of death. Thank you very much. Hare Kṛṣṇa.

(Lecture on *Śrīmad-Bhāgavatam* 6.2.13,
Vṛndāvana, September 15, 1975)

Death Is Coming—Death Is At My Door

We shall declare to the whole world that "Kṛṣṇa is the Supreme. There is no more superior anyone than Kṛṣṇa." This is our Kṛṣṇa consciousness movement. Kṛṣṇa says, *man-manā bhava mad-bhakto mad-yājī māṁ namaskuru*. We are preaching this. In this temple we are asking everyone, "Here is Kṛṣṇa. Always think of Kṛṣṇa. Chant Hare Kṛṣṇa." Then you will have to think, "Hare

Kṛṣṇa." Hare Kṛṣṇa means thinking of Kṛṣṇa. As soon as you hear the name of Kṛṣṇa, *man-manā.* And who will do that? *Mad-bhakta.* Unless you become a devotee of Kṛṣṇa, you cannot waste your time, "Kṛṣṇa, Hare Kṛṣṇa, Hare Kṛṣṇa." That means simply by chanting Hare Kṛṣṇa mantra you become a devotee of Kṛṣṇa. *Man-manā bhava mad-bhakto mad-yājī.*

Everyone should be trained up in this *bhāgavata-dharma.* And "Yes, it is important, that's all right. But let me live for hundred years. Then we shall talk about Kṛṣṇa." And Prahlāda Mahārāja said, "No. You do not know when you will die. At any moment you can die." *Padaṁ padaṁ yad vipadām.* Therefore, before your next death, you realize Kṛṣṇa. Even if you live for a few years and if you take the chance of chanting Hare Kṛṣṇa, still, you are benefited. You are still benefited.

So this chanting of Hare Kṛṣṇa is so important that you can think always that "Death is coming. Death is at my door. Let me finish my chanting. Let me finish my chanting." Always you should think like that, that "Death is already coming, so let me chant."

(Lecture on *Śrīmad-Bhāgavatam* 7.6.1,
Vṛndāvana, December 2, 1975)

Chant Hare Kṛṣṇa—Let Us Die Peacefully

Prabhupāda: I wish to die without a doctor. I may be seriously, but don't call doctor. Chant Hare Kṛṣṇa. Don't be disturbed. Everyone has to die. Let us die peacefully, without doctor. All this medicine, injections, and prohibitions, this, that.

Hari-śauri: Tīrtha Mahārāja had all kinds of machines. Still didn't save him.

Prabhupāda: Chant Hare Kṛṣṇa and depend on Kṛṣṇa. Actually . . . *Nārtasya cāgadam udanvati majjato nauḥ.* That is the Prahlāda Mahārāja's verse. Find out this. *Bālasya neha śaraṇaṁ pitarau nṛsiṁha.* Seventh Canto.

Hari-śauri: "My Lord Nṛsiṁhadeva, O Supreme, because of a

bodily conception of life, embodied souls neglected and not cared for by You cannot do anything for their betterment."
Prabhupāda: That's it.
Hari-śauri: "Whatever remedies they accept, although perhaps temporarily beneficial, are certainly impermanent. For example, a father and mother cannot protect their child, a physician and medicine cannot relieve a suffering patient, and a boat on the ocean cannot protect a drowning man."
Prabhupāda: These are facts.
Gargamuni: That's ultimately, but maybe we could give you some temporary relief so we don't feel . . . Because when you are ill, we feel . . .
Prabhupāda: Yes, that is . . . But for that, no severe treatment should be accepted. Better not to take. Chant Hare Kṛṣṇa.

(Room conversation, January 19, 1977, Bhuvaneśvara)

Death

Once the Bakāsura demon assumed the shape of a very big duck and opened his mouth in order to swallow Kṛṣṇa and all the cowherd boys. When Kṛṣṇa was entering into the demon's mouth, Balarāma and the other cowherd boys almost fainted and appeared as though they had no life. Even if devotees are illusioned by some ghastly scene or by any accidental occurrence, they never forget Kṛṣṇa. Even in the greatest danger they can remember Kṛṣṇa. This is the benefit of Kṛṣṇa consciousness: even at the time of death, when all the functions of the body become dislocated, the devotee can remember Kṛṣṇa in his innermost consciousness, and this saves him from falling down into material existence. In this way Kṛṣṇa consciousness immediately takes one from the material platform to the spiritual world.

In this connection there is a statement about persons who died at Mathurā: "These persons had a slight breathing exhilaration, their eyes were wide open, the colors of their bodies were changed, and they began to utter the holy name of Kṛṣṇa. In this condition they gave up their material bodies." These symptoms are prior manifestations of death.

(*The Nectar of Devotion*, "Further Features of Ecstatic Love for Kṛṣṇa")

Now This Is the Last Day

So to get a material body is not at all pleasure. It is always miserable condition, from the very beginning and up to the point of death, simply miserable condition. This is intelligence, that the miserable condition means we accept this material body. Therefore, to be out of miserable condition means not to accept again this misery. That should be the aim and objective of life—not to accept. That we have repeatedly said. That can be achieved very easily, *tyaktvā dehaḥ punar janma naiti*. After giving up this body, we do not accept anymore material body, provided we become fully Kṛṣṇa conscious. At the time of death, if we simply remember Kṛṣṇa, *yaṁ yaṁ vāpi smaran bhāvaṁ tyajaty ante kalevaram*. That is the highest perfection of life, simply to remember Kṛṣṇa. If we can consciously remember Kṛṣṇa: "Whatever was possible for me, I have tried to execute. Now this is the last day. You do whatever You like." That's all. But Kṛṣṇa is very kind. He will at once take you back to home, back to Godhead. *Ante nārāyaṇa smṛti*. This is the highest perfection of life. Therefore we have to practice, "Hare Kṛṣṇa, Hare Kṛṣṇa, Kṛṣṇa Kṛṣṇa, Hare Hare/ Hare Rāma, Hare Rāma, Rāma Rāma, Hare Hare."

(Lecture on *Śrī Caitanya-caritāmṛta*, *Ādi-līlā* 1.14, Māyāpur, April 7, 1975)

AFTERWORD

This Vibration of Kṛṣṇa's Flute

"The vibration of His flute is just like a bird that creates a nest within the ears of the *gopīs* and always remains prominent there, not allowing any other sound to enter their ears. Indeed, the *gopīs* cannot hear anything else, nor are they able to concentrate on anything else, not even to give a suitable reply. Such are the effects of the vibration of Lord Kṛṣṇa's flute."

PURPORT

The vibration of Kṛṣṇa's flute is always prominent in the ears of the *gopīs*. Naturally they cannot hear anything else. Constant remembrance of the holy sound of Kṛṣṇa's flute keeps them enlightened and enlivened, and they do not allow any other sound to enter their ears. Since their attention is fixed on Kṛṣṇa's flute, they cannot divert their minds to any other subject. In other words, a devotee who has heard the sound of Kṛṣṇa's flute forgets to talk or hear of any other subject. This vibration of Kṛṣṇa's flute is represented by the Hare Kṛṣṇa *mahā-mantra*. A serious devotee of the Lord who chants and hears this transcendental vibration becomes so accustomed to it that he cannot divert his attention to any subject matter not related to Kṛṣṇa's blissful characteristics and paraphernalia.

(*Śrī Caitanya-caritāmṛta, Madhya-līlā* 21.144)

For Eternity in Blissful Existence

Śrīla Śukadeva Gosvāmī has concluded the ninetieth chapter of the Tenth Canto of *Śrīmad-Bhāgavatam* by pointing out five particular excellences of Lord Kṛṣṇa . . .

The fourth excellence of Lord Kṛṣṇa's appearance concerns the glories of His name. It is stated in the Vedic literature that by chanting the different names of Lord Viṣṇu a thousand times, one may be bestowed with the same benefits as by thrice chanting the holy name of Lord Rāma. And by chanting the holy name of Lord Kṛṣṇa only once, one receives the same benefit. In other words, of all the holy names of the Supreme Personality of Godhead, including Viṣṇu and Rāma, the holy name of Kṛṣṇa is the most powerful. The Vedic literature therefore specifically stresses the chanting of the holy name of Kṛṣṇa: Hare Kṛṣṇa, Hare Kṛṣṇa, Kṛṣṇa Kṛṣṇa, Hare Hare/ Hare Rāma, Hare Rāma, Rāma Rāma, Hare Hare . . .

The fifth excellence of Lord Kṛṣṇa's appearance is that He established the most excellent of all religious principles by His one statement in the *Bhagavad-gītā* that simply by surrendering unto Him one can discharge all the principles of religious rites. In the Vedic literature there are twenty kinds of religious principles mentioned, and each of them is described in different *śāstras*. But Lord Kṛṣṇa is so kind to the fallen conditioned souls of this age that He personally appeared and asked everyone to give up all kinds of religious rites and simply surrender unto Him. It is said that this Age of Kali is three-fourths devoid of religious principles. Hardly one fourth of the principles of religion are still observed in this age. But by the mercy of Lord Kṛṣṇa, not only has this void of Kali-yuga been completely filled, but the religious process has been made so easy that simply by rendering transcendental loving service unto Lord Kṛṣṇa by chanting His holy names, Hare Kṛṣṇa, Hare Kṛṣṇa, Kṛṣṇa Kṛṣṇa, Hare Hare/ Hare Rāma, Hare Rāma, Rāma Rāma, Hare Hare, one can achieve the highest result of religion, namely, being transferred to the highest planet within the spiritual world, Goloka Vṛndāvana . . .

In the beginning of *Śrīmad-Bhāgavatam,* Śrīla Vyāsadeva offered his respectful obeisances to the Supreme Truth, Vāsudeva, Kṛṣṇa. After that he taught his son, Śukadeva Gosvāmī, to preach *Śrīmad-Bhāgavatam*. It is in this connection that Śukadeva Gosvāmī glorifies the Lord with the word *jayati*. Following in the footsteps of Śrīla Vyāsadeva, Śukadeva Gosvāmī and all the *ācāryas* in disciplic succession, the whole population of the world should glorify Lord Kṛṣṇa, and for their best interest they should take to this Kṛṣṇa consciousness movement. The process is easy and helpful. It is simply to chant the *mahā-mantra,* Hare Kṛṣṇa, Hare Kṛṣṇa, Kṛṣṇa Kṛṣṇa, Hare Hare / Hare Rāma, Hare Rāma, Rāma Rāma, Hare Hare. Lord Caitanya has therefore recommended that one be callous to the material ups and downs. Material life is temporary, and so the ups and downs of life may come and go. When they come, one should be as tolerant as a tree and as humble and meek as the straw in the street, but certainly he must engage himself in Kṛṣṇa consciousness by chanting Hare Kṛṣṇa, Hare Kṛṣṇa, Kṛṣṇa Kṛṣṇa, Hare Hare/ Hare Rāma, Hare Rāma, Rāma Rāma, Hare Hare . . .

Therefore, regardless of what one is, if one wants the association of Lord Kṛṣṇa in the transcendental kingdom of God for eternity in blissful existence, one must hear about the pastimes of Lord Kṛṣṇa and chant the *mahā-mantra,* Hare Kṛṣṇa, Hare Kṛṣṇa, Kṛṣṇa Kṛṣṇa, Hare Hare/ Hare Rāma, Hare Rāma, Rāma Rāma, Hare Hare . . .

(*Kṛṣṇa,* "Summary Description of Lord Kṛṣṇa's Pastimes")

What Will Please You the Most?

Bahulāśva: What is the thing that will please you most, Śrīla Prabhupāda?

Prabhupāda: Hmm?

Bahulāśva: What is the thing that would please you the most?

Prabhupāda: Chant Hare Kṛṣṇa.

Devotees: Hare Kṛṣṇa!

Prabhupāda: That is the simple thing. You are chanting. I am very much pleased. That's all. I came to your country to chant, that "You chant also along with me." So you are helping me by chanting. So I am pleased.

(Lecture, Detroit, July 16, 1971)

Chant Hare Kṛṣṇa—That Will Please Me

Devotee: How can I please you most?
Śrīla Prabhupāda: [*smiling*] How do you want to please me? [*laughing*] Chant Hare Kṛṣṇa. That will please me. Always, twenty-four hours a day, chant Hare Kṛṣṇa, Hare Kṛṣṇa, Kṛṣṇa Kṛṣṇa, Hare Hare/ Hare Rāma, Hare Rāma, Rāma Rāma, Hare Hare. There is no expenditure. Utilize the tongue Kṛṣṇa has given you. Hare Kṛṣṇa, Hare Kṛṣṇa, Kṛṣṇa Kṛṣṇa, Hare Hare/ Hare Rāma, Hare Rāma, Rāma Rāma, Hare Hare. That will please me. Is that all right? Thank you very much.

(Room conversation, New York, July 5, 1972)

Chanting the Holy Name

mahāprabhoḥ kīrtana-nṛtya-gīta-
vāditra-mādyan-manaso rasena
romāñca-kampāśru-taraṅga-bhājo
vande guroḥ śrī-caraṇāravindam

Chanting the holy name, dancing in ecstasy, singing, and playing musical instruments, the spiritual master is always gladdened by the *saṅkīrtana* movement of Lord Caitanya Mahāprabhu. Because he is relishing the mellows of pure devotion within his mind, sometimes his hair stands on end, he feels quivering in his body, and tears flow from his eyes like waves. I offer my respectful obeisances unto the lotus feet of such a spiritual master.

(*Śrī Śrī Gurv-aṣṭaka*, Śrīla Viśvanātha Cakravartī Ṭhākura)

I Am Simply Running Behind You Shouting, "Kṛṣṇa! Kṛṣṇa!"

ekākī āmāra, nāhi pāya bala, hari-nāma-saṅkīrtane
tumi kāpā kori', śraddhā-bindu diyā, deho' kṛṣṇa-nāma-dhane

I do not find the strength to carry on alone the *saṅkīrtana* of the holy name of Lord Hari. Please bless me by giving me just one drop of faith with which to obtain the great treasure of the holy name of Kṛṣṇa.

kṛṣṇa se tomāra, kṛṣṇa dite pāro, tomāra śakati āche
āmi to kāṅgāla, kṛṣṇa kṛṣṇa boli, dhāi tava pāche pāche

Kṛṣṇa is yours. You have the power to give Him to me. I am wretched and fallen and simply running behind you shouting, "Kṛṣṇa! Kṛṣṇa!"

(*Ohe! Vaiṣṇava Ṭhākura,* Śrīla Bhaktivinoda Ṭhākura)

* * *

Dear Śrīla Prabhupāda, please bless us that we might become meek and humble. Please free us from the evil desire of seeking advantages and honors from others. Please bless us with pure chanting of the holy name. We offer our eternal obeisances at your lotus feet.

(The Editors)

All glories to Śrīla Prabhupāda! Śrīla Prabhupāda *ki jaya*!

Painting by Devahuti Devi Dāsi

A MEDITATION ON ŚRĪ ŚIKṢĀṢṬAKA

The sufferings of the entire human society can at once be brought under control simply by individual practice of "Bhaktiyoga," a simple and easy process of chanting the holy Name of God. Every country, every nation, and every community throughout the world has some conception of the holy Name of God and as such either the Hindus or the Mohammedans or the Christians, every one can easily chant the holy Name of God in a meditative mood and that will bring about the required peace and good will in the present problematic human society.

Any enquiry in this connection will be gladly answered by Sri Swamiji.

The Hindus generally chant the holy Name of God in sixteen chain of transcendental sound composed of 32 alphabets as "Hare krishna, hare krishna, krishna krishna, hare hare, hare rama, hare rama, rama rama, hare hare." The Vedic literatures like the Upanisads and the Puranas do recommend chanting of the abovementioned sixteen holy Names at a stretch and Lord Sri Chaitanya, Who preached this cult of chanting the holy Name of

God, gave special importance on these transcendental sounds. In this age of Kali or the age of hate, hypocrisy, corruption, and quarrel, the only remedial measure is that every man should chant the holy Name of the Lord both individually and collectively.

The Glories of the holy Name have been described by Sri Chaitanya in His eight verses of "Siksastak."

(From the pamphlet Śrīla Prabhupāda brought with him to America in 1965)

Lord Caitanya Mahāprabhu instructed His disciples to write books on the science of Kṛṣṇa consciousness—a task which those who follow Him have continued to carry out down to the present day. The elaboration and exposition on the philosophy taught by Lord Caitanya are in fact the most voluminous, exacting, and consistent, due to the unbreakable system of disciplic succession of any religious culture in the world. Yet Lord Caitanya, in His youth widely renowned as a scholar Himself, left us only eight verses, called *Śikṣāṣṭaka*.

(Purport to *Śrī Śikṣāṣṭaka*, Los Angeles, December 28, 1968)

"O ocean of mercy, Śrī Caitanya Mahāprabhu! Let there be an awakening of Your auspicious mercy, which easily drives away all kinds of material lamentation. By Your mercy, everthing is made pure and blissful. It awakens transcendental bliss and covers all gross material pleasures. By Your auspicious mercy, quarrels and disagreements arising among different scriptures are vanquished. Your auspicious mercy causes the heart to jubilate by pouring forth transcendental mellows. Your mercy always stimulates devotional service, which is full of joy. You are always glorifying the conjugal love of God. May transcendental bliss be awakened within my heart by Your causeless mercy."

(*Śrī Caitanya-candrodaya-nāṭaka* 8.10, quoted in *Śrī Caitanya-caritāmṛta, Madhya-līlā* 10.119)

Śrī Śikṣāṣṭaka Verses

NOTE: The eight verses of *Śrī Śikṣāṣṭaka* below are followed by the translation from *Śrī Caitanya-caritāmṛta, Antya-līlā.* The bold text is the translation from Śrīla Prabhupada's pamphlet. The accompanying verses have been added by the publisher as a meditation.

1

ceto-darpaṇa-mārjanaṁ bhava-mahā-dāvāgni-nirvāpaṇaṁ
śreyaḥ-kairava-candrikā-vitaraṇaṁ vidyā-vadhū-jīvanam
ānandāmbudhi-vardhanaṁ prati-padaṁ pūrṇāmṛtāsvādanaṁ
sarvātma-snapanaṁ paraṁ vijayate śrī-kṛṣṇa-saṅkīrtanam

Let there be all victory for the chanting of the holy name of Lord Kṛṣṇa, which can cleanse the mirror of the heart and stop the miseries of the blazing fire of material existence. That chanting is the waxing moon that spreads the white lotus of good fortune for all living entities. It is the life and soul of all education. The chanting of the holy name of Kṛṣṇa expands the blissful ocean of transcendental life. It gives a cooling effect to everyone and enables one to taste full nectar at every step.

Glory to the Sri Krishna Samkirtan which cleanses the heart of all the dust accumulated for years together . . .

śṛṇvatāṁ sva-kathāḥ kṛṣṇaḥ,
puṇya-śravaṇa-kīrtanaḥ
hṛdy antaḥ stho hy abhadrāṇi,
vidhunoti suhṛt satām

Śrī Kṛṣṇa, the Personality of Godhead, who is the Paramātmā [Supersoul] in everyone's heart and the benefactor of the truthful devotee, cleanses desire for material enjoyment from the heart of the devotee who has developed the urge to hear His messages, which are in themselves virtuous when properly heard and chanted.

(*Śrīmad-Bhāgavatam* 1.2.17)

. . . and thus the fire of conditional life of repeated birth and death, is extinguished.

tasmāt saṅkīrtanaṁ viṣṇor
jagan-maṅgalam aṁhasām
mahatām api kauravya
viddhy aikāntika-niṣkṛtam

Śukadeva Gosvāmī continued: My dear King, the chanting of the holy name of the Lord is able to uproot even the reactions of the greatest sins. Therefore the chanting of the *saṅkīrtana* movement is the most auspicious activity in the entire universe. Please try to understand this so that others will take it seriously.

(*Śrīmad-Bhāgavatam* 6.3.31)

Such Samkirtan movement is the prime benediction for humanity at large because it spreads the rays of the benediction Moon.

hare kṛṣṇa hare kṛṣṇa kṛṣṇa kṛṣṇa hare hare
hare rāma hare rāma rāma rāma hare hare
iti ṣoḍaśakaṁ nāmnāṁ kali-kalmaṣa-nāśanam
nātaḥ parataropāyaḥ sarva-vedeṣu dṛśyate

Hare Kṛṣṇa, Hare Kṛṣṇa, Kṛṣṇa Kṛṣṇa, Hare Hare/ Hare Rāma, Hare Rāma, Rāma Rāma, Hare Hare. These sixteen names composed of thirty-two syllables are the only means of counteracting the evil effects of the Kali-yuga. After searching through all the Vedic literature, one cannot find a method of religion for this age so sublime as the chanting of the Hare Kṛṣṇa mantra."

(*Kali-santaraṇa Upaniṣad*)

It is the life of transcendental knowledge, it increases the ocean of transcendental bliss, and it helps to have a taste of the full nectarine for which always anxious we are.

ramante yogino 'nante
satyānanda-cid-ātmani
iti rāma-padenāsau
paraṁ brahmābhidhīyate

The mystics derive unlimited transcendental pleasures from the Absolute Truth, and therefore the Supreme Absolute Truth, the Personality of Godhead, is also known as Rāma.

(*Padma Purāṇa*)

2

nāmnām akāri bahudhā nija-sarva-śaktis
tatrārpitā niyamitaḥ smaraṇe na kālaḥ
etādṛśī tava kṛpā bhagavan mamāpi
durdaivam īdṛśam ihājani nānurāgaḥ

My Lord, O Supreme Personality of Godhead, in Your holy name there is all good fortune for the living entity, and therefore You have many names, such as "Kṛṣṇa" and "Govinda," by which You expand Yourself. You have invested all Your potencies in those names, and there are no hard and fast rules for remembering them. My dear Lord, although You bestow such mercy upon the fallen, conditioned souls by liberally teaching Your holy names, I am so unfortunate that I commit offenses while chanting the holy name, and therefore I do not achieve attachment for chanting.

O my Lord! Your holy name alone can render all benediction upon the living being and therefore You have hundreds and millions of Names like Krishna, Govinda, etc.

nāma-cintāmaṇi-kṛṣṇaś
caitanya-rasa-vigrahaḥ
pūrṇaḥ śuddho nitya-mukto
'bhinnatvān nāma-nāminoḥ

There is no difference between the holy name of the Lord and the Lord Himself. As such, the holy name is as perfect as the Lord Himself in fullness, purity and eternity. The holy name is not a material sound vibration, nor has it any material contamination. This is because the name of Kṛṣṇa and Kṛṣṇa Himself are identical.

(*Padma Purāṇa*)

In these transcendental Names You have invested all Your transcendental potencies . . .

kali-kāle nāma-rūpe kṛṣṇa-avatāra
nāma haite haya sarva-jagat-nistāra

In this Age of Kali, the holy name of the Lord, the Hare Kṛṣṇa *mahā-mantra,* is the incarnation of Lord Kṛṣṇa. Simply by chanting the holy name, one associates with the Lord directly. Anyone who does this is certainly delivered.

(*Śrī Caitanya-caritāmṛta, Ādi-līlā* 17.22)

. . . and there are no hard and fast rules for chanting these holy Names.

yena tena prakāreṇa
manaḥ kṛṣṇe niveśayet
sarve vidhi-niṣedhā syur
etayor eva kiṅkarāḥ

Somehow or other one should fix his mind on Kṛṣṇa. All the rules and prohibitions mentioned in the *śāstras* should be the servants of this principle.

(*Bhakti-rasāmṛta-sindhu* 1.2.24)

O my Lord! You have so kindly made easy approach to You by Your holy Names but unfortunate as I am, I have no attraction for them.

tad aśma-sāraṁ hṛdayaṁ batedaṁ
yad gṛhyamāṇair hari-nāma-dheyaiḥ
na vikriyetātha yadā vikāro
netre jalaṁ gātra-ruheṣu harṣaḥ

If one's heart does not change, tears do not flow from his eyes, his body does not shiver, and his bodily hairs do not stand on end as he chants the Hare Kṛṣṇa *mahā-mantra,* it should be understood that his heart is as hard as iron. This is due to his offenses at the lotus feet of the Lord's holy name.

(*Śrī Caitanya-caritāmṛta, Ādi-līlā* 8.25)

caitanya-nityānande nāhi e-saba vicāra
nāma laite prema dena, vahe aśrudhāra

If one chants the exalted holy name of the Lord again and again and yet his love for the Supreme Lord does not develop and tears do not appear in his eyes, it is evident that because of his offenses in chanting, the seed of the holy name of Kṛṣṇa does not sprout. But if one chants, with only some slight faith, the holy names of Lord Caitanya and Nityānanda, very quickly he is cleansed of all offenses. Thus as soon as he chants the Hare Kṛṣṇa *mahā-mantra,* he feels the ecstasy of love for God.

(*Śrī Caitanya-caritāmṛta, Ādi-līlā* 8.29–31)

3

tṛṇād api sunīcena
taror iva sahiṣṇunā
amāninā mānadena
kīrtanīyaḥ sadā hariḥ

One who thinks himself lower than the grass, who is more tolerant than a tree, and who does not expect personal honor but is always prepared to give all respect to others can very easily always chant the holy name of the Lord.

One can chant the holy Names of the Lord in an humble state of mind thinking himself as lower than the straw on the streets, . . .

Raising my hands, I declare, "Everyone please hear me! String this verse on the thread of the holy name and wear it on your neck for continuous remembrance."

(*Śrī Caitanya-caritāmṛta, Ādi-līlā* 17.32)

kva cāhaṁ kitavaḥ pāpo
brahma-ghno nirapatrapaḥ
kva ca nārāyaṇety etad
bhagavan-nāma maṅgalam

Ajāmila continued: I am a shameless cheater who has killed his brahminical culture. Indeed, I am sin personified. Where am I in comparison to the all-auspicious chanting of the holy name of Lord Nārāyaṇa?

(*Śrīmad-Bhāgavatam* 6.2.34)

. . . tolerant more than the tree, devoid of all sense of false prestige and being ready to offer all kinds of respects to others.

titikṣavaḥ kāruṇikāḥ
suhṛdaḥ sarva-dehinām
ajāta-śatravaḥ śāntāḥ
sādhavaḥ sādhu-bhūṣaṇāḥ

The symptoms of a *sādhu* are that he is tolerant, merciful, and friendly to all living entities. He has no enemies, he is peaceful, he abides by the scriptures, and all his characteristics are sublime.

(*Śrīmad-Bhāgavatam* 3.25.21)

In such a state of mind one can chant the holy name of the Lord constantly.

prabhu kahe,—"kabhu tomāra nā habe abhimāna
nirantara kaha tumi 'kṛṣṇa' 'kṛṣṇa' nāma"

Being meek and humble, the *brāhmaṇa* Vāsudeva worried that he would become proud after being cured by the grace of Śrī Caitanya Mahāprabhu.

To protect the *brāhmaṇa,* Śrī Caitanya Mahāprabhu advised him to chant the Hare Kṛṣṇa mantra incessantly. By doing so, he would never become unnecessarily proud.

(*Śrī Caitanya-caritāmṛta, Madhya-līlā* 7.146–147)

4

na dhanaṁ na janaṁ na sundarīṁ
kavitāṁ vā jagad-īśa kāmaye
mama janmani janmanīśvare
bhavatād bhaktir ahaitukī tvayi

O Lord of the universe, I do not desire material wealth, materialistic followers, a beautiful wife, or fruitive activities described in flowery language. All I want, life after life, is unmotivated devotional service to You.

Oh the Almighty Lord, I have no desire for accumulating wealth . . .

sthānābhilāsī tapasi sthito 'haṁ
tvāṁ prāptavān deva-munīndra-guhyam
kācaṁ vicinvann api divya-ratnaṁ
svāmin kṛtārtho 'smi varaṁ na yāce

"My dear Lord, I have practiced austerities and penances because I was desiring to receive something from You, but in exchange

You have allowed me to see You, who are never visible even to the great sages and saintly persons. I had been searching out some pieces of broken glass, but instead I have found the most valuable jewel. I am therefore fully satisfied, my Lord. I do not wish to ask anything more from Your Lordship."

(*Śrī Caitanya-caritāmṛta, Madhya-līlā* 22.42)

. . . nor I have any desire to enjoy beautiful woman;

yuvatīnāṁ yathā yūni
yūnāṁ ca yuvatau yathā
mano 'bhiramate tadvan
mano me ramatāṁ tvayi

My Lord, I know that young girls have natural affection for young boys, and that young boys have natural affection for young girls. I am praying at Your lotus feet that my mind may become attracted unto You in the same spontaneous way. Just as the minds of young girls take pleasure in young boys, and young boys take pleasure in young girls, kindly allow my mind to take pleasure in You alone.

(*Viṣṇu Purāṇa*)

. . . neither I want any number of followers of mine.

janmaiśvarya-śruta-śrībhir
edhamāna-madaḥ pumān
naivārhaty abhidhātuṁ vai
tvām akiñcana-gocaram

My Lord, Your Lordship can easily be approached, but only by those who are materially exhausted. One who is on the path of [material] progress, trying to improve himself with respectable parentage, great opulence, high education, and bodily beauty, cannot approach You with sincere feeling.

(*Śrīmad-Bhāgavatam* 1.8.26)

What I want only is that I may have your causeless devotional service in my life birth after birth.

yāvat te māyayā spṛṣṭā
bhramāma iha karmabhiḥ
tāvad bhavat-prasaṅgānāṁ
saṅgaḥ syān no bhave bhave

Dear Lord, as long as we have to remain within this material world due to our material contamination and wander from one type of body to another and from one planet to another, we pray that we may associate with those who are engaged in discussing Your pastimes. We pray for this benediction life after life, in different bodily forms and on different planets.

PURPORT

This is the best benediction that a devotee can ask of the Supreme Lord ... Caitanya Mahāprabhu prays, *mama janmani janmanīś-vare bhavatād bhaktir ahaitukī tvayi:* "My dear Lord, life after life may I be fixed in Your pure devotional service." The conclusion is that a pure devotee is not anxious to stop the repetition of birth and death, but is always eager to associate with other devotees who are engaged in chanting and hearing about the glories of the Lord.

(*Śrīmad-Bhāgavatam* 4.30.33)

5

ayi nanda-tanuja kiṅkaraṁ
patitaṁ māṁ viṣame bhavāmbudhau
kṛpayā tava pāda-paṅkaja-
sthita-dhūlī-sadṛśaṁ vicintaya

O My Lord, O Kṛṣṇa, son of Mahārāja Nanda, I am Your eternal servant, but because of My own fruitive acts I have fallen into this horrible ocean of nescience. Now please be causelessly merciful to Me. Consider Me a particle of dust at Your lotus feet.

Oh the son of Maharaj Nanda, I am your eternal servitor . . .

jīvera 'svarūpa' haya—kṛṣṇera 'nitya-dāsa'
kṛṣṇera 'taṭasthā-śakti' 'bhedābheda-prakāśa'

"It is the living entity's constitutional position to be an eternal servant of Kṛṣṇa because he is the marginal energy of Kṛṣṇa . . .
(*Śrī Caitanya-caritāmṛta, Madhya-līlā* 20.108)

. . . and although I am so, some how or other I have fallen on the ocean of birth and death.

kṛṣṇa bhuli' sei jīva anādi-bahirmukha
ataeva māyā tāre deya saṁsāra-duḥkha

"Forgetting Kṛṣṇa, the living entity has been attracted by the external feature from time immemorial. Therefore the illusory energy [*māyā*] gives him all kinds of misery in his material existence.
(*Śrī Caitanya-caritāmṛta, Madhya-līlā* 20.117)

kṛṣṇa bhuliya jīva bhoga vañcha kare
pāśate māyā tāre jāpaṭiyā dhare

As soon as you forget Kṛṣṇa, becoming envious and rebellious and you want to enjoy, to act independently, then immediately you are captured by *māyā* and you are punished.
(Quoted by Śrīla Prabhupāda, source unknown)

Please therefore pick me up from the ocean of death and fix me up as one of the atoms of your lotus feet.

namo deva dāmodarānanta viṣṇo
prasīda prabho duḥkha-jālābdhi-magnam

kṛpā-dṛṣṭi-vṛṣṭyātidīnaṁ batānu-
gṛhāṇeśa mām ajñam edhy akṣi-dṛśyaḥ

O unlimited Viṣṇu! O master! O Lord! Be pleased upon me! I am drowning in an ocean of sorrow and am almost like a dead man. Please shower the rain of mercy on me; uplift me and protect me with Your nectarean vision.

(*Śrī Dāmodarāṣṭaka*)

6

nayanaṁ galad-aśru-dhārayā
vadanaṁ gadgada-ruddhayā girā
pulakair nicitaṁ vapuḥ kadā
tava nāma-grahaṇe bhaviṣyati

My dear Lord, when will My eyes be beautified by filling with tears that constantly glide down as I chant Your holy name? When will My voice falter and all the hairs on My body stand erect in transcendental happiness as I chant Your holy name?

Oh my Lord when shall my eyes be decorated with tears of love flowing incessantly by chanting your holy Name? And when all the holes of hairs on my body will have eruptions by the recitation of your Name?

While reading the manuscript, Śrī Caitanya Mahāprabhu saw a verse on that page, and as soon as He read it He was overwhelmed by ecstatic love.

(*Śrī Caitanya-caritāmṛta, Antya-līlā* 1.98)

Then Śrī Caitanya Mahāprabhu said, "My dear Rūpa, please recite that verse from your drama which, upon being heard, makes all people's unhappiness and lamentation go away."

(*Śrī Caitanya-caritāmṛta, Antya-līlā* 1.118)

tuṇḍe tāṇḍavinī ratiṁ vitanute tuṇḍāvalī-labdhaye
karṇa-kroḍa-kaḍambinī ghaṭayate karṇārbudebhyaḥ spṛhām
cetaḥ-prāṅgaṇa-saṅginī vijayate sarvendriyāṇāṁ kṛtiṁ
no jāne janitā kiyadbhir amṛtaiḥ kṛṣṇeti varṇa-dvayī

I do not know how much nectar the two syllables 'Kṛṣ-ṇa' have produced. When the holy name of Kṛṣṇa is chanted, it appears to dance within the mouth. We then desire many, many mouths. When that name enters the holes of the ears, we desire many millions of ears. And when the holy name dances in the courtyard of the heart, it conquers the activities of the mind, and therefore all the senses become inert.

(*Śrī Caitanya-caritāmṛta, Antya-līlā* 1.120)

"My spiritual master taught Me a verse from *Śrīmad-Bhāgavatam.* It is the essence of all the *Bhāgavatam's* instructions; therefore he recited this verse again and again."

(*Śrī Caitanya-caritāmṛta, Ādi-līlā* 7.93)

evaṁ-vrataḥ sva-priya-nāma-kīrtyā
jātānurāgo druta-citta uccaiḥ
hasaty atho roditi rauti gāyaty
unmāda-van nṛtyati loka-bāhyaḥ

"When a person is actually advanced and takes pleasure in chanting the holy name of the Lord, who is very dear to him, he is agitated and loudly chants the holy name. He also laughs, cries, becomes agitated, and chants just like a madman, not caring for outsiders."

(*Śrīmad-Bhāgavatam* 11.2.40)

7

yugāyitaṁ nimeṣeṇa
cakṣuṣā prāvṛṣāyitam

śūnyāyitaṁ jagat sarvaṁ
govinda-viraheṇa me

My Lord Govinda, because of separation from You, I consider even a moment a great millennium. Tears flow from My eyes like torrents of rain, and I see the entire world as void.

Oh Govinda, feeling your separation, I am considering a moment as 12 twelve years or more than that . . .

kṛṣṇa-bhakti-rasa-bhāvitā matiḥ
krīyatāṁ yadi kuto 'pi labhyate
tatra laulyam api mūlyam ekalaṁ
janma-koṭi-sukṛtair na labhyate

"Pure devotional service in Kṛṣṇa consciousness cannot be had even by pious activity in hundreds and thousands of lives. It can be attained only by paying one price—that is, intense greed to obtain it. If it is available somewhere, one must purchase it without delay."

(*Śrī Caitanya-caritāmṛta, Madhya-līlā* 8.70)

. . . and tears flowing down my cheeks like the torrents of rains. I am feeling all vacant in the world without your presence.

ayi dīna-dayārdra nātha he
mathurā-nātha kadāvalokyase
hṛdayaṁ tvad-aloka-kātaraṁ
dayita bhrāmyati kiṁ karomy aham

"O My Lord! O most merciful master! O master of Mathurā! When shall I see You again? Because of My not seeing You, My agitated heart has become unsteady. O most beloved one, what shall I do now?"

(*Śrī Caitanya-caritāmṛta, Madhya-līlā* 4.197)

kibā mantra dilā, gosāñi, kibā tāra bala
japite japite mantra karila pāgala

"My dear lord, what kind of mantra have you given Me? I have become mad simply by chanting this *mahā-mantra*!"

PURPORT

Śrī Caitanya Mahāprabhu prays in His *Śikṣāṣṭaka:*

yugāyitaṁ nimeṣeṇa
cakṣuṣā prāvṛṣāyitam
śūnyāyitaṁ jagat sarvaṁ
govinda-viraheṇa me

"O Govinda! Feeling Your separation, I am considering a moment to be like twelve years or more. Tears are flowing from my eyes like torrents of rain, and I am feeling all vacant in the world in Your absence." It is the aspiration of a devotee that while he chants the Hare Kṛṣṇa *mahā-mantra* his eyes will fill with tears, his voice falter, and his heart throb. These are good signs in chanting the holy name of the Lord. In ecstasy, one should feel the entire world to be vacant without the presence of Govinda. This is a sign of separation from Govinda. In material life we are all separated from Govinda and are absorbed in material sense gratification. Therefore, when one comes to his senses on the spiritual platform he becomes so eager to meet Govinda that without Govinda the entire world becomes a vacant place.

(*Śrī Caitanya-caritāmṛta, Ādi-līlā* 7.81)

8

āśliṣya vā pāda-ratāṁ pinaṣṭu mām
adarśanān marma-hatāṁ karotu vā
yathā tathā vā vidadhātu lampaṭo
mat-prāṇa-nāthas tu sa eva nāparaḥ

Let Kṛṣṇa tightly embrace this maidservant who has fallen at His lotus feet, or let Him trample Me or break My heart by never being visible to Me. He is a debauchee, after all, and can do whatever He likes, but still He alone, and no one else, is the worshipable Lord of My heart.

I do not know any one except Krishna as my Lord and He shall remain as such even if he handles me roughly by His embrace or He may make me broken hearted by not being present before me.

tat te 'nukampāṁ su-samīkṣamāṇo
bhuñjāna evātma-kṛtaṁ vipākam
hṛd-vāg-vapurbhir vidadhan namas te
jīveta yo mukti-pade sa dāya-bhāk

"My dear Lord, any person who is constantly awaiting Your causeless mercy to be bestowed upon him, and who goes on suffering the resultant actions of his past misdeeds, offering You respectful obeisances from the core of his heart, is surely eligible to become liberated, for it has become his rightful claim."

(*Śrīmad-Bhāgavatam* 10.14.8)

He is completely free to do anything but he is always my worshipful Lord, unconditionally.

sa vai puṁsāṁ paro dharmo
yato bhaktir adhokṣaje
ahaituky apratihatā
yayātmā suprasīdati

"The supreme occupation (*dharma*) for all humanity is that by which men can attain to loving devotional service unto the transcendent Lord. Such devotional service must be unmotivated and uninterrupted to completely satisfy the self."

(*Śrīmad-Bhāgavatam* 1.2.6)

* * *

vande śrī-kṛṣṇa-caitanya-
devaṁ taṁ karuṇārṇavam
kalāv apy ati-gūḍheyaṁ
bhaktir yena prakāśitā

I offer my respectful obeisances unto Lord Śrī Caitanya Mahāprabhu. He is an ocean of transcendental mercy, and although the subject matter of *bhakti-yoga* is very confidential, He has nonetheless manifested it so nicely, even in this Age of Kali, the age of quarrel.

(*Śrī Caitanya-caritāmṛta, Madhya-līlā* 22.1)

nāma-saṅkīrtanaṁ yasya
sarva-pāpa praṇāśanam
praṇāmo duḥkha-śamanas
taṁ namāmi hariṁ param

I offer my respectful obeisances unto the Supreme Lord, Hari, the congregational chanting of whose holy names destroys all sinful reactions, and the offering of obeisances unto whom relieves all material suffering.

(*Śrīmad-Bhāgavatam* 12.13.23—this is the concluding verse of *Śrīmad-Bhāgavatam*)

GLOSSARY

Ācārya—Spiritual leader who teaches by personal example.
Advaita—One of Lord Caitanya's principal associates; a member of the Pañca-tattva. He is considered to be an incarnation of both Lord Śiva and Lord Mahā-Viṣṇu.
Ahaṅkāra—"False ego," the first and most subtle of the separated elements of material creation. By its influence, conditioned souls assume temporary material identities.
Ajāmila—A *brāhmaṇa* whose attraction to a prostitute led him into sinful life but who was saved by his deathbed cries for his son Narāyaṇa, cries that brought the messengers of Lord Narāyaṇa to stop those of Yamarāja from dragging him to hell.
Anartha—Unwanted things; material desire.
Anartha-nivṛtti—The cleansing of unwanted things from the heart.
Aparādha—An offense, especially against the Supreme Lord or His devotees.
Arjuna—A great bowman, he figured prominently in winning the Kurukṣetra battle, with Kṛṣṇa driving his chariot. It was to Arjuna that Kṛṣṇa spoke the *Bhagavad-gītā* just before the battle.
Āsakti—Attachment for Kṛṣṇa.
Asura—Demon or ungodly person, who opposes the demigods and the service of the Lord.
Avatāra—A "descent" of the Supreme Lord to the material world in one of His many forms.
Avidyā—Ignorance.

Balarāma—Kṛṣṇa's elder brother, and His first plenary expansion.
Battle of Kurukṣetra—A great fratricidal war fought 5,000 years ago between the Pāṇḍavas (Arjuna and his brothers) and their cousins, the Kurus, at which Lord Kṛṣṇa spoke the *Bhagavad-gītā* to Arjuna.

Bhagavad-gītā—The essential teachings on progressive spiritual life and pure devotion to the Supreme Lord spoken by the Supreme Lord Himself, Kṛṣṇa, to His friend Arjuna at Kurukṣetra in the last moments before the great battle.

Bhakti—Devotional service to the Supreme Lord. *Bhakti* in practice is the prime means of spiritual success, and perfected *bhakti,* pure love of God, is the ultimate goal of life.

Bhakti-rasāmṛta-sindhu—Lit., "The Ocean of the Pure Nectar of Devotional Service"; a treatise on the science of devotional service (*bhakti*), written by Śrīla Rūpa Gosvāmī.

Bhaktisiddhanta Sarasvatī—The spiritual master of His Divine Grace A. C. Bhaktivedanta Swami Prabhupāda.

Bhaktivinoda Ṭhākura—An *ācārya* in the Gauḍīya Vaiṣṇava disciplic succession; the father of Bhaktisiddhānta Sarasvatī Ṭhākura.

Bhakti-yoga—The execution of devotional service rendered to the Supreme Lord with love.

Bhāva—Ecstasy in love of God.

Brahmā—The first finite living being in the material creation. At the beginning of creation, and again at the start of each day of his life, Brahmā engineers the appearance of all the species and the planets on which they reside. He is the first teacher of the *Vedas* and the final material authority to whom the demigods resort when belabored by their opponents.

Brahmacārī—A celibate boy in the student phase of spiritual life, receiving education at the residence of a spiritual master.

Brāhmaṇa—A member of the most intelligent class among the four occupational divisions in the *varṇāśrama* social system.

Brahminical—Having the qualities of a *brāhmaṇa,* such as truthfulness, cleanliness, control of the senses, tolerance.

Caitanya Mahāprabhu—The form in which the Personality of Godhead Kṛṣṇa made His advent in CE 1486 at Māyāpur, West Bengal, and acted in the guise of His own devotee. He taught the pure worship of Rādhā and Kṛṣṇa, primarily by *saṅkīrtana,* the congregational chanting of Their names.

Caitanya-caritāmṛta—The biography and philosophy of Caitanya Mahāprabhu, written by Śrīla Kṛṣṇadāsa Kavirāja Gosvāmī.

Caṇḍāla—The most degraded class of man, an outcaste.

Dharma—"Religious principles," or, more properly, individual duty. In another sense, dharma is the inseparable nature of a thing that distinguishes it, like the heat of fire or the sweetness of sugar.

Durgā—Lord Śiva's eternal consort, of many names and forms, who joins him in his incarnations. She is the creator and controller of the material world.

Ekādaśī—A day on which Vaiṣṇavas fast from grains and beans and increase their remembrance of Kṛṣṇa. It falls on the eleventh day of both the waxing and waning moons.

Gadādhara—One of the principal associates of Caitanya Mahāprabhu; a member of the Pañca-tattva. He is considered to be an incarnation of the Lord's internal potency.

Gaṅgā or **Ganges**—The great sacred river flowing from the peaks of the Himālayas to the Bay of Bengal and delivering from sin everyone who comes in contact with her.

Gaura—A name of Śrī Caitanya Mahāprabhu meaning "golden."

Gaurāṅga—A name of Śrī Caitanya Mahāprabhu meaning "golden-limbed."

Gaura-Nitāi—Lord Caitanya (Gaura) and Lord Nityānanda (Nitāi).

Gaurasundara—A name of Śrī Caitanya Mahāprabhu meaning "beautiful golden one."

Gāyatrī—A prayer chanted silently by *brāhmaṇas* at sunrise, noon, and sunset.

Goloka Vṛndāvana—The eternal abode of the Supreme Lord in His original form of Kṛṣṇa. It is located above all the other Vaikuṇṭha planets. It has three parts—Vṛndāvana, Mathurā, and Dvārakā.

Gosvāmīs—The six Gosvāmīs of Vṛndāvana, who are direct followers of Lord Caitanya in disciplic succession, and who systematically presented His teachings.

Hari—The Supreme Lord, Kṛṣṇa or Viṣṇu.

Haribol—Lit., "chant the name of Hari."

Haridāsa Ṭhākura—A great devotee of Lord Caitanya Mahāprabhu; known as the *nāmācārya,* the master who taught the chanting of the holy names by his own example.

Harmonium—A small organlike instrument typically used in *kīrtana.*

Jagāi and Mādhāi—Two debauchees whom Lord Nityānanda converted into Vaiṣṇavas.

Jagannātha—"Lord of the universe," an ancient Deity of Kṛṣṇa. He was established along with His brother Balarāma and sister Subhadrā in the holy city of Purī, on the coast of Orissa. Caitanya Mahāprabhu resided in Purī and worshiped Lord Jagannātha.

Jīva-tattva—The category of ordinary souls, who, although emanating from God, are not in the category of God.

Jñānī—A practitioner of *jñāna-yoga* (the spiritual discipline of cultivating knowledge of pure spirit), or, more generally, any learned person.

Kali-yuga—The fourth of four repeating ages that form the basic cycles of universal time. In each Kali-yuga the world degrades into quarrel and dishonesty. The present Kali-yuga began 5,000 years ago and will continue for another 427,000 years.

Kaniṣṭha-adhikārī—Neophyte.

Karatālas—Hand cymbals used during *kīrtana.*

Karmī—One whose aim in life is to achieve material elevation by acting dutifully, especially by performing Vedic sacrifices.

Līlā—"Pastimes," the eternal activities of the Supreme Lord in loving reciprocation with His devotees. Unlike the affairs of materially conditioned souls, the Lord's *līlās* are not restricted by the laws of nature or impelled by the reactions of past deeds.

Madhyama-adhikārī—A devotee whose advancement in spiritual life is midway between the neophyte (*kaniṣṭha*) and advanced (*uttama*) levels.

Mahā—A Sanskrit prefix meaning "great" or "large."

Mahābhārata—The epic history of "greater India" composed by Dvaipāyana Vyāsa. One chapter is the *Bhagavad-gītā.*

Mahāprabhu—Supreme master of all masters; refers to Lord Caitanya.

Maṅgala-ārati—The first Deity worship of the day, performed an hour and a half before sunrise.

Māyā—Illusion; the energy of the Supreme Lord that deludes the living entities into forgetting their spiritual nature and forgetting God.

Māyāpur—A town in West Bengal, India, where Lord Caitanya appeared.

Māyāvādī—Proponents of the impersonal philosophy of "oneness," which holds that the Absolute Truth, one without a second, is formless and changeless, and that whatever has name and form is an illusion falsely imposed on that Truth.

Mleccha—A class of persons outside the social and spiritual divisions of Vedic culture, whose standards and practices are considered abominable.

Mokṣa—Liberation from the cycle of birth and death.

Mṛdaṅga—A two-headed clay drum, traditionally used in *kīrtana.*

Mukti—Liberation from the cycle of birth and death.

Mūrti—A form, usually referring to a Deity.

Nāmācārya—One who teaches by their example the pure chanting of the holy name of the Lord.
Nāmāparādha—Offense to the holy name.
Nārada—A great devotee of Lord Kṛṣṇa who travels throughout the spiritual and material worlds singing the Lord's glories and preaching the path of devotional service.
Nārāyaṇa—The Personality of Godhead as the Lord of Vaikuṇṭha, the infinitely opulent spiritual world.
Nityānanda—The incarnation of Lord Balarāma who is a principal associate of Lord Caitanya.
Nṛsiṁhadeva—The pastime incarnation of the Supreme Lord Viṣṇu as half man, half lion. He appeared in order to deliver the saintly child Prahlāda from the persecutions of his father, Hiraṇyakaśipu. When Hiraṇyakaśipu demanded of Prahlāda, "If your God is everywhere, is He also in this pillar?" Lord Nṛsiṁha burst out of the pillar and ripped Hiraṇyakaśipu apart.

Pañca-tattva—The "five truths" of the Godhead manifested personally as Lord Caitanya and His four primary associates, namely, Nityānanda Prabhu, Advaita, Gadādhara, and Śrīvāsa.
Paṇḍita—A scholar.
Paramahaṁsa—"Perfect swan," a completely pure devotee of the Supreme Lord, beyond any influence of material illusion.
Paramātmā—The "Supersoul," the aspect of the Supreme Lord who accompanies every conditioned soul as the indwelling witness and guide.
Paraṁ Brahma—The supreme personal form of the Absolute Truth.
Paramparā—An authorized Vaiṣṇava disciplic succession. More ordinarily, any tradition.
Patita-pāvana—Savior of the fallen souls.
Prabhu–Lit., "master." Added to a devotee's name by another devotee to show respect.
Prahlāda Mahārāja—One of the greatest devotees of Lord Viṣṇu. As the five-year-old son of the mighty demon

Hiraṇyakaśipu, he openly dared to worship the Personality of Godhead and preach His glories. Hiraṇyakaśipu tried many ways to kill the boy, but failed to harm him. Finally Lord Viṣṇu appeared as Lord Nṛsiṁha, killed Hiraṇyakaśipu, and enthroned Prahlāda as king of the demons.

Prasāda(m)—The remnants of food and other items offered to the Supreme Lord. By accepting Kṛṣṇa's *prasāda* one can rapidly become purified and achieve pure love of God.

Purāṇas—The eighteen very old books which are histories of this and other planets.

Rādhārāṇī—Kṛṣṇa's original pleasure potency, from whom all His internal energies expand. She is His eternal consort in Vṛndāvana and the most dedicated and beloved of His devotees.

Rāma—A name of Lord Kṛṣṇa, meaning "the source of all pleasure." As part of the Hare Kṛṣṇa *mahā-mantra,* refers to the highest eternal pleasure of Lord Kṛṣṇa; may also refer to Lord Balarāma or Lord Rāmacandra.

Ratha-yātrā—The yearly festival in Purī, Orissa, during which Lord Jagannātha, His brother Lord Baladeva, and Their sister Subhadrā move in procession, each on their own cart, from their temple to the Guṇḍicā temple, which represents Vṛndāvana. Lord Caitanya Mahāprabhu would observe this Guṇḍicā-yātrā with great festivity in the company of His devotees.

Sādhu—A saintly person.

Sādhu-saṅga—The association of saintly persons.

Sahajiyā—A class of pseudodevotees who take the conjugal pastimes of Kṛṣṇa and the *gopīs* cheaply and who do not follow the proper regulations of *vaidhi-bhakti* (devotional service conducted under discipline and according to rules).

Samādhi—Fully matured meditation, the last of the eight steps of the yoga system taught by Patañjali. A perfected devotee of the Supreme Lord also achieves the same *samādhi.*

Saṁsāra—The cycle of repeated birth and death, which

continues until one gives up one's rebellion against the Supreme Lord.

Saṁskāra—Vedic purificatory rites of passage.

Satya—The first of four repeating ages that form the basic cycles of universal time. During its 1,728,000 years, purity and spiritual competence are prominent.

Śikṣāṣṭaka(m)—Eight verses of instruction in devotional service written by Lord Caitanya.

Śiva—The special expansion of the Supreme Lord who is uniquely neither God nor *jīva*. He energizes the material creation and, as the presiding deity of the mode of ignorance, controls the forces of destruction.

Śrīmad-Bhāgavatam—Also known as the *Bhāgavata Purāṇa,* it teaches unalloyed devotional service to Kṛṣṇa, the Supreme Personality of Godhead.

Śrīvāsa—An associate of Caitanya Mahāprabhu; a member of the Pañca-tattva; said to be the incarnation of a pure devotee.

Supersoul—An expansion of the Supreme Lord as an all-pervading personal presence in the universe and in the heart of every living entity; Paramātma.

Tapasya—Austerity and penance.

Tilaka—Auspicious marks, of sacred clay and other substances, applied daily on the forehead (and sometimes on various limbs as well) to dedicate one's body to God.

Tretā—The second of the four repeating ages that form the basic cycles of universal time. During its 1,296,000 years, the mode of passion comes into prominence. The system of Vedic fire sacrifices is developed elaborately during the Tretā-yuga.

Tulasī—The sacred plant most beloved of Kṛṣṇa. *Tulasī* is a form of the *gopī* Vṛndā, the expansion of Śrīmati Rādhārāṇī who owns the Vṛndāvana forest. Without the leaves of the *tulasī* plant, no offering of food is accepted by Lord Viṣṇu, and no worship to Him is complete.

Upaniṣads—The philosophical chapters of the *Vedas,* organized into 108 books. They are also called Vedānta, meaning "the culmination of Vedic knowledge," and were explained systematically by Dvaipāyana Vyāsa in his *Vedānta-sūtra.*

Vaikuṇṭha—Lit., the place free from anxiety. The kingdom of God, full of all opulence and unlimited by time and space.
Vaiṣṇava—A devotee of the Supreme Lord Viṣṇu. Since Kṛṣṇa and Viṣṇu are different aspects of the same Supreme Person, devotees of Kṛṣṇa are also Vaiṣṇavas.
Vedas—The original revealed scriptures, eternal like the Supreme Lord and thus in need of no author. Because in Kali-yuga the *Vedas* are difficult to understand or even study, the *Purāṇas* and epic histories, especially *Śrīmad-Bhāgavatam,* are essential for gaining access to the teachings of the *Vedas.*
Vedic—Pertaining to the *Vedas,* or more broadly, following or derived from the Vedic authority.
Viṣṇu—The Supreme Lord in His opulent feature as the Lord of Vaikuṇṭha, who expands into countless forms and incarnations.
Viṣṇudūtas—The messengers of Lord Viṣṇu who take perfected devotees back to the spiritual world at the time of death.
Vṛndāvana—Kṛṣṇa's most beloved forest in Vraja-bhūmi, where He enjoys pastimes with the cowherd boys and the young *gopīs;* also, the entire district of Vraja.

Yajña—Vedic sacrifice, or any work done for the pleasure of the Supreme Lord Viṣṇu.
Yamadūtas—The agents of Yamarāja, the superintendent of death and karmic justice.
Yamarāja—The judge of sinful persons at death.
Yamunā—The holiest of rivers, flowing through Vraja-bhūmi and thus touched by the dust of Kṛṣṇa's feet. The Yamunā personified is also known as Kālindī. After Kṛṣṇa established His capital at Dvārakā, she became one of His eight principal queens.

Centers of the International Society for Krishna Consciousness

Founder-*Ācārya:* His Divine Grace A. C. Bhaktivedanta Swami Prabhupāda

For further information on classes, programs, festivals, residential courses, and local meetings, please contact the center nearest you.

EUROPE

UNITED KINGDOM AND IRELAND

Belfast, Northern Ireland — Sri Sri Radha-Madhava Mandir, Brooklands, 140 Upper Dunmurry Lane, Belfast BT17 OHE; Tel. +44-28-90620530; belfast@iskcon.org.uk; www.iskconuk.com/belfast

Birmingham, England — 84 Stanmore Road, Edgebaston, Birmingham B16 9TB; Tel. +44-121-4204999; birmingham@iskcon.org.uk; www.iskconbirmingham.org

Cardiff, Wales — The Soul Centre, 116 Cowbridge Road East, Canton, Cardiff, CF11 9DX; Tel. +44-2920-390391; the.soul.centre@pamho.net

Coventry, England —Radha Krishna Centre, Kingfield Road, Radford, Coventry, West Midlands; (mail: 19 Gloucester Street, Coventry, CV1 3BZ); Tel. +44-24-76552822 or 5420; kov@krishnaofvrindavan.com; www.krishnaofvrindavan.com

✦ **Dublin, Ireland** — Govinda's Kirtan Centre, 83 Middle Abbey Street, Dublin 1, Rep. of Ireland; Tel. +353-1-862120452, +353 (0)87 992 1332; dublin@krishna.ie, syamananda@govindas.ie; www.krishna.ie; Govinda's: Tel. +353 1 475 0309; info@govindas.ie; www.govindas.ie

Lanarkshire, Scotland — Karuna Bhavan, Bankhouse Rd, Lesmahagow, Lanarkshire, ML11 0ES; Tel. +44 1555 894790; karunabhavan@aol.com; www.iskcon.org.uk/scotland

Leicester — 31 Granby Street, Leicester, LE1 6EP; Tel. +44 (0)116 276 2587/+44 (0)7597 786676; info@iskconleicester.org; www.iskconleicester.org

✦ **London, England (city)** — 10 Soho Street, London W1D 3DL; Tel. +44-20-74373662; shop: 72870269; Govinda's Restaurant: 74374928; london@pamho.net; www.iskcon-london.org

London (Kings Cross) — Matchless Gifts, 102 Caledonian Road, Kings Cross, London N1; Tel. +44 (0)20 7168 5732; foodforalluk@gmail.com; www.matchlessgifts.org.uk

London, England (south) — 42 Enmore Road, South Norwood, London SE25 5NG; Tel. +44-20-86564296

Manchester, England — 20 Mayfield Road, Whalley Range, Manchester, M16 8FT; Tel. +44-161-2264416; contact@iskconmanchester.com; www.iskconmanchester.com

Newcastle, England — 304 Westgate Road, Newcastle-upon-Tyne, Tyne & Wear NE4 6AR; Tel. +44-191-2721911; info@iskconnewcastle.org; www.iskconnewcastle.org

✦ **Swansea, Wales** — The Hare Krishna Temple, 8 Craddock Street, Swansea SA1 3EN; Tel. +44-1792-468469; iskcon.swansea@pamho.net; restaurant: govindas.swansea@pamho.net; www.iskconwales.org.uk

Watford, England — Bhaktivedanta Manor, Dharam Marg, Hilfield Lane, Aldenham, near Watford, Herts WD25 8EZ; Tel. +44 1923 851000; info@krishnatemple.com; accommodations.requests@pamho.net; www.krishnatemple.com

RURAL COMMUNITIES

Upper Lough Erne, Northern Ireland (Govindadwipa) — Hare Krishna Temple, Inis Rath Island, Derrylin, Co. Fermanagh BT92 0BY; Tel. +44-28-67723878; tp@krishnaisland.com; www.krishnaisland.com

RESTAURANTS

Cardiff — Tel. +44 (0)2920 390391; iskcon.wales@pamho.net; www.iskconwales.org.uk

Dublin, Ireland — Govinda's, 4 Aungier St, Dublin 2; Rep. of Ireland; Tel. +353 1 475 0309; info@govindas.ie; www.govindas.ie

Dublin, Ireland — Govinda's, 18 Merrion Row, Dublin 2, Rep. of Ireland; Tel. +353 1 6615095; praghosa.sdg@pamho.net; www.govindas.ie

Hare Krishna meetings are held regularly in more than forty towns in the UK. For more information, contact: ISKCON Reader Services, +44 (0)1923 851000, readerservices@pamho.net. Visit us on the web at www.iskcon.org and for UK info and projects at www.iskconuk.com

GERMANY

Abentheuer — Böckingstrasse 4a, 55767 Abentheuer; Tel. +49-6782-2214; www.goloka-dhama.de

Berlin — ISKCON, Berliner Allee 209, 13088 Berlin; mail@tempelberlin.de; www.tempelberlin.de

Cologne — ISKCON, Taunusstrasse 40, 51105 Köln; Tel. +49-221-8303778; restaurant: +49-221-9750323; keshava.bbs@gauradesh.com; www.krishna-tempel.de

Hamburg — ISKCON, Eiffestrasse 422, 20537 Hamburg; Tel. +49-40-4102848; vaidyanath.acbsp@pamho.net; www.bhaktiyogazentrum.de

Heidelberg — ISKCON, Forum 5, Wohnung 4, 69126 Heidelberg; Tel. +49 (06252) 128108; www.iskcon-heidelberg.de

Leipzig — ISKCON, Stöckelstrasse 60, 04347 Leipzig; Tel. +49-34-12348055; krishnabrief@gmail.com; www.krsna-is-cool.de

Munich — ISKCON, Wachenheimer Strasse 1, 81539 München; Tel. +49-89-68800288; iskcon.muenchen@krishnatempel.de; www.krishnatempel.de

Wiesbaden — Hari Nam Desh, Aarstrasse 8, 65329 Burg Hohenstein; Tel.+49-61-20904107; iskcon.wiesbaden@web.de; www.iskconwiesbaden.de

RURAL COMMUNITY

Jandelsbrunn — Simhachalam, Zielberg 20, 94118 Jandelsbrunn; Tel. +49-8583-316; info@simhachalam.de; www.simhachalam.de

HUNGARY

Budapest — Hungarian Society for Krishna Consciousness, Lehel ú. 15-17, 1039 Budapest; Tel. +36-1-212-6270; info@krisna.hu; www.krisna.hu

✦ **Debrecen** — Péterfia u. 57., 4024 Debrecen; Tel. +36-52-458092; debrecen@pamho.net; www.krisna.hu

Eger — Szechenyi u. 64., 3300 Eger; Tel. +36-36-313761; eger@pamho.net; www.krisna.hu

Kecskemét — Felsöcsalános 116, 6000 Kecskemét (mail: Pf. 546, 6001 Kecskemét); Tel. +36-76-480920; kecskemet@pamho.net; www.krisna.hu

Pécs — Damjanich u. 22., 7624 Pécs; Tel. +36-72-515991; pecs@pamho.net; www.krisna.hu

RURAL COMMUNITY

Somogyvámos — Krisna-völgy, Fő u. 38., 8699 Somogyvámos; Tel. +36-85-540002; krisna-volgy@pamho.net; www.krisna-volgy.hu

RESTAURANT

Budapest — Govinda Restaurant, Vigyázó Ferenc utca 4., 1051 Budapest; Tel. +36-1-2691625; govinda@invitel.hu

ITALY

Bergamo — Villaggio Hare Krishna (da Medolago strada per Terno d'Isola), 24040 Chignolo d'Isola (BG); Tel. +39-035-4940706

Milan — via Valpetrosa 5, 20123 Milano; Tel. +39-02-862417; Fax +39-035-4940705

✦ **Rome** — Govinda Centro Hare Krsna, via Santa Maria del Pianto 16, 00186 Roma; Tel. +39-06-68891540; govinda.roma@harekrsna.it

RURAL COMMUNITY

✦ **Florence** — Villa Vrindavan, Via Scopeti 108, 50026 San Casciano in Val di Pesa (FI); Tel. +39-055-820054; info@villavrindavana.org

ADDITIONAL RESTAURANT

Milan — Govinda's, via Valpetrosa 5, 20123 Milano; Tel. +39-02-862417

SPAIN

Barcelona — Plaza Reial 12, Entlo 2, 08002 Barcelona; Tel. +34-93-3025194; templobcn@hotmail.com

Madrid — Espíritu Santo 19, 28004 Madrid; Tel. +34-91-5213096

RURAL COMMUNITY

Brihuega (New Vraja Mandala) — (Santa Clara) 19411 Brihuega; Tel. +34-949-280436

RESTAURANT

Barcelona — Restaurante Govinda, Plaza de la Villa de Madrid 4-5, 08002 Barcelona; Tel. +34-93-3187729

SWEDEN

✦ **Gothenburg** — Karl Johansgatan 57, 41455 Göteborg; Tel. +46-31-879648; restaurant: +46-31-421462; info@harekrishnagoteborg.com; www.harekrishnagoteborg.com. Restaurant: govindas.gothenburg@pamho.net; www.govindas.gastrogate.com

✦ **Lund** — Bredgatan 28, 22221 Lund; Tel. +46-46-399500, +46-46-120413 (restaurant); vedicstudieslund@pamho.net.

Malmö — Box 8119, 20041 Malmö; info@harekrishna.nu

Stockholm (country) — New Radhakund, Korsnäs Gård, 14792 Grödinge; Tel. +46-8-53029800; info@pamho.net; www.krishna.se

RURAL COMMUNITY

Järna — Almviks Gård, 15395 Järna; Tel. +46-8-55152050; almviks.gard@pamho.net; www.almviksgard.se

RESTAURANT

Malmö — Govindas, Brogatan 11, 21144 Malmö; Tel. +46-40-308108

OTHER COUNTRIES

✦ **Durbuy, Belgium** — Radhadesh, Château de Petite Somme, 6940 Septon (Durbuy); Tel. +32-86-322926; info@radhadesh.com; www.radhadesh.com

Helsinki, Finland — Ruoholahdenkatu 24 D (III krs) 00180 Helsinki; www. harekrishna.fi

Kaunas, Lithuania — 37, Savanorių pr., 3000 Kaunas; Tel. +370-7-222574

Ljubljana, Slovenia — Zibertova 27, 1000 Ljubljana; Tel. +386-1-4312124; iskcon.ljubljana@pamho.net; www.harekrisna.net

Paris, France — 230 Avenue de la Division Leclerc, 95200 Sarcelles; Tel. +33-1-43030951, +33-1-39885358, +33-1-34458912; paris@pamho.net; www.krishnaparis.com

Prague, Czech Republic — Jilova 290, Prague 5-Zlicin 15521; Tel. +42-02-57950391; info@harekrsna.cz

✦ **Riga, Latvia** — 56, K. Baron St., 1011 Riga; Tel. +371-2-272490

Sarajevo, Bosnia-Herzegovina — Gornjo Vakufska 12, 71000 Sarajevo; Tel. +387-71-201530

Skopje, Macedonia — Borka Taleski 43, 1000 Skopje; Tel. +38970371717; vaideha@mt.net.mk; www.nitaigaurasundar.net.tf

Sofia, Bulgaria — 119 Kliment Ohridski Street, kv. Malinova Dolina, 1756 Sofia; Tel. +359-2-9616050; oks_sofia@abv.bg

Tallinn, Estonia — Luise Street 11a, 10142 Tallinn; Tel. +372-6460047; tallinn@pamho.net

Warsaw, Poland — ul. Zakręt 11, Mysiadło k. Warszawy, 05-500 Piaseczno; Tel. +48-22-7507797; kryszna@post.pl; www.harekryszna.pl

Zagreb, Croatia — Centar Za Vedske Studije, Bizek II 36, 10090 Zagreb (mail: P.O. Box 68, 10001); Tel. +385-1-3492468; zg@vvz.hr; www.vvz.hr

Zurich, Switzerland — Bergstrasse 54, CH-8032 Zürich; Tel. +41-44-2623388; kgs@pamho.net; www.krishna.ch

RURAL COMMUNITIES

Lucay le Mâle, France — La Nouvelle Mayapura, Domaine d'Oublaisse, 36360, Lucay le Mâle; Tel. +33-2-54402395; www.newmayapur.fr

ADDITIONAL RESTAURANTS

Prague, Czech Republic — Govinda's, Soukenicka 27, 11000 Prague-1; Tel. +420-2-24816631; info@vedavision.cz

Tallinn, Estonia — Damodara, Lauteri St. 1, 10114 Tallinn; Tel. +372-6442650

ASIA

INDIA

Kolkata, WB — 3C Albert Road (behind Minto Park, opp. Birla High School), 700017 Kolkata; Tel. +91-33-2287-3757, 6075, 8242; info@iskconkolkata.com; www.iskconkolkata.net

✦ **Mayapur, WB** — ISKCON, Shree Mayapur Chandrodaya Mandir, 741313 Shree Mayapur Dham, Dist. Nadia, ; Tel. +91-3472-245239, 245240, or 245233; mayapur.chandrodaya@pamho.net

✦ **Mumbai (Bombay), Maharashtra** — Hare Krishna Land, Juhu, Mumbai 400049; Tel. +91-22-2620-6860; iskcon.juhu@pamho.net, guesthouse.mumbai@pamho.net; www.iskconmumbai.com

Mumbai, Maharashtra — 7 K. M. Munshi Marg, Chowpatty 400007; Tel. +91-22-2369-7228; rgsevaka@pamho.net; www.radhagopinath.com

✦ **New Delhi, UP** — Hare Krishna Hill, Sant Nagar Main Road, East of Kailash, 110065; Tel. +91-11-2623-5133, 4, 5, 6, 7; delhi@pamho.net, Guesthouse: guest.house.new.delhi@pamho.net

Tirupati, AP — K.T. Road, Vinayaka Nagar, 517 507; Tel. +91-877-2230114 or 2230009; iskcon.tirupati@gmail.com; iskcontirupati.com

✦ **Vrindavan, UP** — Krishna-Balaram Mandir, Bhaktivedanta Swami Marg, Raman Reti, Mathura Dist., 281124; Tel. +91-565-254-0021; vrindavan@pamho.net; guesthouse: Tel. +91-565-254-0022; ramamani@sancharnet.in

RURAL COMMUNITIES

Govardhan Ecovillage, Maharastra — Galtare, Hamrapur (P.O), Wada (Taluka) Thane (District) – 421303 Maharashtra; Tel. +91-9167204666; contactus@ecovillage.org.in; www.ecovillage.org.in

Mayapur, WB — (contact ISKCON Mayapur)

RESTAURANT

Kolkata, WB — Govinda's, ISKCON House, 22 Gurusaday Road, 700019; Tel. +91-33-24756922, 24749009

NORTH AMERICA

CANADA

Calgary, Alberta — 313 Fourth Street N.E., T2E 3S3; Tel. +1 (403) 265-3302; vamanstones@shaw.ca; www.calgary.iskcon.ca

Edmonton, Alberta — 9353 35th Ave., T6E 5R5; Tel. +1 (780) 439-9999; edmonton@iskcon.ca; www.edmonton.iskcon.ca

Montreal, Quebec — 1626 Pie-IX Boulevard, H1V 2C5; Tel. +1 (514) 521-1301; iskconmontreal@gmail.com; www.iskconmontreal.ca

Toronto, Ontario — 243 Avenue Rd., M5R 2J6; Tel. +1 (416) 922-5415; www.toronto.iskcon.ca

Vancouver, B.C — 5462 S.E. Marine Dr., Burnaby V5J 3G8; Tel. +1 (604) 433-9728; vancouver@iskcon.ca; www.vancouver.iskcon.ca

USA

Berkeley, CA — 2334 Stuart Street, 94705; Tel: +1 (510) 540-9215; info@iskconberkeley.net; www.iskconberkeley.net

Boston, MA — 72 Commonwealth Ave., 02116; Tel. +1 (617) 247-8611; www.iskconboston.org

Chicago, IL — 1716 W. Lunt Ave., 60626; Tel. +1 (773) 973-0900; chicago@iskcon.net

✦ **Los Angeles, CA** — 3764 Watseka Ave., 90034; Tel. +1 (310) 836-2676; nirantara@juno.com; restaurant: arcita@webcom.com

✦ **New York, NY** — 305 Schermerhorn St., Brooklyn, 11217; Tel. +1 (718) 855-6714; ramabhadra@aol.com

✦ **Spanish Fork, UT** — Radha Krishna Temple, 311 West 8500 South, Spanish Fork, 84660; Tel. +1 (801) 798-3559; carudas@earthlink.net; www.utahkrishnas.org

San Diege, CA — 1030 Grand Ave., (Pacific Beach) 92109; Tel. +1 (858) 483-2500; krishna.sandiego@gmail.com; www.krishnasd.com

Washington, D.C. — 10310 Oaklyn Dr., Potomac, MD 20854; Tel. +1 (301) 299-2100; info@iskconofdc.org; www.iskconofdc.org

RURAL COMMUNITIES

Alachua, Florida — New Raman Reti, 17306 NW 112th Blvd., 32615; Tel. +1 (386) 462-2017; alachuatemple@gmail.com; alachuatemple.com

✦ **Moundsville, West Virginia (New Vrindaban)** — R.D. No. 1, Box 319, Hare Krishna Ridge, 26041; Tel. +1 (304) 843-1600; Guest House, +1 (304) 845-5905; mail@newvrindaban.com; www.newvrindaban.com

AUSTRALASIA

AUSTRALIA

Brisbane — 95 Bank Road, Graceville, QLD 4075; Tel. +61-7-33795455; brisbane@pamho.net; www.iskcon.org.au

Melbourne — 197 Danks Street, Albert Park, VIC 3206; Tel. +61-3-96995122; melbourne@pamho.net

Sydney — 180 Falcon Street, North Sydney, NSW 2060; Tel. +61-2-99594558; info@iskcon.com.au; www.iskcon.com.au

RESTAURANTS

Brisbane — Govinda's, 99 Elizabeth Street, 1st floor, QLD 4000; Tel. +61-7-32100255; www.brisbanegovindas.com.au

Sydney — Govinda's, 112 Darlinghurst Rd., Darlinghurst NSW 2010; Tel. +61 (02) 9380-5155; info@govindas.com.au

NEW ZEALAND

Auckland, NZ — The Loft, 1st Floor, 103 Beach Road; Tel. +64-9-3797301; www.theloft.org.nz

Christchurch, NZ — 83 Bealey Avenue; Tel. +64-3-3665174; iskconchch@clear.net.nz

AFRICA

Accra, Ghana — Samsam Road, Off Accra-Nsawam Highway, Medie, Accra North; Tel. +233302981099; srivas_bts@yahoo.co.in

Cape Town, South Africa — 17 St. Andrews Road, Rondebosch 7700; Tel. +27 (21) 689 1060/6861179; iskcon.cape@pamho.net

✦ **Durban, South Africa** — 50 Bhaktivedanta Swami Circle, Unit 5 (mail: P.O. Box 56003), Chatsworth, 4030; Tel. +27 (31) 403 3328; iskcon.durban@pamho.net

✦ **Johannesburg, South Africa** — 7971 Capricorn Ave., (entrance of Nirvana Drive East), Ext 9; Lenasia, Johannesburg; Tel. +27 (11) 854 1975/7969; iskconjh@iafrica.com

Kinshasa, RD Congo — Commune de Mont Ngafula Mbudi Safrica, avenue du Fleuve N1, Kinshasa; Tel. +243-997132360; srikrishnardcongo@yahoo.fr

✦ **Phoenix, Mauritius** — Sri Sri Radha Golokananda Mandir, Hare Krishna Land, Pont Fer; Tel. +230 696 5804; iskcon.hkl@intnet.mu

RURAL COMMUNITIES

Mauritius (ISKCON Vedic Farm) — Hare Krishna Road, Vrindavan, Bon Accueil; Tel. +230-418-3955; sriniketandas@yahoo.com; www.iskconmauritius.org